ST. MARY'S COL
ST. MAR

557 Russell + Russell 11-91 (Sweeringen)

THE
MORAL AND POLITICAL PHILOSOPHY
OF JOHN LOCKE

BY

STERLING POWER LAMPRECHT, Ph.D.

NEW YORK

RUSSELL & RUSSELL · INC

1962

REISSUED, 1962, BY RUSSELL & RUSSELL, INC.
L. C. CATALOG CARD NO: 62—13837

PRINTED IN THE UNITED STATES OF AMERICA

21880

PREFACE

The following study of the moral and political philosophy of John Locke aims to supply a lack in the existing discussions of the subject. Only one previous monograph on Locke's ethics has appeared—Professor M. M. Curtis's *Outline of Locke's Ethical Philosophy*, Leipzig, 1890—which contains much helpful material. The present essay, in addition to differing widely from some of Professor Curtis's conclusions, attempts to view Locke more closely in his relations to his predecessors and contemporaries. Hence a rather full exposition has been given both of the traditions in moral and political philosophy from Hooker to Locke, and of the controversies into which Locke was himself drawn on certain points of ethical theory. Not only does such a study throw further light on Locke's epistemology, that aspect of his thought which usually attracts the most attention, but also it should have considerable interest in itself.

The bibliography which is appended in no way pretends to be an exhaustive list of even the most important works which bear upon Locke's moral and political philosophy. It includes only those books which have been mentioned in the course of the discussion and is designed to indicate the editions which have been used and to assist in the verification of references. Wherever possible the references to the works of Locke and the other writers have been to chapters and sections rather than to pages. Where that procedure has been impossible, the fact has been distinctly noted.

I wish to express my great indebtedness to Professor John Dewey. I received special help from him in writing Chapter I of Book II, but profited throughout by his general advice and wise counsel. I found it a constant pleasure to work under his inspiring instruction. Also I wish to thank Professor Frederick J. E. Woodbridge, both for the light he has frequently thrown for me on this period in the history of philosophy and for his personal services in reading the proof and editing the dissertation.

TABLE OF CONTENTS

BOOK III. THE SOCIAL AND POLITICAL
PHILOSOPHY OF LOCKE

THE MORAL AND POLITICAL PHILOSOPHY
OF JOHN LOCKE

INTRODUCTION

1. Locke has always held an important place in all histories of modern philosophy, and his wide influence on the development of thought since his day has been generally recognized. But it has been his epistemology to which attention has been chiefly directed; and his moral theories, and to some extent his political theories, have been correspondingly neglected. Such disproportionate emphasis upon one phase of his contribution to philosophy is not altogether surprising. Epistemological problems have been the storm center of controversy both in England and Germany ever since the *Essay concerning Human Understanding* precipitated them in so striking a form. Ind̶ ̶ philosophy has often been treated as if it were synonymous with epis̶ temology; and ethics has been relegated even ̶where it has been mentioned at all, to an appendix. Recently, however, a reaction has ̶ ̶ ̶ ̶ ̶ ̶steadily been going on against too exclusive an absorption in epistemological matters, and moral and political questions are regaining the importance which they once held in philosophical discussions. It seems desirable, therefore, to consider more fully than has yet been done the ethics of Locke and the relation of his ethics to the development of thought in his century.

The sources for information concerning the ethics of Locke are not as plentiful as the historian might well desire. Various phases of his social and political philosophy he discussed in his *Letters for Toleration, Treatises of Government*, and *Thoughts concerning Education*. But nowhere did he present a systematic statement of his general ethical position, of the fundamental ethical principles upon which all social and political principles must rest. He was repeatedly urged to write a treatise on morality by his friend Molyneux,[1] whose expectations he had stimulated by his repeated assertions in the *Essay* that ethics should be classed with mathematics among the demonstrable sciences.[2] Molyneux insisted that such a task as a treatise on morality would be "worthy of your consideration," and well suited to "so clear and distinct a thinker as you are." Locke humbly replied that "though . . . I

[1] *Cf.* Molyneux's letters to Locke: *Works*, Vol. IX, pp. 291, 299, 329. The same request was repeated by others of his admirers, *e. g.*, Mrs. Katherine Trotter Cockburn in the introductory letter to her *Defence of Mr. Locke's Essay* in 1702.

[2] *Cf.* below, Book II, Chapter II, § 3.

saw that morality might be demonstratively made out, yet whether I am able so to make it out, is another question."[3] He promised indeed to employ his leisure hours in thinking of the matter, and may possibly have designed a short fragment among his papers entitled *Of Ethics in General*[4] in answer to Molyneux's request. Yet he never actually published any work dealing directly with ethical theory. Had he ventured to do so, his exact position on certain questions would not be so difficult to determine to-day, and some of the ambiguities and inconsistencies in his theories might have been removed. As such a treatise was not framed, the historian's evidence for an outline of his thoughts on ethics consists mainly of the various isolated passages in the *Essay* in which he dealt with moral problems, and a number of brief selections from his *Journals* and *Common-place Books* printed by his biographers, together with the assumptions upon which his discussions of social and political matters seem to have rested.

2. The reasons which deterred Locke from publishing a treatise on the principles of morality are probably two. In the first place, he came to be more and more absorbed in controversial writings in defending the *Essay*, *The Reasonableness of Christianity*, and the first *Letter concerning Toleration* against the attacks of Stillingfleet, Edwards, and Proast respectively. He was so vitally interested in the issues involved in those controversies that he gave over to wearisome, and at times petty, refutation the leisure which might otherwise have been employed on more constructive tasks. In the second place, he had a simple religious trust in the complete adequacy of the revelation of moral principles in Scripture. He was to be sure a confident rationalist, insisting that revelation can never contradict the sure results of reason, and will not even, especially where the revelation is traditional instead of original, carry the same conviction which reason carries.[5] He granted that, because of the imperfections of language, the written revelation in Scripture is exposed to misunderstanding; and he drew the lesson therefrom that men should be "more careful and diligent" in using their powers of reason, and less "magisterial, positive, and imperious" in interpreting revealed truths.[6] Yet though he was fond of proclaiming the glory of reason in general, he often fell back upon revelation when any particular, concrete point needed to be proved. All through *The Reasonableness of Christianity* he emphasized the insufficiency of natural religion,[7] and of "natural morality" also, as morality established by reason might be called. "It would seem, by

[3] Locke: *Works*, Vol. IX, pp. 294-295.
[4] King: *Life of Locke*, pp. 308-313. *Cf.* below, Book II, Chapter V, Section 2.
[5] *Essay* IV, 18, 1-4. *Cf. Works*, Vol. VII, p. 142. (In this and similar references to Locke and other authors, Roman numerals indicate the book, Arabic numerals the chapters, and superior figures the section.)
[6] *Essay* III, 9, 23.
[7] *Works*, Vol. VII, pp. 5, 102, 135-156, 157-158.

the little that has hitherto been done in it, that it is too hard a task for unassisted reason to establish morality in all its parts, upon its true foundation, with a clear and convincing light; and it is at least a surer and shorter way, to the apprehensions of the vulgar and the mass of mankind, that one manifestly sent from God, and coming with visible authority from Him, should, as a king and lawgiver, tell them their duties, and require their obedience, than leave it to the long and sometimes intricate deductions of reason, to be made out to them."[8] Therefore, as he concluded, revelation is a better basis for morality than reason, at least for most men, for "the day-laborers and tradesmen, the spinsters and dairy-maids," who "want leisure or capacity for demonstration."[9] There was no satisfactory body of ethics "before our Saviour's time;"[10] and all the wise men since Christ have not been able by reason to equal in any way the teachings of the New Testament. Men not only are feeble in intellectual grasp and vigor, but also are swept away by passions and vices. If revelation did not furnish them with an indubitable knowledge of true morality, they might not ever gain such knowledge at all. Thus in spite of his respect for reason, Locke came to the position that "the gospel contains so perfect a body of ethics that reason may be excused from that inquiry."[11]

3. Nevertheless, though Locke in replying to one of his critics had to acknowledge that he had not demonstrated morality,[12] certainly the dominant interest and underlying motive in his work were practical rather than speculative, ethical rather than epistemological. He explicitly stated that his purpose in writing the *Treatises of Government* was "to establish the throne of our great restorer, our present King William,"[13] *i. e.*, to justify the democratic principles involved in the Revolution of 1688 rather than to develop a scientific set of ideas. Likewise he disclosed that he wrote the *Thoughts concerning Education* in order to help in the proper education of the son of one of his friends, and that he published them in the hope that still others might derive benefit therefrom.[14] Certainly he had no other aim in the *Letters for Toleration* than to promote that ideal cause which throughout his life he had deeply at heart, and mocked at those who placed ceremonial purity ahead of true morality.[15] Even in his most abstract work, the *Essay concerning Human Understanding*, the primary motive was practical. Locke wrote in the *Epistle to the Reader*[16] that the epis-

[8] *Idem*, Vol. VII, p. 139.
[9] *Idem*, Vol. VII, p. 146.
[10] *Idem*, Vol. VII, p. 141.
[11] In a letter to Molyneux. *Idem*, Vol. IX, p. 377.
[12] *Works*, Vol. IV, p. 187.
[13] Preface. *Works*, Vol. V, p. 209.
[14] The Epistle Dedicatory.
[15] *Cf. Works*, Vol. VI, pp. 7, 23.
[16] *Essay;* Epistle to the Reader 4.

temological problems of the *Essay* were forced upon his consideration by difficulties which arose in a discussion with some friends; and Tyrrell explained that this discussion was "about the principles of morality and revealed religion."[17] It was in order to reach a sound foundation upon which morality and religion could be based, therefore, that Locke entered upon the task of examining the origin and limits of human knowledge. This task proved to be a greater one than he had at first supposed it would be, and consumed large portions of his time over a period of twenty years before his results were published in the bulky *Essay*. Yet never in all this time did Locke forget the practical motive with which he began. He said in 1677 that painstaking study is important because "we can make little further progress in doing than we do in knowing."[18] And he made the prior importance of conduct to mere thinking still more emphatic in a passage at the outset of the *Essay* itself: "If we can find out those measures whereby a rational creature, put in that state in which man is in this world, may and ought to govern his opinions and actions depending thereon, we need not to be troubled that some other things escape our knowledge."[19]   Thus even in the most abstruse and abstract of Locke's writings, the practical and ethical interest predominated.

4. The extent to which Locke was dependent upon the work of his predecessors has been a disputed point. Most critics have maintained that he was the originator of a wholly new tradition, building up his philosophy without so much as consulting the writings of others. This view of Locke's rather complete independence from historical relations to earlier thinkers is doubtless a misunderstanding, and can be explained as due to three causes.

In the first place, Locke was prone to insist in an exaggerated fashion that he had spun his philosophy out of his own "coarse thoughts,"[20] and emphasized the difference between his own direct and fresh observation of facts and the hide-bound traditionalism of the Schools. But he thereby simply intended to express his strong feelings of revolt against the type of philosophy current in the universities of his day, in which the method and subject matter of medieval thought were still employed. He was quite willing to acknowledge his great debt to Descartes[21] and others for the emancipation which they brought him from the narrow channels of academic teaching at Oxford. And it was only because he was aware of the important novelties which in the *Essay* he was introducing into epistemological theory, that he modestly gave expres-

---

[17] This information is derived from a marginal note made by Tyrrell in his own copy of the *Essay* which is now preserved in the British Museum. *Cf.* Bourne, *Life of Locke*, Vol. 1, p. 249. Also Fraser's edition of the *Essay*, Vol. 1, p. 9, note 2.

[18] King: *Life of Locke*, p. 93.

[19] *Essay;* Introduction 6.

[20] *Essay:* Epistle to the Reader 6.

[21] *Works*, Vol. IV, p. 48.

sion to what has been to many of his readers a misleading emphasis. The controversy which he had with Stillingfleet led him further to explain what he meant by writing out of his own "coarse thoughts." Stillingfleet accused him both of trying to invent "a new way of certainty by ideas," and also of merely reiterating what everyone knew quite well before the *Essay* appeared. He retorted to this charge with delightful irony that he was unfortunately not "as well read as your lordship" in the literature of the subject, and then added in a more serious way on the next page that he had come to regard his own theory as original with himself only after he "had in vain hunted for it in the books of others." [22] The discrepancy between these two comments on his relation to other writers is only apparent, and can be explained even aside from pointing out the ironical quality of the first of the two remarks. He had indeed hunted in the works of others such as Descartes; and not having found there what satisfied him as being a correct view of human knowledge, he then turned to observation of his own mind in order to frame his theory. When, however, Stillingfleet asserted that his theory was only a repetition of an established view, he could not deny the charge categorically; for he was but slightly familiar with the writings of the medieval schoolmen and ecclesiastics to whom Stillingfleet was referring. He was none the less acquainted with other writers of the more modern period, and wrote his *Essay* to supply what seemed to him the deficiencies in them.

In the second place, Locke did not state his position in the *Essay* in a well-balanced form. He took occasion to deal only with the new features which he was aiming to contribute to a theory of knowledge. He did not think it worth while or necessary to specify those other matters upon which he was in entire agreement with current and commonly accepted views. He seems to have taken it for granted that his readers would understand that he assented to that part of the established tradition which he did not deny.[23] Only when Stillingfleet began to attack him as a dangerous innovator did he explain his position more adequately. His three lengthy letters to Stillingfleet disclose much more than does the *Essay* the extent to which he was familiar with earlier writers. However, just as his method of including little but his original ideas in the *Essay* misled Stillingfleet, it has misled others since. Nevertheless he was not in all respects an innovator, but built largely on the work of his predecessors.

In the third place, Locke's *Essay* shows fewer traces of his familiarity with the writings of earlier thinkers than any of his other works. And the *Essay* is also that one of his works which is most read, even, in too

[22] *Idem*, Vol. IV, pp. 134-139.
[23] The new and old elements in Locke's epistemology are distinguished and discussed below. *Cf.* Book II, Chapter I.

many cases, which is exclusively read. Generalizing from the *Essay*, many critics have thus been led to suppose that he was unfamiliar with his predecessors. Yet the *Treatises of Government*, the *Thoughts concerning Education*, and many allusions in his *Journals* and *Commonplace Books* show quite conclusively that he did not escape the influence of the intellectual inheritance of his time. He explicitly mentioned the names of numerous men to whom he was indebted for instruction or from whom he greatly differed. One of his biographers goes so far as to claim that he never ventured to write until "he had acquainted himself with nearly every work of importance that had been offered to the world" on the subject he was considering.[24] And though this estimate is guilty of overstatement of the extent of Locke's reading, it is certainly correct in maintaining that Locke was familiar with many of the great philosophers of the past. He did scorn the medieval period as being one of barren and futile disputations; but he used to great profit some of the leading authors both of classical antiquity[25] and, more especially, of his own century. As the particular authors whom he knew best and followed most will be discussed in the next four chapters, they need not, however, be reviewed here.

An insistence upon Locke's dependence on his predecessors is even more important in a discussion of his moral and political philosophy than in an account of his epistemology. For, though his theory of knowledge has frequently been misunderstood through failure to appreciate its relations to the rationalism of the seventeenth century,[26] yet in many ways Locke, even more than Descartes or Hobbes, stands at the threshold of a new era in epistemological speculation. He opened up new paths of inquiry and formulated new problems for his successors to examine. His connections with subsequent developments are probably more important than his connections to earlier situations. But in ethics almost the opposite is the case. Here he represents rather the conclusion of a period. His moral and political philosophy may well be viewed as the summation of the best thought of the seventeenth century. Though he added new ideas of his own and developed the old ideas which he took over from others, he is rather the ripe fulfilment of the past than the herald of the future. Consequently his historical antecedents are important for an understanding of the significance of his ethical position.

---

[24] Bourne: *Life of Locke*, Vol. 1, p. 72.

[25] As Locke's relation to classical antiquity will not be dealt with elsewhere, it may be mentioned briefly here. In his *Thoughts concerning Education*, Locke spoke of a knowledge of Latin as "absolutely necessary to a gentleman" (§§ 163–168), and said that "no man can pass for a scholar that is ignorant of the Greek tongue" (§ 195). Among the Greeks he evidently thought most highly of Aristotle, especially of the *Politics*. Cf. *Works*, Vol. X, pp. 306–307. He also claimed acquaintance with Plato and others. Cf. King: *Life of Locke*, pp. 297–298. His knowledge of Latin authors seems to have been of the more literary men rather than of the philosophers. His admiration for Cicero will be referred to in the next chapter.

[26] Cf. below, Book II, Chapter I.

Book I

The Traditions in Moral and Political Philosophy Before the Time of Locke

CHAPTER I

EARLY WRITERS ON THE LAW OF NATURE

1. The tradition which seems to have had the most outstanding effect upon Locke's ethical philosophy was that which based morality upon "the law of nature." This tradition was very old and widespread. It sprang from the teachings of the Roman stoics, dominated the thought of the medieval scholastics, and then found striking expression in several of the greatest moralists of the seventeenth century. Locke probably was not acquainted with the stoics except as their ideas were embodied in Cicero, whom he often quoted;[1] and he surely had slight contact with any of the scholastics. But he was familiar with some of those writers of the seventeenth century who, after the disintegrating and chaotic moral effect of Protestant sectarianism, revived the conception of the law of nature as a unifying and catholic principle. Among these writers there were two on the continent who stand out prominently, the Dutch jurist Grotius and the German jurist Pufendorf. Both of these men Locke knew quite well and admired greatly, even recommending their works as an indispensable part of the education of a gentleman.[2] In England itself the writers who discussed the law of nature were quite numerous. In the last decade of the sixteenth century there had appeared the work of Richard Hooker, who not only antedated but prepared the way for Grotius. Locke was fond of quoting his words, usually adopting the current designation of him as "the judicious Hooker."[3] Then throughout the second half of the seventeenth century a group of less notable writers appeared. Culverwel and Cumberland used the law of nature as the basis of their replies to Hobbes. There is no direct evidence to indicate whether or not Locke was acquainted with their treatises. Yet it was an intimate friend of Locke, Tyrrell, who in 1692 published an abridgment of Cumberland's work. Also both Culverwel and Cumberland, as intellectual leaders, had many followers among the clergy, who popularized their ideas and made their fundamental principle a common possession of most educated men.[4] Benjamin Whichcote,

---

[1] *Some Thoughts concerning Education*, §§ 184–186, 188–189. Also King: *Life of Locke*, pp. 5, 45, 130. *Works*, Vol. III, pp. 271–272. Vol. X, p. 306. *Essay* II, 28, 11.

[2] *Some Thoughts concerning Education*, § 186. King: *op. cit.*, p. 5. Also *Works*, Vol. III, p. 272; Vol. X, p. 308.

[3] *Of Civil Government*, §§ 5, 15, 60, 61, 74, 90, 91, 94, 111, 134, 135, 136. *Works*, Vol. III, p. 272; Vol. X, p. 308.

[4] *E. g.*, Samuel Parker: *Demonstration of the Law of Nature and of the Christian Religion*, 1681. Also the works of John Wilkins (†1672), Henry More (†1687), and John Tillotson (†1694).

for example, who is said to have been Locke's favorite preacher,[5] spoke much of the law of nature, as his *Discourses*, printed long after his death, disclose. Locke recommended the sermons of Whichcote, Barrow, and Tillotson as "masterpieces."[6] Thus there is no doubt that Locke was very familiar with this whole tradition in moral and political philosophy.

2. The term "the law of nature" on which morality was made to rest did not of course have the same meaning in the many discussions devoted to it through the centuries by its various adherents. But in those writers of the seventeenth century who have just been mentioned, it had come to have a fairly consistent signification. At least there were certain points of general agreement which were characteristic of the period before Locke.

(*a*) In the first place, the law of nature was said to be identical with the law of reason. This identification had been a traditional one through many centuries. But in the Middle Ages it had meant several different things. Sometimes the law of nature was a sort of impersonal cosmic force, regulating the ordered relations of all things, animate and inanimate alike; and the law of reason was identified with it because, according to the tradition of Greek philosophy, order of any kind is witness to the existence of reason. At other times the law of nature was a law common to all living beings (inanimate objects were here excluded); and the law of reason was identified with it because that with which nature had endowed all life was supposed to be noble and worthy of eulogy.[7] In the former case reason became an attribute of the universe in general; in the latter case it became a kind of animal instinct. But in the writers of the seventeenth century reason is that faculty of the human mind which sets man off, not only from inanimate nature, but also from the lower animals,— it is that divine faculty which man is supposed to share with God. Hence when the law of nature and the law of reason are identified, reason is proclaimed to be that which has been designed by nature and by God to be man's moral guide. Those creatures who do not possess the faculty of reason cannot comprehend what law means, and hence are not to be held responsible for obedience to any law: they are completely outside the realm of moral distinctions. Man, however, is endowed with reason; hence he can comprehend what law means, and especially can know that law which flows from the nature of his own being. "The law of nature is that law which is intrinsical and essential to a rational creature."[8] It is "the dictate

⁵ Fraser's edition of Locke's *Essay*, Vol. I, p. xxiv.

⁶ *Works*, Vol. X, p. 306.

⁷ Carlyle: *A History of Medieval Political Theory in the West*, Vol. I, pp. 37-40; Vol. II, pp. 30, 103-104.

⁸ Culverwel: *Of the Light of Nature*, p. 57.

of right reason, showing the moral malignity, or the moral necessity that there is in any act, by either the repugnancy, or congruity, it hath to rational nature itself."[9] No man can deny the indubitable and self-evident character of the law of nature, without at once ceasing to be rational and descending to the level of the brutes. "Every man of a mature age, and entire sense, has so much natural light in him, as that, with necessary care and due consideration, he may comprehend at least those general precepts and principles which are requisite in order to pass our lives here honestly and quietly."[10] The more theologically inclined writers, to be sure, were quick to add that it was yielding to temptation and committing sin which made men unable thereafter to discern the law of nature.[11] But all alike agreed wherever reason was present, there would be an immediate apprehension of the law of nature, which is the moral law.[12]

(b) Secondly, the law of nature is immutable. Its immutability is a necessary correlate of its rationality; for reason issues, not in changing whims, but in fixed decrees. Morality does not rest on anything transient; it cannot vary from one generation to another; it has nothing relative about it; rather it is forever the same, at all places and at all times. Consequently, the moral law cannot depend upon any enactment, human or divine. It is not a statutory affair. It follows from the nature of reason, not from any will. No man, however much a king, can create right and wrong. The law of nature stands as the eternal standard behind all monarchs and all codes, setting forth "propositions of unchangeable truth and certainty" which "lay obligations upon all outward acts of behaviour, even in a state of nature, prior and antecedent to all laws of human imposition whatsoever, and are clearly distinct from every consideration of all such compacts and agreements as constitute civil government."[13] Even God himself cannot by arbitrary fiat alter the basis of moral law. For the law of reason is the criterion by conformity to which God's will is judged to be good.[14]

There is involved in this insistence on the priority of the law of nature to all human and divine wills no denial that morality lies in obedience to God's commands.[15] God's will is true and righteous altogether,—i. e., it is in joyful harmony with the law of nature.

[9] Grotius: *Concerning the Rights of War and Peace*, I, 1, 10, *Cf.* also p. xiv.

[10] Pufendorf: *The Whole Duty of Man, according to the Law of Nature*, I, 1, 4.

[11] Whichcote: *Works*, Vol. I, p. 131; Vol. II, p. 64. Also, *Cf.* Vol. I, pp. 132, 140, 199.

[12] Hooker, though he would assent to the statements of the men who came after him, employed a slightly different terminology. He preferred to use the term "law of nature," more as science today uses "natural law," for the laws according to which inanimate objects operate. Yet he recognized the law of reason as the injunctions which man realizes himself morally bound to obey. *Cf. Of the Laws of Ecclesiastical Polity*, I, 3, 1-4, 6, 1-5, 8, 9.

[13] Cumberland: *A Philosophical Enquiry into the Laws of Nature*, pp. 2-3.

[14] Grotius: *op. cit.* 11, 10. *Cf.* also Whichcote: *op. cit.*, Vol. I, pp. 252-253; Vol. III, p. 128.

[15] Grotius: *op. cit.*, I, 1, 10. Culverwel: *op. cit.*, p. 79. Cumberland: *op. cit.*, p. 28.

All the philosophers of the seventeenth century granted that God as the creator of the world and the giver of reason to mankind is responsible for man's rational and moral nature and his consequent subjection to law. But God acted as he did, not arbitrarily, but from the necessity imposed on him by reason. Therefore, the ultimate source of moral distinctions is that reason which God himself is not free to disobey. And though in the beginning he alone existed and alone possessed reason, yet the law of nature was determined by the nature of reason simply as reason, and not as the reason of God. The law would continue now to be binding on all rational beings even if God ceased to exist. The priority of reason to will is what makes the law of nature supreme above God as well as above earthly rulers. Nevertheless the divine law is identical with the law of nature, so that the religious man will always find added incentive for doing right in the fact that he is thus obeying God.

The writers on the law of nature who have been mentioned differ on one point. Though they all agree that reason declares the law of nature, they do not agree whether reason also makes it binding on man. Grotius and Cumberland, as thorough rationalists, implicitly assume that as soon as a principle is proved reasonable, man is morally bound to obey it. But Culverwel and Pufendorf are not so intellectualistic in their psychology. Every complete law consists of two parts,—precept and sanction. And though reason can declare the law of nature, it cannot create the obligation to obey. The law of nature becomes binding on man only when it is commanded by God. "That the same [i. e., the law of nature] may obtain the force of laws, it must necessarily be presupposed that there is a God who governs all things by his providence, and that he has enjoined us mortals to observe these dictates of our reason as laws."[16]   Hence, however independent of God's will the existence of the law may be, its controlling force arises by God's positive injunction.[17]

(c) Thirdly, the law of nature is universal. Its universality follows as a corollary from its rationality and immutability. Since that which reason lays down is always the same, all rational beings will know the one fixed moral law. We find the civil codes of all nations more or less approximating each other in their essential features; for underlying them all, as the common standard to which they tend to conform, is the law of nature. Even where the divine will is revealed in some form of positive law (as in the Mosaic code or the Gospel), such revelation is only a reaffirmation, needed because of men's sinful conduct or careless thinking, of that law of nature which all rational beings

[16] Pufendorf *op. cit.*, I, 3, [10]. *Cf.* I, 2, [7]. Also Culverwel: *op. cit.* p. 75.

[17] The question of future rewards and punishments is likely to arise here, and tends to give a hedonistic flavor to the moral law. *Cf.* Culverwel: *op. cit.*, p. 54. Cumberland: *op. cit.*, pp. xvii, 28. Hooker, I, 9, [1].

could know by their own effort. Moreover, individuals as well as nations are naturally led to identical decisions on moral questions; for reason is universal and alike in all individuals, and apprehends the same law. Though on other subjects the greatest disagreement is found, yet in their views of the moral law, men show a fundamental unanimity. "Every one being who exercises right reason, judgment, and the natural desire which these direct, must and ought to agree with all other beings, who judge likewise by right reason about the same thing."[18]

(d) In the fourth place, the law of nature is applicable to every state or condition under which men may live. According to the view of the Middle Ages, the law of nature, which had been the rule of life in the Garden of Eden before the Fall, had been not only supplemented, but also actually superseded, in man's corrupt state after the Fall, by "the law of nations;" and hence many institutions (e. g., slavery and war) which had been forbidden by the law of nature were permitted by the law of nations.[19] Such a virtual setting aside of the law of nature for a lower standard was not acceptable to the seventeenth century writers. To be sure, they retained much of the medieval belief in a primitive "state of nature." Cumberland confused the logical priority of the law of nature with its temporal priority.[20] Whichcote would derive the law of nature from a consideration of "man's constitution in the state of innocency."[21] Pufendorf, though he denied that all men had once been at the same historical period in the state of nature, held that such a primitive state frequently prevailed between certain groups of men.[22] However, there never is a suggestion of the older view which regarded the law of nature as belonging to an order which had long since passed away. The older view made the law of reason, which is identical with the law of nature, inapplicable to current problems. But the writers of the seventeenth century, especially Grotius and Pufendorf, wished to use reason to remedy social abuses and political institutions. Hence they held that the law of nature is valid under all conditions of life, whether a primitive state of nature or a highly organized civil structure. In order to be moral, one must be rational. Indeed, the more intricate and complex human living becomes, the more need there is for reason as a guide. Though the law of nature may be supplemented by positive laws on points where it is itself indifferent, it can never be superseded. Contemporary social evils cannot be condoned on the ground that the law of nature, and hence of reason, reflects only an

[18] Cumberland: op. cit., pp. 1, 152. Cf. Grotius: op. cit., I, 1, [12].
[19] Carlyle: op. cit. Vol. I, pp. 44, 109-110; Vol. II, pp. 111-113.
[20] Cumberland: op. cit., p. 2.
[21] Whichcote: op. cit., Vol. III, p. 54.
[22] Pufendorf: op. cit., Vol. II, 1, [5-7].

ideal state of affairs in the distant past.   The reforming spirit demands
an application of that law to all conditions of life.[23]

(e) In the fifth place, the law of nature is a social principle, i. e.,
it directs men to act for the interests of the social group.   This social
character of the law of nature follows from the conception of reason,
not as a law of the nature of things in general, but as a human faculty.
"The law of nature is the product of human nature."[24] Since man alone
has reason, he alone is that about which the law of nature is concerned.
His conduct should be such as to develop his own natural powers.
Whatever improves and perfects his abilities and capacities is good.[25]
And when human nature is examined, it is seen to be predominantly
social.   Man is not happy alone.   "He greedily affects society, that
is, community."[26] Moreover, man not only enjoys the company of
his fellows, but he needs it.   He cannot by himself attain much
development.   In the first few years of his life, he is utterly helpless,
and subsists through the care of others; and even in his maturer
years, he can accomplish nothing alone, but only in cooperation
with his fellows.   "There is nothing in the world more beneficial to
mankind than men themselves."[27] Thus in order to realize his own
powers, man is driven to enter upon a social life.   Still further, the
interests of the individual and of the group do not conflict at all.
"The fullest, most vigorous endeavor of each and all rational agents,
in promoting the common good of the whole rational system, con-
tributes effectually to the good of each single part in such a system:
under which whole or system, the single, individual happiness of
each and all of us is essentially contained."[28] Thus the law of nature
becomes identified with that which furthers the common good.   The
moral is the social.   "This is a fundamental law of nature, that every
man ought, as much as in him lies, to preserve and promote society:
that is, the welfare of mankind."[29] Whatever is necessary for the
continued existence of society, or will advance the interests of that
society, is good.   Similarly whatever harms the group, or destroys
confidence in social life, is evil.   In their common participation in the
common good, men best obey the law of nature.

3. There have thus been reviewed five points on which the writers
of the seventeenth century agreed in their interpretation of the law
of nature.   The law of nature is the dictate of reason, more ultimate
than any positive enactment, universally present to rational beings,

[23] Cumberland: op. cit., p. ix. Pufendorf: op. cit., I, 2, [16], 3, [9]; II, 1, [8].
[24] Grotius: op. cit,, p. vii.
[25] Cumberland: op. cit., p. 250.
[26] Grotius: op. cit. p. iii.
[27] Pufendorf: op. cit., I, 3, [3]. Cf. II, 1, [9]. Also Hooker: op. cit., I, 10, [1].
[28] Cumberland: op. cit., p. xxvi. Cf. also p. 9.
[29] Pufendorf: op. cit., I, 3, [9]. Cf. I, 2, [16]. Also Grotius: op. cit., I, 1, [12].

morally binding under all conditions of life, and leading inevitably to a thoroughly social ideal.

Beyond these specified points, however, there was little agreement. How does reason discover the law of nature? What are the data with which reason must operate to reach its conclusions? Just what is reason anyhow? To these questions the advocates of the principle of natural law gave no definite answer. Grotius and Pufendorf are mainly occupied with political problems; Culverwel is rhetorical rather than scientific; Cumberland is as confused as he is verbose. All alike seem to have failed to appreciate the necessity of a frank consideration of epistemological questions. A rationalistic ethics requires a theory of knowledge. And their theories of knowledge are only implicit and incidental,—indeed are often different on successive pages of the same work. But since Locke later realized the importance for morals of a careful epistemological foundation, the epistemological suggestions of these earlier writers must here be examined.

(a) One way in which the law of nature may be discovered is from the universal consent of nations. As has been shown above, the law of nature is universally known wherever reason prevails. Hence to establish particular moral rules, one needs only to show their common acceptance. If nations widely separated from each other in time and space are nevertheless found to hold the same moral principles, such unanimity is too striking to be accidental,—it must be the effect of a universally operating cause. Such a universally operating cause could be found nowhere except in the voice of reason. As the same kind of seed bears the same kind of fruit in many different soils, so the same rational faculty leads to the same law of nature in many diverse civilizations.[30] However, if universal agreement by all nations is not found, agreement "by the most civilized" is adequate.[31] Grotius, in making this last admission, seems to have been unaware to what extent he was betraying his whole case.

(b) The proof of the law of nature from its universal acceptance hardly touches the real epistemological difficulties. For why do the various nations agree? How does each nation, or how does each man in each nation, reach the same conclusion? Even if the conclusions reached are the same, the process of discovery is not yet revealed. Moreover, if the agreement of only the most civilized nations, or of the most rational men, is to be sought, how are the relative civilizations and degrees of rationality to be judged?

To meet such difficulties, another suggestion is offered. Hooker had contented himself merely by insisting that "the main principles

[30] Culverwel: *op. cit.*, p. 109. *Cf.* Grotius: *op. cit.*, II, 20, [45]. Also Hooker: *op. cit.*, I, 8, [2-3]. Pufendorf rejected this argument, probably under the influence of Hobbes.

[31] Grotius: *op. cit.*, I, 1, [12].

of reason are in themselves apparent." When these principles are
proposed, "the mind doth presently embrace them as free from all
possibility of error, clear and manifest without proof." [32] With this
idea of the law of nature as an axiom of reason, Grotius and Pufendorf agreed. But the English writers of the second half of the seventeenth century wanted something more definite. They held that
there are certain fundamental principles impressed on every human
mind, from which reason can develop the law of nature. Thus they
added a rather crude theory of innate ideas to the accepted rationalistic position. "There are stamped and printed upon the being of
man some clear and indelible principles, some first and alphabetical
notions, by putting together of which it can spell out the law of
nature. . . Reason, thus, by warming and brooding upon these
first and oval principles of her own laying, it being itself quickened
with a heavenly vigor, does thus hatch the law· of nature." [33] The
first principles of knowledge, therefore, do not need to be discovered
or invented: they are given. They do not need to be criticized or
questioned; for what is innate is also indubitably true.

This doctrine of characters imprinted on the mind of man was
not stated by any of the writers on the law of nature in as crude a
fashion as it had been by Lord Herbert. [34] Indeed it was at times
almost entirely contradicted. Culverwel ridiculed the supposition
that a child in the cradle is aware of any first principles. Rather
the self-evident and indubitable principles are consciously present
only when the faculty of reason develops. [35] And he even anticipated
Locke's epistemology when he asserted that reason, "the pinnacle of
certainty," is but "fantastical and poetical" unless its operations are
based in sense-experience. [36] Cumberland also insisted that he did
not intend to base his argument on "innate ideas," which, though they
may possibly be born with us, are not acceptable to most philosophers.
Rather he wished to begin "with those principles which are discovered
and understood upon the evidences of sense and daily experience." [37]
Likewise, Pufendorf denied that new-born babes have "plain and
distinct notions concerning what is to be done or avoided." [38]

Yet the procedure of all of these moralists belies their concessions
to empiricism. No use is made of the data of sense experience, and
the principles of reason are developed in a purely *a priori* fashion.
Pufendorf immediately added to the passage last quoted that reason

[32] Hooker: *op. cit.*, I. 8, 5.
[33] Culverwel: *op. cit.*, p. 81. *Cf.* Cumberland: *op. cit.*, pp. 284–285. Also Whichcote: *op. cit.*, Vol. III, pp. 22, 122–123.
[34] *Cf.* below, Book I,Chapter II, § 3.
[35] Culverwel: *op. cit.*, pp. 126–128.
[36] Culverwel: *op. cit.*, p. 202.
[37] Cumberland: *op. cit.*, p. xvi.
[38] Pufendorf: *op. cit.*, I, 3, 12.

is so able to apprehend with plain and clear evidence the law of nature that that law comes to be regarded as equivalent to a connate principle. Certainly it so came to be regarded by these seventeenth century upholders of natural law. The bulk of their work rests on the naïve acceptance of those innate impressions which at moments of epistemological frankness they somewhat repudiated.

If the law of nature is derived by reason from indelible imprints on the mind, the task of the moralist is simple. He has only to gather and note down his own clear notions.[39] Whatever he cannot conceive to have been determined by personal prejudice will be a "natural precept." But the outcome of this moral philosophy reveals the weakness of the position. There are only two possible alternatives open, either of which is futile. One alternative is to remain in the realm of vague generalities, defending natural law in general, extolling the power of reason, without specifying any particular concrete maxims. This alternative is the one of which the seventeenth century was most often guilty. The other alternative is to attempt definite statements concerning actual problems, at the cost of becoming dogmatic. When morals are spun out of one's inner endowments, every one can frame his own system for himself. A great deal of contradiction is likely to result, and there will be no means of settling any dispute. Culverwel mentions three of his "first and indelible principles":[40] "We must seek good and avoid evil," "We must seek happiness," and "Do not do to others what you do not wish to have done to yourself." But he does not tell what things are good and what are evil; he does not define happiness; and he mentions no way of confuting one who, like Hobbes, is bent solely on selfish aims. Whichcote, typical of most Christian preachers, simply fits the traditional ethics of the church into his barren philosophical scheme. "Humility, patience, meekness, and such like virtues favor nature, whereas passion, pride, and envy do waste and destroy nature."[41] But such a verdict is convincing only to one who has already accepted the Christian standpoint. Consequently, the bare principle of natural law is in itself so lacking in content as to be useless, and the epistemology on which it rests is so tied up with rank dogmatism as to be quite unconvincing.

4. Grotius and Pufendorf, and even Hooker to some extent, were interested in political affairs, and attempted to construct a philosophy of the state. Certain of their views are important because of their relation to Locke's *Treatises of Government*.

(a) The need for a powerful social organization was recognized. Not only is it true, as has already been shown in discussing the law

---

[39] *Cf.* Culverwel: *op. cit.* p. 83.
[40] Culverwel: *op. cit.*, pp. 81–82.
[41] Whichcote: *op. cit.* Vol. III, p. 53.

of nature, that men are naturally inclined to each other, and that they need each other's help in order to attain the kind of a life that they desire; but also it is true that men are naturally selfish and sensual, and that they would, if unrestrained, be constantly quarreling with each other. "Strifes and troubles would be endless, except they gave their common consent all to be ordered by some whom they should agree upon."[42] Thus men need defense and security against each other. The law of nature, however morally binding, is often violated unless some political power is erected to enforce it. The state is justified by the valuable service it renders.

(b) The particular fashion by which the state came into being was discussed. What just basis is there for the exercise of power by one man over his fellows? Such power does not come as an extension of parental authority. To be sure, parents properly have complete control over their children when the children in early life are of unripe judgment, and even retain partial control while the children, though mature, continue to abide in the father's house. Yet any person, as soon as he becomes a reasonable being and wishes to direct his own life, is free to do so and is equal in his rights to all of his fellows.[43] Political power is quite distinct from parental authority. Hooker recognized but one legitimate claim by which a ruler can justify his government over his subjects,—an express agreement between ruler and ruled. He opposed Aristotle's view that the noble and wise have an inherent right to govern, even without the assent of the common people. Usurped power is altogether unlawful. No one who has not the consent of the social group is morally entitled to exercise power over it.[44] Grotius and Pufendorf also accepted this "contract theory" of the origin of the state. But unlike Hooker they recognized other legitimate bases of political power. A ruler can justify his government on the ground that he obtained it through a just war of conquest, that he came to the rescue of a people when nothing but his assistance could have saved them, that he admitted them to dwell on his territory on condition that they be subservient, etc.[45] Yet in all these cases except that of a rule based on just conquest, the people have some voice in the matter. Only in the one case where they have by some crime justly exposed themselves to the wrath of

[42] Hooker: op. cit. I, 10, ⁴, ⁶. Pufendorf, in discussing Hobbes's state of war, insisted that the state of nature is one of peace. Cf. Of the Law of Nature and Nations, II, 2, ⁵⁻⁷. But he used the phrase, "state of peace," only by way of antithesis to Hobbes's extreme position. He did not mean to deny that man's selfishness led to much inconvenience and discord when it was unrestrained by civil authority. His views came out more clearly in his shorter work where he did not set them over against the doctrine of Hobbes. Cf. The Whole Duty of Man, II, 5,⁴⁻⁷.

[43] Grotius: op. cit. II, 5, ¹⁻⁶. Pufendorf: The Whole Duty of Man, II, 3, ⁵⁻⁸.

[44] Hooker: op. cit. I, 10,⁴. Cf. Grotius: op. cit. I, 3,⁸. Pufendorf: op. cit. I, 2, ⁸; II, 6,⁷⁻⁹.

[45] Grotius: op. cit., I, 3,⁸. Pufendorf: op. cit., I, 2, ⁵, II, 9,⁷.

an invading army, have the people lost all claim to some part in the establishment of the government over them.

(c) The degree of authority which a ruler is entitled to exercise varies from case to case. Where the government is founded on contract, the people may grant their ruler full power in perpetuity, full power for a limited time, limited power in perpetuity (i. e., "usufructuary right"), or limited power for a limited time. Where the government is founded on just conquest, the victor's power is quite absolute.[46] Consequently, different governments are justified in aiming at different ends. When the state rests on a contract, the ruler must fulfil his part of the bargain. He must aim to secure the welfare of the people, their security and peace, or any other benefits specified in the contract. But the ruler often has rights over against his subjects. Some governments are for the joint welfare of governors and governed; and some, for the sole benefit of the supreme governor himself. The nature of the origin of the state determines the extent of the power and the obligation of the ruler.[47]

(d) Yet once the government is established, it is supreme. The sovereign power does not rest in the people,—great mischief would result from the adoption of such a principle. The sovereign power rests in the ruler alone, or in the government as constituted by the contract. Once a people have chosen a form of government and transferred power to a ruler, they are bound to obedience. They cannot resume at pleasure rights which they have bargained away. They cannot withdraw from the contract on the ground that the government is unsatisfactory; for all governments have their inconveniences, yet are better than a wholly unorganized society. Nor can a people claim to be free from obligation to obey the ruler on the ground that they were not party to a contract made generations before their birth. For the consent of those who live today was involved in the consent of those who founded the society of which we are a part. "We were then alive in our predecessors, and they in their successors do live still."[48] Thus a government, once formed, has rights over generations yet unborn. It is "unaccountable to all the world."[49]

(e) This theory of the supremacy of the state forced Grotius and Pufendorf to examine the alleged right of subjects to resist their rulers,—i. e., "the right of revolution." They did not question that an individual is entitled to use force in defense of his own rights, when other individuals so assault them that recourse to a judge is impossible.[50] But the use of force to oppose the legally constituted

[46] Grotius: op. cit., I, 3,¹¹. Pufendorf: op. cit., II, 9,⁷.
[47] Grotius: op. cit., I, 3,⁸.
[48] Hooker: op. cit., I, 10,⁸.
[49] Pufendorf: op. cit., II, 9,³. Cf. II, 6, ⁸. Also Grotius: op. cit., I, 3,⁸.
[50] Grotius: op. cit., I, 3,¹⁻³. Pufendorf: op. cit., I, 5,¹⁶⁻¹⁸.

rulers is quite another matter. In discussing this point, Grotius and his followers should have been ready to fall back upon the law of nature as a solution. But they did so only partially. They were unwilling to carry their fundamental ethical principle out to its logical conclusion. They recommended that the minor faults of a prince be overlooked, especially as no one can claim to be in all things perfect. But if the commands of a ruler are clearly contrary to the law of nature, obedience is as wrong as open rebellion would be. A good subject, placed in such a position, will adopt one of two remedies. Either he will flee out of the country, or he will use passive resistance. In the latter case, he will patiently submit to the penalties attached to a failure to perform the commands of the prince. And since acceptance of the penalties is offered as an alternative to performance of the commands, he who uses passive resistance cannot be accused of disobedience to the prince. The majesty of the state is maintained, and the peace of the commonwealth is not disturbed.[51]

On the use of actual armed resistance, Grotius and Pufendorf seem to have been quite unwilling to render an explicit answer. Grotius would never permit rebellion except when it is made in the interests of the whole people, without any great commotion or bloodshed, and without the destruction of many innocent persons. He even seems to have made this limited right of rebellion contingent upon an original reservation of such right to the people at the time when the state was first founded. And finally he did not so much express approval of rebellion under such circumstances as say that he did "not dare condemn indifferently" the use of arms as a last refuge.[52] In other sections of his treatise Grotius was somewhat more explicit. A free people may resist, and even punish by death, a prince who violates his contract with them. And a king who seeks "with a mind truly hostile, the destruction of the whole body of the nation," may be resisted; for the violence of revolt would in such a case be not greater than the violence of submission.[53] Pufendorf was even less willing to face the issue clearly. The section in his longer work which deals with this subject[54] is utterly equivocal. If a prince maliciously tries to destroy an innocent subject and there is no possiblity of escape, many persons, he asserted, would sanction armed resistance. But he avoided agreement by insisting that it is hardly possible to find instances of such a prince. He went so far as to suggest that it is better to obey a command contrary to the law of nature than to resist; and he even advised men to prefer to be killed than to kill. Thus

[51] Grotius: *op. cit.*, I, 4,¹⁻². Pufendorf: *op. cit.* II, 9,⁴.
[52] Grotius: *op; cit.*, I, 4,⁷.
[53] Grotius: *op. cit.*, I, 4,⁸⁻¹⁴.
[54] Pufendorf: *Of the Law of Nature and Nations*, VII, 8,⁵.

the right of revolution is either reduced to a negligible minimum or entirely denied.

5. In criticism of the writers who based their moral and political philosophy on the principle of the law of nature, not much need here be said. Two important steps forward in ethical theory were made, — (1) in setting forth as the ultimate test of right and wrong a law of reason, which is morally prior to all positive enactments, divine as well as human, and is applicable to all conditions of life,—and (2) in recognizing man's social nature and needs, and the consequent necessity for some form of social organization or government. However, there were many weak points which were to require further serious consideration. There was a crying need for an epistemology which would fill in the abstract law of nature with an empirical content. Above all, there was need for a consistent application of reason to political problems without so much conservative bias. Grotius and Pufendorf were primarily jurists; and they had legal, at times almost legalistic, minds. They valued the established order, placing peace ahead of liberty, and thus inevitably tending to sanction the *status quo*. Living as they did in an era of incessant and ruinous warfare, they were led to overstress the dangers of violence. They applied the law of nature rigorously to the relations between different nations where there was no other available means of maintaining peace; but they fell back on external compulsion as a surer means of keeping peace within any one nation. Looking upon questions of origin rather than present utility as the important factor, they were prejudiced in their treatment of popular sovereignty, the supremacy of the state, the extent of the power of a ruler, the right of revolution. Determining the law of nature by the universal consent of nations, they continually tended to slip into the error of confusing morality with legal precedent. As long as questions of origin and contract were stressed, it would be difficult to decide just what rights the people in the various states of Europe were entitled to exercise, which rulers were absolute and which limited in power. On Grotius's own statement, the right of revolution would hinge largely on historical evidence. Yet in spite of such legalism, the advocates of the law of nature furnished a principle which in other hands was to become a means of more successful achievement.

CHAPTER II

THE DEISTS OF THE SEVENTEENTH CENTURY

1. Another source whence Locke drew inspiration and material for his ethical philosophy was the deistic movement. Indeed he stood so close to the deists that he has sometimes been classified as one of their number. Yet his historic relations to the development of deism have not usually been properly defined.

Locke has generally been treated as one who came at the beginning of the deistic movement and prepared the way for the theological radicalism which was to develop in the two or three generations after his death. Though he was decidedly a liberal for his day and stood with the broadest of the churchmen, he was not one of those who felt hostility to traditional Christianity. He did, to be sure, attempt to reduce the required credal statements of the Church to a bare minimum; he rejected many articles of Calvinistic theology, such as predestination and original sin; he took a skeptical attitude to such a central doctrine as that of the Trinity; he set up an empirical test for knowledge which made it difficult to insist upon those doctrines which rested on mysteries;[1] and he stood for the complete and generous toleration of all Protestant sects. And yet at the same time he retained many of the accepted doctrines of orthodoxy, such as the virgin birth and justification by faith; he regarded the Scriptures as the infallible revelation of the divine will; he accepted the belief in miracle and the supernatural origin of the Christian religion. He was essentially constructive in his emphasis, and took a sympathetic attitude toward historic Christianity. Thus he presents a sharp contrast to the radicals who flourished in the eighteenth century. And consequently he is usually treated as a forerunner of deism, who only suggested the direction which theological speculation was about to take. That is, he is regarded as more of a cause than an effect in the history of the development of deism.

Yet such a view of Locke's relation to deism is only half of the truth. For deism, though mainly an eighteenth century product, was not wholly so. Most of the important deistic works came out after Locke's

---

[1] Probably it was Locke's theory of knowledge with its insistence on the empirical test for the validity of ideas, rather than any specifically religious views, which forwarded the deistic movement. His epistemology furnished the later deistic writers with a working tool in their controversies, and with an excuse for sheltering themselves behind the prestige of his revered name. His influence is especially to be seen in Toland's *Christianity not Mysterious* (1696), pp. 7-22, and in Wollaston's *Religion of Nature Delineated* (1724), pp. 69-87.

Essay appeared in 1690. But the beginning of the deistic movement dates far back into the seventeenth century. It began to be a factor in English thought when Lord Herbert of Cherbury first published his *De Veritate* in 1624. This early work was followed by Herbert's second important book, *De Religione Gentilium*, in 1663. Then Blount's writings began to appear in 1679, and a collected edition of them was edited by his pupil Gildon in 1693. Few other books [2] or pamphlets prior to 1690 have survived to indicate the exact extent to which Herbert's teachings were adopted,—a fact which no doubt is at least partly due to the zeal with which heretical works in this period were deliberately destroyed. But various attacks on deism—by Stillingfleet in 1677, by Assheton in 1685, and by Prideaux in 1697—clearly indicate that other deistic writings had been put forth. Deism may not have been presented to the public in many books or lengthy treatises. It may have been disseminated only in pamphlets, in personal letters, in sermons, and in conversation.[3] But at least the movement was a more important factor in the thought of the two generations preceding Locke than could be inferred from its literary remains.

Locke was certainly influenced considerably by the early deists. From his reference to Lord Herbert in the *Essay*,[4] it is possible to infer that he had not had his attention called to the *De Veritate* until after he had formed his own views.[5] But he must have been more familiar with the currents of thought contemporary with himself. He confessedly put forth his work on *The Reasonableness of Christianity* as a means of mediating between the warring theological schools.[6] Certainly his insistence on the messiahship of Jesus and the necessity for revelation was designed to offset the deistic tendency to neglect the historical origins and supernatural character of the Christian faith; it has even been conjectured that he had Blount particularly in mind.[7] Yet he also, at the same time, wished to help the deists in denying the indispensability of a host of speculative dogmas which were being more and more questioned by educated men. In a letter to Limborch he wrote that he deliberately ventured to shock the or-

[2] Hobbes's writings are not here included in the list of deistic literature prior to 1690. For though he is usually classified as a deist, his position in ethics is so unique as to require separate treatment. Blount was a follower of Hobbes in political matters, and edited a volume of extracts from the *Leviathan*. But his other works are generally more akin to the position of Lord Herbert.

[3] Even John Leland, whose book *A View of the Principal Deistical Writers* (1754-1756) is the earliest history of deism, mentioned only Lord Herbert, Hobbes, and Blount in the period before 1690. Gildon included in *The Oracles of Reason* letters signed by R. A. Richardson, Rob. Yaxly, and Au. Rogers. But if these were names of some fellow deists, they have now ceased to be anything but mere names.

[4] *Essay*, I, 2,¹⁵.

[5] It is quite possible, however, that Locke had been familiar with Herbert's *De Religione Gentilium* for some time. This work, being more concerned with religion than *De Veritate* was, would appeal more to Locke's interest. An early essay by Locke, entitled *Sacerdos* (King: *Life of Locke*, p. 186), suggests Herbert's book very strongly, and was written just about the time when Herbert's book appeared. But this conjecture is supported by no external evidence whatever, and hence cannot be relied on.

[6] *Works*, Vol. VII, p. 188.

[7] Gillett: *The Moral System*, p. 35.

thodox by some of his doctrines in the first part of *The Reasonableness of Christianity*, in order that he might render his book useful to the deists.[8] Hence, though he felt that the deists misunderstood historic Christianity in many of their attacks, yet he sympathized with their liberal programme. His interest in theology was quite keen; and as a close observer of contemporary movements, he could hardly have failed to know much of the deistic literature. Which particular writers he was familiar with, no one can now ascertain. But the general influence of the movement on his religious and moral ideas is quite clear.

2. There is no one ethical system which can be pointed to as typically deistic. For deism was, of course, not an ethical, but a theological, movement; and men who agreed in certain theological doctrines might differ in their moral philosophy. The main purposes of Lord Herbert and the other early deists were to find a common basis on which the warring Christian sects might unite, to set aside Scripture as an infallible revelation from God, and to refute certain of the more supernaturalistic articles of the established theologies. Any discussion of ethics was almost incidental. Yet in spite of a lack of attention to strictly moral philosophy, the early deists enunciated a few principles which had important effects.

3. The whole philosophy of the deists, as of the writers on the law of nature, was quite rationalistic. Indeed if their theories of knowledge were alone to be considered, the two groups of writers might with good warrant be classified together. Lord Herbert even claimed that he published his first work with the approval of Grotius.[9] Hence no extended comment on the rationalism of the deists is here required.

The deists, like the other writers, had turned to reason for something universal and absolute, something which stood above the passions of party strife. Reason alone can win men away from the multiplicity of sects to the one true faith. The lower animals, who have to care only for their subsistence in the present, may have a suitable guide to action in their instincts; but man, who has also to anticipate future needs and to prepare for the life to come, must be ruled by reason. All the best men of all ages have followed reason. Reason leads to that which has been known always, everywhere, and by all. It alone destroys misleading prejudices. It alone serves as an adequate moral guide. And though it is "not sufficient to bring us to a perfect knowledge of all things," it is "able to furnish us with enough to make us happy."[10]

---

[8] Letter to Limborch, Oct. 29, 1697. *Works*, Vol. X, pp. 63–64. Also *Cf. Works*, Vol. VII, p. 229, where Locke speaks of "deists and Christians" with equal deference.

[9] In his *Autobiography*, p. 93, Herbert wrote that Grotius was one of the first to read the manuscript of *De Veritate*, that he spoke of it with "more commendations than it is fit for me to repeat," and that he "exhorted me earnestly to print and publish it."

[10] Gildon: preface to *Oracles of Reason*, pp. 1–3. *Cf.* Herbert: *Ancient Religion of the Gentiles*, pp. 255–268, 299–300.

Reason meant, for the early deists, the knowledge of innate principles. This doctrine Lord Herbert stated in a cruder and more extreme form than any other important writer of the century.   There are five definite articles written in the hearts of all men,[11] which "not only we, but all mankind in general, must needs acknowledge."[12] These undeniable propositions are: "that there is one supreme God; that he ought to be worshiped; that virtue and piety are the chief parts of divine worship; that we ought to be sorry for our sins, and repent of them; and that the divine goodness doth dispense rewards and punishments both in this life and after it."[13]   Since our faculties are conformed to the nature of the world without us, these innate propositions convey certain knowledge.   They are "orthodox and catholic," and are sufficient without further additions to procure eternal happiness.[14]   From them all particular rules for concrete moral situations can be deduced.   These five propositions were repeated by other writers in substantially the same form.[15]   Thus they represent the type of rationalism characteristic of the early deists of the seventeenth century.

4. The early deistic writers were the first moralists in modern times to reject entirely the Scriptural sanction in ethics.   Other writers of the seventeenth century had granted that morality could be proved by reason, but had also added that the divine revelation in Scripture would be found to be perfectly harmonious therewith.[16]   Thus, in spite of the admission of the right of reason to examine fundamental issues, the conclusions of reason were usually determined in advance. Reason had to operate within the limits of an external authority, and was constrained to agreement with the letter of Scripture.   For every moral precept in the Bible, some justification had to be found.

The difficulties into which the deists drove their more orthodox contemporaries can be seen in the replies made to the deistic position by Stillingfleet, Assheton, and Prideaux.   Stillingfleet's *Letter to a Deist* is especially illuminating.   His opponent had evidently maintained that Scripture contains things "inconsistent with the wisdom or goodness of God according to a rational persuasion."[17]   He defended Scripture against this attack by three curious arguments.   First,

[11] Herbert: *op. cit.*, pp. 11, 356.

[12] *Idem*, p. 3.

[13] *Idem*, pp. 3-4.   These five articles were more fully treated in the earlier work, *De Veritate*, pp. 210-222.

[14] Herbert: *The Ancient Religion of the Gentiles*, p. 364.

[15] *E. g.*, by "A. W." in a letter to Blount, which Gildon reprinted in the *Oracles of Reason*, p. 197. However, later deists, writing after 1690, were unwilling to subscribe to innate truths.   Wollaston, in 1724, in deference to Locke's criticism in the *Essay*, spoke of the acceptance of "principles that are born with us" as a superficial view, and regarded the alleged innate maxims as due to "the impressions of education."   *Cf. The Religion of Nature Delineated*, pp. 35-36.

[16] *Cf.* Tillotson, John Howe, Edward Fowler, *etc.*   Even Hobbes, though probably only as a matter of discreet policy, endeavored to find sanction for his views in quotations from the Bible.

[17] Stillingfleet: *A Letter to a Deist*, p. 106.

some seemingly immoral provisions are justified on the ground that they have prophetical value. "May not God make use of one vice, whose evil is notorious, to represent another by, whose evil they are more hardly convinced of?"[18] Secondly, some concessions are made to human weakness. "God doth not always require that from men which is best pleasing to himself,"[19] but is willing to accept a lower standard. Thirdly, Scripture makes some recommendations concerning even wrong customs. God does not mean to permit an evil but he does insist on regulating the evil if the evil is going to be done.[20] On one of these three grounds any passage of Scripture can be made acceptable. Thus the more orthodox theologians would say of the whole Bible what Prideaux concludes of the New Testament: "It is so far from having any such flaw therein, that it is the perfectest law of righteousness which was ever yet given unto mankind, and both in commanding of good, as well as in forbidding of evil, vastly exceeds all others that went before it, and prescribes much more to our practise in both, than the wisest and highest moralist was ever able without it to reach in speculation."[21]

With such a Scriptural tradition the deists entirely broke. For them there was no external authority. Reason was given free play. The need vanished of a casuistry which had to go through violent contortions in order to reconcile a supposedly divine command with a developing conscience. The vehemence of the protests against their assaults on the Bible reveals to what extremes the deists must have gone. Perhaps in no respect have the deists as much significance for the history of ethical theory as in their definite rejection of Scripture as a guide in morals.

5. The early deists believed quite frankly in a primitive state of nature. In spite of their theological radicalism, they here remained within the Christian tradition. Since God endowed all men alike with reason and certain fixed innate principles of unquestionable truth, all men naturally began with a clear knowledge on religious and moral questions. Hence before the present corruption of men's minds, there was an earlier period when wisdom and righteousness prevailed. At this fortunate era, "there was no worship of God but in a rational way," and virtue and piety were everywhere taught and practised.[22] Thus instead of a doctrine of the total depravity of man, the deists went to the other extreme, holding to the natural goodness of man's untutored nature.

[18] *Idem.*, p. 130.
[19] *Idem.*, p. 112.
[20] *Idem.*, p. 106.
[21] Prideaux: *A Letter to the Deists*, p. 59.
[22] Blount: *Great is Diana of the Ephesians*, p. 3. *Cf.* also the same view in the later work of Toland: *Christianity not Mysterious*, p. xiii.

The deists consequently had to give an explanation of the origin of error and of evil. The golden age was destroyed by the inordinate ambitions of a few schemers. Certain crafty, intriguing princes imposed superstitious inventions on the common people, in order to procure greater credit and esteem for themselves. Then false prophets and scheming priests introduced vain ceremonies, spread erroneous doctrines, and inculcated immoral practises, in order to establish their own greedy power over their fellows. "The primitive institution of idolatry received its birth from princes, at whose charge it was afterwards educated by ecclesiastics; the one made the idol, and the other ordained the worship of it."[23] Lord Herbert endeavored in his *De Religione Gentilium* to trace the historical steps by which the original purity of the one true religion was followed by the degradation of many false religions.

Yet however corrupted man has become, he still possesses the saving power of reason. Through all the perversions of faith and practise among the heathen, the five innate articles of true religion continued to be held. These fundamental propositions "never were or ever can be concealed from any age or country."[24] Hence in reason lies the possibility of a genuine reformation both in religion and in morals. The natural goodness of man's primitive make-up has never been lost, and is available as a basis for any new effort to establish a high standard of moral living.

6. At no point is the ethical work of the deists more inadequate than in their explanation of the relation of man's duty to God's will. Coming to ethics from the theological standpoint, they unfortunately tended to make ethics a mere appendix to their theological system. The belief in innate principles impressed on the human mind by God so bound morals and theology together that ethics did not gain emancipation from doctrinal ties. The very denial that God can be properly worshiped by sacrifices and ceremonies led to an emphasis on obedience to God's moral commands. Nowhere did the deists explicitly make the nature of goodness dependent upon God's arbitrary fiat. But they did insist upon the intimate connection of man's duty with the divine will. They seem to have resolved the moral life into a matter of imitating the divine perfections. Sometimes morality is placed in an almost mystic allegiance to God. "All vice and wickedness is but a denial and disowning of God to be the supreme, infinite good." He who gives way to lust makes matter more important than God; he who feels envy puts some created thing ahead of God; he who seeks revenge is attacking what God has made.[25] Many of such pas-

---

[23] Blount: *op. cit.*, p. 7. *Cf.* Blount: *Anima Mundi*, p. 13. Also Herbert: *Ancient Religion of the Gentiles*, pp. 3, 12-254, 270-296.

[24] Herbert: *op. cit.*, p. 354.

[25] Blount: *The Oracles of Reason*, pp. 88-89, 95.

sages in the writings of the early deists may have been designed simply
for their homiletical value rather than also as definitions of philosophical
positions. Yet they seem to have erected a theological sanction for
morality which was one of the most important consequences of deism.

7. The deists also suggested in many places a hedonistic basis for
their moral teachings. Those who wrote in the seventeenth century
are not as frankly hedonistic as those in the eighteenth.[26] But surely
a strain of hedonism is to be expected in writers who were so repre-
sentative of the reaction against strict Puritanism. Gildon included
in *The Oracles of Reason* a letter which quotes with approval a long
passage from Epicurus, to show that pleasure is the beginning and
the end of a happy life.[27] Lord Herbert certainly assumed a rather
hedonistic position by an appeal to the sanction of future rewards
and punishments. The rules of virtue and piety "are necessary for
living well and happily here, and to all eternity hereafter."[28] Men
cannot, even by lives of virtue, attain in this world the happiness for
which they hope; and many blessings are here bestowed without
consideration for the merits of the recipients. To be sure, conscience
grants some rewards for virtue and inflicts some punishments for vice
here and now. But men will not receive their full deserts until the
next world.[29] The rewards and punishments of the future are so
important as to have a determining influence on men's conduct in
the present. Hence even though the hedonistic position was not
definitely and consciously adopted by the early deists, the attainment
of happiness was utilized as a sanction for morality. And again the
theological approach of the deists to ethics lent its color to the conclusion reached.

8. In criticism of the ethical principles of the deists, little need be
said. Since their purpose was not to write treatises on moral philosophy, their fragmentary and inadequate discussion of moral problems
cannot be held as a fault against them. They had greater influence
on the history of ethics than they deserved. In their rationalism they
were in complete harmony with the currents of thoughts in their
century, and reveal the same general inadequacies of that position.
Their only prominent merit, in so far as ethical theory is concerned,
was their thorough-going rejection of the Scriptural sanction. Their
complacently optimistic estimate of man's naturally moral character
is most extravagant; and yet this error was to help later moralists
make an effective denial of Hobbes's equally extreme pessimistic
view. In other respects their ethical contribution was quite confused.
They had no one unifying conception like the law of nature which

[26] *Cf.* Wollaston: *The Religion of Nature Delineated,* pp. 58-64.
[27] Gildon: *The Oracles of Reason,* pp. 106-110.
[28] Herbert: *op. cit.,* p. 299.
[29] *Idem.,* pp. 327-333.

would serve as an ultimate criterion. Sometimes harmony with the will of God was suggested as a standard; and sometimes, the attainment of happiness, especially in the future life. To be sure, these suggestions were not developed into an explicit theory. But they serve to erect a theological background for ethics which was destined to continue for some time still in English thought. And in any case they were symptomatic of a confusion of mind which only too frequently accompanies a pious religious attitude. The deists' scientific interest stopped short with their attack on certain doctrines. When they went on into the ethical realm, their sharp definition of terms gave place to merely devotional writing. And though devotional writing would naturally have influence with such reverent minds as that of Locke, yet it is not a satisfactory substitute for a sound philosophical position. Probably it was just the equivocations in the thought of the deists which were partly responsible for Locke's wavering and unsettled explanations of the foundations of the moral law.

CHAPTER III

HOBBES

1. Evidence for the influence of Hobbes upon Locke is almost altogether internal, but is none the less certain. It is probably safe to say that every British moralist for a century after Hobbes was influenced by him. The course of English moral and political philosophy from the middle of the seventeenth century to the middle of the eighteenth has often been treated by historians as the persistent attempt to refute Hobbes's doctrines. No one who, like Locke, lived in close contact with practical problems of governmental administration and parliamentary strife could possible have escaped some knowledge of what Hobbes stood for. Locke, to be sure, professed that he was not "well read" in Hobbes;[1] and when he was accused of having borrowed the thesis of *The Reasonableness of Christianity* from the *Leviathan*, he denied that he knew that his thesis was to be found in the older work.[2] But such professions, however sincere, were probably exaggerations. They were made in the heat of controversy, in order to answer certain attempts to disparage his work by linking him with men who were popularly regarded as dangerous heretics. Hobbes and Spinoza[3] he spoke of as "justly decried names;" and he did not wish to be classed with them. Yet he referred to Hobbes several times in such a way as to show that he was familiar with Hobbes's general principles. He knew that Hobbes made the keeping of contracts contingent upon the power of the commonwealth to punish,[4] based morality upon the principle of self-preservation,[5] and denied the possibility of the freedom of the will.[6] Furthermore it is difficult to believe that he was not, in certain sections of the *Treatises of Government*, consciously opposing the doctrines of the *Leviathan*. Finally the similarities between his discussion of pleasures and pains and that of Hobbes, as well as between his solution of the problem of freedom in the first edition of the *Essay* and that of Hobbes,

---

[1] *Works*, Vol. IV, p. 477.

[2] *Idem*, Vol. VII, p. 420.

[3] Spinoza had slight influence on Locke. Locke probably never read Spinoza's *Ethics;* for if he had, he would hardly have referred to the possibility of a mathematical demonstration of morality as something never yet attempted. He may have seen the *Theologico-Political Tractate*, and been shocked by its attitude toward Scripture. He may also have read the *Political Treatise*, which was largely in harmony with Hobbes, except on questions of liberty of thought and of speech. But Locke's views on toleration clearly had other sources than Spinoza.

[4] *Essay*, I, 2, [5].

[5] King: *Life of Locke*, p. 103.

[6] *Works*, Vol. X, p. 255.

are too striking to be dismissed as mere coincidences. Consequently it seems necessary to conclude that he knew Hobbes's philosophical position, attacked those points which he most disliked, and even accepted, when he was forced to do so by Hobbes's keen logic, some of the less objectionable features of his predecessor's system.[7] Hence even if Locke was not acquainted with all of Hobbes's many (and largely parallel) treatises, he certainly knew the teaching and felt the influence of the older philosopher. The main points in Hobbes which bear upon Locke's ethics are here briefly outlined.

2. Hobbes designed to write a complete system of philosophy on a unified plan, in which he would treat successively of body in general, of that particular body which we call man, and finally of the body politic. The link which bound these three parts of his philosophy together was his mechanistic point of view. He resolved all the changes which go on in the world into motion. And since all of man's passions and actions involve some kind of change, they too must be explained in terms of motion. Thus Hobbes was led to a quite materialistic psychology, which, since it had important effects on his ethical and political theories, calls for special consideration.

When motions from the external world are transmitted through the senses to the brain (or "some internal substance of the head"), they give rise to various "conceptions" under which term Hobbes meant to include sensations, imaginations, thoughts, emotions, *etc*. These conceptions are particular kinds of motions, set up from without. They are not copies or duplications of the motions which produced them, but are "apparitions" or "phantasms."[8] These motions frequently do not stop in the head, but proceed to the heart, which is the seat of the vital motions, such as the circulation of the blood, breathing, nutrition, *etc*., and have the effect of either furthering or hindering the vital motions. In so far as they further the vital motions they are called pleasure, and in so far as they hinder they are called pain. Thus pleasure and pain, which figure so prominently in ethical considerations, are a matter of the harmony or conflict of the internal motions of the body. Moreover, these motions which are designated as pleasures and pains are found to be respectively motions towards or motions away from the external objects which aroused them. In other words, the motion called pleasure is the same thing as appetite or desire; and the motion called pain is the same thing as aversion.[9]

[7] Professor Curtis in his *Outline of Locke's Ethical Philosophy* (1890), p. 22, denies that there is "a trace of indebtedness of Locke to Hobbes." Certainly he errs if negative influence is to be regarded as indebtedness. And even if positive influence alone is meant, as seems probable, there are strong reasons for dissenting from Professor Curtis's view.

[8] *Human Nature*, 2. *Leviathan*, 1.

[9] *Human Nature*, 7, 1–2. *Leviathan*, 6. Hobbes was certainly guilty of confusion at this point in his identification of pleasure with desire. Desire is for an object yet to be attained; pleasure is often found in an object already attained. Locke later fell into this same error, probably as a result of Hobbes's influence, but finally worked his way to a sounder position. *Cf*. below, Book II, Chapter VI, § 4.

With such a view of the constitution of man, Hobbes was logically bound to be egoistic. Man, as part of the world of material forces, naturally seeks what pleases him, and avoids what pains him. He cannot possibly do otherwise, inasmuch as his desires are all connected up entirely with those objects which by furthering the vital motions around the heart arouse pleasure. All his emotions, too, however altruistic they may seem, must be interpreted as self-regarding.[10] No one can either seek or even want anything which is not bound up with his own private pleasure.

This materialistic and egoistic psychology had several consequences for ethical theory which are important to note. (1) Good and bad, in order to have any legitimate meaning, must be defined in terms of pleasure and pain. Moral obligation must fall within the limits of psychological possibility. Since man is so made that he can seek only what pleases him, it cannot be said that he ought to seek anything else. Therefore all the objects which affect a man can be classified as good or bad for him according as he desires them or is repelled by them. Each man's good will be relative to himself; yet in every case it will be a matter of pleasure. And since pleasure is the phantasm of that which furthers the vital motions, the fundamental goods will be the things necessary to a man's preservation, and the secondary goods will be the things which heighten the quality of his living.[11] (2) There is no *summum bonum* or greatest good. Since the good is the pleasant and the pleasant is a certain favorable kind of motion, the good is dependent upon continued motion. A happy life can never be found in repose. There is no utmost end which can make men permanently happy. When one desire has been satisfied, new desires will be aroused. "Felicity . . consisteth, not in having prospered, but in prospering."[12] (3) The will is not a separate thing from the desires. It is not a mysterious faculty which interferes in the orderly sequence of bodily motions. The desires and emotions do not proceed from the will, but are the will. In those cases where a man has but one desire, that desire immediately determines his action, and hence is his will. In those other cases, where, as more frequently happens, a man has alternating and conflicting desires, a suspension of action takes place which is called deliberation. Then finally some one desire is so strong as to end deliberation and result in action. This last desire, "immediately adhering to the action," is what in such cases is meant by the will. Thus in either case, the will is not a faculty apart from desires, but is identical with that one of the desires which prevails.[13] (4) The will cannot be spoken of as voluntary. For the

[10] *Leviathan*, 6.
[11] *Human Nature*, 7, [3]. *Leviathan*, 6.
[12] *Human Nature*, 7, [4-6]. *Leviathan*, 11.
[13] *Human Nature*, 12,[1-2]. *Leviathan*, 6.

will is a matter of the play of bodily motions, and that desire which gains control is simply the strongest of the competing motions. Only actions can be spoken of as voluntary and involuntary, according as they result from the will or inner determination of the man himself or result from some external necessity of nature. The will, however, is itself always a determined thing.[14]

3. When Hobbes turned from his discussion of the nature of man to his social philosophy or study of the body politic, the ethical consequences of his materialistic and egoistic psychology became still more clear. Since men are naturally self-seeking, they will often run counter to each other's interests. "Men by natural passion are divers ways offensive one to another."[15] They think only of themselves and their own private advantage, so that, if unrestrained by superior force, they will try to triumph over and oppress their fellow men. And since their good lies in the objects of their desires, there is no reason why they should not. A man is naturally entitled to whatever he is able to get; he need recognize no rights of others. "Every man by nature hath right to all things." Whatever he can possess either through brute strength or through cunning, he is entitled to enjoy. Whatever he wills is good for him. There is no law to which he is subject except the law of his own desires.[16]

Consequently, though Hobbes, like nearly all the writers of the seventeenth century, believed in a primitive state of nature, he differed from them in the description he gave of it. He was not, as the deists were, under the influence of the Christian tradition; and having no theological doctrine to defend, he was not led by any *a priori* conceptions to adopt their light-hearted view of what the state of nature must have been. He did not even depict the state of nature as Grotius and Pufendorf did, as the state where reason and peace, at least partially, prevailed. He formulated his theory of the state of nature, not by reconstructing the past so as to harmonize history with preconceived dogma, but by drawing logical conclusions from what he regarded the facts of human nature to be. Hence he viewed the state of nature as a state of war,—the war of all against all. An unorganized existence is full of inadequacies and perils for every one concerned. Impulse governs, and bitter conflict is inevitable. Every man possesses, as "the right of nature," the liberty to use all his resources to gain his own ends, no matter what the result is upon others. *Natura dedit omnia omnibus.* As long as men remain in the state of nature, there is no moral law at all. "Nothing can be unjust. The notions of right and wrong, justice and injustice, have there no

[14] *Human Nature*, 12,3-4. *Leviathan*, 6.
[15] *De Corpore Politico*, Part I, 1, 4.
[16] *De Corpore Politico*, Part I, 1, 10. *Philosophical Rudiments*, 1,7-10.

place. . . Force and fraud are in war the two cardinal virtues."
Even contracts solemnly entered into may be freely broken by anyone
clever enough to profit thereby.[17]

Hobbes was eager to insist upon the utter unsatisfactoriness of
this state of nature. He had lived through the chaos of the English
revolution and knew well what strife and incessant warfare meant.
He longed above all else for security. In the state of nature, no man
can be sure of obtaining his own good; for he is at the mercy of his
fellows. "In such condition, there is no place for industry; because the
fruit thereof is uncertain; and consequently no culture of the earth;
no navigation, nor use of the commodities that may be imported by
sea; . . no knowledge of the face of the earth; no account of
time; no arts; no letters; no society; and which is worst of all, continual fear, and danger of violent death; and the life of man, solitary,
poor, nasty, brutish, and short."[18] The state of nature involves such
misery that everyone will endeavor, for his own good, to escape therefrom, and to attain some means of peace and security.

4. Hobbes, like so many of his contemporaries, used the phrase
"the law of nature." And he too identified it with "the dictate of right
reason."[19] Reason is just as much a part of the nature of man as his
passion or impulse, and is shared as a common possession by all men
alike. Moreover, reason is the only part of man's nature which can
be spoken of as in any sense laying down a law. For passions are
essentially unruly and chaotic, recognizing no authority except their
own urgency. Reason, however, is disciplinary and directive, specifying the conditions necessary to be observed for the attainment of
the desired goal.[20] Hence it alone of all man's faculties defines a
law. And its law may well be called the law of nature.

But in all other respects than in treating the law of nature as the
dictate of reason, Hobbes differed greatly with the other writers of
the century. According to him, the law of nature is not to be found
in "the consent of all nations, or the wisest and most civil nations;"
for the nations are often in conflict and each claims to be the wisest.
Nor is the law of nature in the common consent of mankind; for then
no man could violate the law of nature, since his own consent is part
of the common consent. "To receive the laws of nature from the
consents of them who oftener break than observe them is in truth
unreasonable."[21] Nor finally is the law of nature found in any innate
imprints on the mind of man; for Hobbes nowhere recognized any
such inborn principles.

---

[17] *De Corpore Politico*, Part I, 1, [10], 2, [10]. *Leviathan*, 13–14.
[18] *Leviathan*, 13. *De Corpore Politico*, Part I, 1,[12–13]. *Philosophical Rudiments*, 1,[12–14].
[19] *Philosophical Rudiments*, 1, [15]. *De Corpore Politico*, Part I, 1, [14].
[20] *De Corpore Politico*, Part I, 2, [1]. *Philosophical Rudiments*, 2, [1].
[21] *Philosophical Rudiments*, 2, [1]. *De Corpore Politico*, Part I, 2, [1].

Rather the law of nature is, for Hobbes, that dictate of reason which specifies "what are the conditions of society or of human peace."[22] It is the procedure by which, and by which alone, escape from the state of nature would be effected. When men exercise their natural rights as they freely wish, they defeat their own ends and imperil their own existence. Reason, "conversant about those things which are either to be done or omitted for the constant preservation of life," suggests as a law that which affords the only way out to peace. Among its articles are these: that men relinquish at least a part of the right they by nature have to all things; that they perform their covenants; that they exhibit due gratitude for favors received; that they render themselves helpful to others; that they recognize the rights of others equally with their own *etc.*[23] These articles of the law of nature are in no sense arbitrary, but are discovered by reason from a survey of human nature. Hence they are immutable and eternal.[24]

Nevertheless, the law of nature is not binding in the state of nature. It seems strange in reading Hobbes to find that what he called the law of nature has no constraining power in what he called the state of nature. Yet he doubtless used such terminology in order to emphasize his disagreement with the principles advocated by Grotius. Where there is no power present in society which can guarantee that others will be forced to obey the law of nature, a man is not under obligation to that law himself. *Inter arma silent leges.* Though the law of nature alone can save men from the state of war, yet it has no moral force until the situation which it would remedy has been superseded. Any one who yields obedience to the law of nature while he still lives in the state of nature will only "procure his own certain ruin, contrary to the ground of all laws of nature."[25] In other words, the laws of nature "are not properly laws, but qualities that dispose men to peace and obedience. When a commonwealth is once settled, then are they actually laws, and not before."[26] The laws of nature have binding moral force only when they have actual civil force behind them too.

Hobbes was willing, however, to grant the law of nature a certain slight function even in the state of nature. It cannot control men's actions, but it should "oblige the conscience." In other words, men should be desirous of obeying the law of nature, as soon as conditions arise which make it prudent for them to do so. The law of nature binds *in foro interno* always, but it binds *in foro externo* only in so far as men are safe in following it.[27]

[22] *Philosophical Rudiments*, I, ¹.
[23] *Leviathan*, 14–15. *Philosophical Rudiments*, 2–3. *De Corpore Politico*, Part I, 2–4.
[24] *Philosophical Rudiments*, 3, ²⁹. *Leviathan*, 15.
[25] *Philosophical Rudiments*, 5, ¹⁻². *De Corpore Politico*, Part I, 6, ¹⁻²; Part II, 1, ⁶. *Leviathan*, 15–17.
[26] *Leviathan*, 26.
[27] *Leviathan*, 15. *Philosophical Rudiments*, 3, ²⁷.

5. Since the state of nature is intolerable and the law of nature has in itself no power to compel obedience, men seek to bring about a state of civil government. This civil state is not a natural thing; it is an artificial product. Yet expediency compels men to create it, and successful exercise of power justifies its existence. Only when there is "some mutual and common fear to rule them," will men live in peace.[28] Only when there is some central authority able to enforce laws, will men give up the full extent of the rights to which they are by nature entitled. Only when there is an overwhelmingly superior power which is able to restrain men in the ways in which they are so objectionable to one another, to crush the individual's lust for power, and to put an end to all strife, will men ever be able to attain an era of concord, of secure enterprise, of human welfare.[29]

Thus the state rests on a contract. Hobbes emphasized this contract as much as any other writer in the history of political theory. All existing civil societies are based on solemn agreements between ruler and ruled. The agreement of a people with a prince may have been entered into freely, with no pressure on his part, simply that the people might secure protection against each other; or it may have been entered into under threat of death, through the power of conquest, in order that the people might secure protection against the prince himself.[30] But in either case the contract or covenant is binding. The power of the sovereign is to be justified, not by how it was secured, but by its ability to control. It may be true that "there is scarce a commonwealth in the world whose beginnings can in conscience be justified."[31] Certainly "the original of all great and lasting societies consisted not in the mutual good will men had toward each other, but in the mutual fear they had of each other."[32] Yet a wise ruler will not seek justification for the source of his power, nor approbation of his past acts; rather he will rest his claims to obedience upon the security and peace which his enforcement of law guarantees. The contract on which the state rests was the result of distressing fear. But that fear, so far from invalidating the right of the ruler, gives him indisputable sovereignty.

Hobbes's view of the contractual origin of civil society led him to emphasize one quality which a successful commonwealth must possess. He did not deny that a commonwealth may have any one of a number of forms of government; for though he himself for several reasons [33] preferred a monarchy to either an oligarchy or a democracy, yet he

28 De Corpore Politico, Part I, 6, 4.
29 Leviathan, 17. Philosophical Rudiments, 5. De Corpore Politico, Part I, 6, 8–11.
30 Philosophical Rudiments, 8, 1. De Corpore Politico, Part II, 3, 2.
31 Leviathan: Conclusion.
32 Philosophical Rudiments, 1, 2.
33 De Corpore Politico, Part II, 5, 4–8. Philosophical Rudiments, 10, 4–19. Leviathan, 19.

granted that the body politic may, at the time of the original contract, create whatever form of government, monarchic, aristocratic,
or democratic, they are able to create and happen to prefer. But he
did insist that this government, of whatever form it may be, must
be absolute. Contrary to Grotius and Pufendorf, he did not regard
the contract as capable of limiting the power of the rulers. While
the earlier writers made the governors of a state supreme, Hobbes
made them also absolute. A limited monarch is a contradiction in
terms. For the sovereign must be able to guarantee security against
any combination of foes, to enforce any law and execute any punishments, to appoint any necessary officials, to determine policies for
any emergency which may arise, *etc.* To limit a sovereign would be
only partially to abolish the state of nature; and hence there would
still be left something of the state of war which might flare up at any
time and overwhelm civil society altogether.[34]

And since the sovereign power is absolute, it must also be above
all law. That which creates law is not itself bound to obedience.
Every ruler will of course be brought to judgment by God; but he
cannot be judged by any of his subjects. He is unpunishable. His
form of government, once brought into being, cannot even be altered
by his people. All his subjects are under obligation to obey him, since
he has power to compel them; but he is under no obligation to them,
since they have no power to compel him. Though a ruler ought of his
own accord to obey the law of nature, yet such obedience is voluntary,
and no infraction of it can be punished except by God alone.[35]

His theory of political absolutism forced Hobbes to consider the
problem of the rights of the individual conscience. With this problem
he had great difficulty, but offered two solutions. In the first place,
he believed that "the profit of the sovereign and subject goeth always
together."[36] "Governing to the profit of the subjects is governing to
the profit of the sovereign."[37] Hence there is no reason why an issue
of conscience should arise between a ruler and any of his subjects.
However, the actual political situation in England was such that this
solution must have seemed, even to Hobbes himself, almost wholly
verbal. In the second place, Hobbes believed that, if an issue of
conscience did arise, the will of the sovereign should prevail. No
man is infallible in his reasoning; and consequently there is need for
an "interpreter of right reason."[38] Such an interpreter is afforded in
the sovereign. Most men are not competent to decide truly concerning
good and evil. Where, therefore, a conflict of conscience arises, the

[34] *De Corpore Politico,* Part II, 1. *Philosophical Rudiments,* 5–6. *Leviathan,* 18, 20.
[35] *Leviathan,* 18. *Philosophical Rudiments,* 6, [14], 7, [2], 12, [4], 13, [2].
[36] *De Corpore Politico,* Part II, 5, [1].
[37] *Idem,* Part II, 9, [1].
[38] *Philosophical Rudiments,* 15, [17]. *Cf.* also 12, [1].

subject should subordinate his conscience to the will of the ruling power. The sin, if any is committed, is not his who obediently performs the act, but is his who commands the act.[39] All subjects may then conscientiously obey all the civil laws, and will be themselves innocent of all reproach. To disobey or to defy the established government is a far worse sin than any which might be committed by complying with law,—indeed it is the worst possible sin. For it would be a step towards anarchy, and would thus lead to a restoration of the hideous state of nature in which moral distinctions do not exist at all. Between the lawless state of nature and complete subservience to established civil law there is no middle ground. Thus Hobbes tolerated no breach to be made in his thorough-going political absolutism. He was more unwilling than Grotius had been to admit a possible moral justification for rebellion. And it was probably his influence which later led Pufendorf, who followed Grotius closely on most points, to adopt a more conservative attitude in condemning all armed resistance to the established civil power.

6. Hobbes's writings certainly deserve the attention which has been directed to them ever since they first called forth a storm of opposition. It was fortunate for the subsequent development of ethical thought in England that he made so radical and consistent a presentation of the tenets of a materialistic, egoistic, and politically absolutistic philosophy. His work served as a corrective to the light-hearted optimism which did not grapple seriously enough with the unpleasant aspects of the moral life of man. Hobbes for the first time raised such fundamental questions of psychology, as, for example, whether man is really the delightfully beautiful creature which deism made him out to be. It was necessary to consider man's nature more carefully and to reflect upon the possible value of coercion, of governmental restraint. Moreover, Hobbes for the first time gave a fruitful definition of the law of nature as that which reason finds to be requisite for the existence of an orderly society. He did not derive the law of nature from innate imprints, from common consent, or from a sort of timeless contemplation of human nature. All such methods of deriving it looked to the past, and Hobbes looked to the future. He derived the law of nature from human needs, from a consideration of the best means of getting from an unsatisfactory present to a particular kind of desired future. Hence he showed how to give empirical content to a law which until his time had been uselessly abstract.

But Hobbes set more problems than he solved. In the first place, if, as he said, the law of nature is not binding in the state of nature, how can it ever become binding in any condition of life? Moral obligation is not first created by legal enactment. If Hobbes had said that men were not in duty bound to be too trusting in their fellows, and need not under conditions of savage strife take risks which they could safely take in a smoothly running social order, he could have made out a good case. But he started with a state utterly devoid of moral obligation, and ended with a state in which moral obligation was present. Such a transition is impossible. If a man is free from all ethical claims upon him before he enters into political society, he remains free afterwards. He can simply use the advantages of that society without having to render compensation therefor. If contracts do not hold in a state of nature, the social contract is itself null and void. Hobbes seems to have confused moral obligation with power sufficient to compel obedience to the obligation, or duty with the motive power to perform that duty. Thus he tended to make right a matter of might, and confused the moral with the positive law. If men had ever existed in Hobbes's state of nature,—as they undoubtedly have not,—they would never have escaped therefrom.

In the second place, why is not the law of nature binding in the state of nature before the dawn of civil society? Hobbes made the law of nature identical with the dictate of reason operating in the interests of man; and surely he would not want man to refrain, even in the state of nature, from using every means to promote his own welfare. Hobbes should at least have made the law of nature progressively binding on man, as society becomes more orderly and peaceful. In that case, however, both his state of nature and his absolute monarchy would have come to be non-existent extremes between which the real life of man falls. Just as monarchs were viewed as subject to the law of nature even though they remain, after all other men are in civil society, in the state of nature, so men ought to have been made equally subject at all times to the same law. But Hobbes was unwilling to take the logical step here. For had he taken it, he would have weakened his defense of political absolutism, and might have had to recognize the right of revolution.

In the third place, where does ultimate political authority reside? Hobbes was the first one in modern times to make the question of sovereignty acute. No such notion as that of sovereignty had existed for medieval thought. Law was supreme, and all men, ruler as well as ruled, were under law.[40] Though the idea of sovereignty was suggested by Grotius, he remained on the whole within the medieval position. But Hobbes thrust the problem into a conspicuous position where it could no longer be avoided. Does the King possess the final political power? or does Parliament? or do the people? The conflict

[40] Cf. Gierke: Political Theories of the Middle Ages, pp. 71–86. Also Maitland: The Constitutional History of England, p. 101.

of king and Commons was raging in England when Hobbes wrote; and he merely made the moral questions involved explicit. If the battle is not simply to the strongest, where is the moral right to ultimate control to be located? Hobbes suggested one solution to this problem. But with the rise of political parties men of different mind would not allow his solution to go unquestioned.

To these problems, which Hobbes so violently raised, Locke later directed his thoughtful attention.

CHAPTER IV

FILMER

1. While in any general history of the political thought of the seventeenth century, Sir Robert Filmer deserves only a minor place, yet he probably merits more attention than he usually receives. The quite disparaging remarks by which most critics entirely dispose of him in a casual way are uncalled for. It may be true that he made no important contribution of a positive nature to a philosophy of the state. There is hardly anything of permanent value in his *Patriarcha*. But he brought forward in his *Observations on Aristotle* and especially in his *Observations on Hobbes, Milton, Grotius, and Hunton* several acute criticisms of current views. He was keener at destructive than at constructive work. It seems at times as if those critics who brush him aside in a footnote were acquainted with only one, and that the least creditable, of his works.

Moreover, in any attempt to outline the influences which helped to form Locke's moral and political views, Filmer must certainly have more than an incidental mention. Hobbes, because of his rejection of the claims of the Church to large grants of power, could not serve as a rallying-point for the English Tories, who were high churchmen in theology as well as absolutists in politics. But Filmer did provide a suitable rallying-point for these monarchists in the second half of the seventeenth century. So Locke took the trouble to refute in wearisome detail the principles which Filmer advanced. Locke's philosophy of the state developed in the midst of a combat with the men who shared Filmer's attitude to the royal power. The topics which Locke treated and the form in which his conclusions were cast reflect the influence of this struggle. The closing paragraph of the preface to Locke's *Treatises of Government* indicates that he was familiar with at least the more important of Filmer's writings. Hence, as an aid to the understanding of Locke's work, a short summary of Filmer's views is here given.

2. Filmer accepted the general supposition current in the seventeenth century that political problems can only be solved by examining the origin of the state.[1] But he entirely rejected the theory held alike

---

[1] Hobbes warned statesmen not to seek to justify their various governments by considerations of genesis and origin. But he does not seem to have realized that the same warning might be given to political philosophers in reference to their theories of civil society in general. Not until the utilitarian school arose, did anyone reject the notion that governments were to be justified on the grounds of their origin.

by two such contrasted thinkers as Grotius and Hobbes, that government arose from a voluntary contract made by persons who previously lived in the freedom and independence of a state of nature. He saw more clearly than those greater predecessors of his the implications for political philosophy of the belief in man's original equality, and endeavored to prove that that belief would lead, if logically developed, to a recognition of the right of revolution. And as he denied utterly the right of revolution, he also denied man's original equality and the political contract. Of course this argument would have force against those only who regarded governments as possessing the right to unquestioned and unchallenged rule. But as Grotius and Hobbes, the former only a trifle less outspokenly than the latter, maintained that governments, once established, not only were supreme, but were also permanently entitled to the obedience of their subjects, the argument did have force against them. Starting with the assumption of the soundness of absolute monarchy, he was necessarily led to deny the political contract, the state of nature, and the original equality of mankind.

In demonstrating the inconsistency between the idea of an original state of nature and the idea of a fixed and absolute government, Filmer had to vary the course of his argument to meet the differences between Grotius's and Hobbes's views. On the one hand, he insisted against Grotius that, if the law of nature were binding in the state of nature, no contract of permanently valid force could be supposed to have been effected. For (1) the contract would in that case have to be supposed to have been made by the "unanimous consent" of all persons concerned. No man could be bound by an agreement to which he was not a party. Yet it is hardly possible that all men did at the same instant in the past agree to change from their free state to civil society.[2] (2) The contract to leave the state of nature would not have been made unless there had been great inconveniences in that state. Such inconveniences would not have been present unless there had been war. War would not have been just unless certain men possessed a title over their fellows. But all men in the state of nature are supposed to have been equal. Therefore, either no occasion for a contract would have occurred, or the contract was founded on injustice, in which case it can have no binding power.[3] (3) If men were free to change from the state of nature to subjection to a common ruler, they are free to change back again. "It is as lawful for men to alter their wills as their judgments."[4] A group of men may have delegated some of their power to others; but they would hardly have

---

[2] Filmer: *Observations on Hobbes, Milton, Grotius, and Hunton*, pp. 70-71.
[3] *Idem*, p. 66.
[4] *Idem*, p. 70.

renounced all their rights and enslaved themselves entirely. (4) If a government depends on a contract made in the past, the extent of its power can not be known unless the exact terms of the contract are preserved. To assume that the grant of power was complete is a precarious foundation for any government.[5]

On the other hand Filmer insisted with equal force against Hobbes that if the state of nature was lawless, no binding contract and no legitimate government could have been made at all. To be sure he agreed much more with Hobbes than with Grotius; for he like Hobbes refused to recognize a law of nature as obligatory in the absence of civil power to enforce it. Laws which rest on a common sentiment without force at their disposal are not really laws, but only customs; and customs can be freely violated unless "the approbation of the supreme power" gives them legality.[6] But nevertheless, though agreeing with Hobbes's identification of right with might, he denied Hobbes's theory of the origin of government by contract in a state of nature. Contracts entered into by those who do not live under law are, as Hobbes himself admitted, of no value. The parties to such contracts may violate their pledges whenever they are able to do so profitably and successfully. A man may temporarily, for his own advantage, cease to exercise his full rights; but he cannot be regarded as having relinquished them permanently. He may utilize a government erected on a contract in so far as it serves his purposes; but he may also disobey and even overthrow it at will.[7] Thus if, as Hobbes acknowledged, governments are absolute, they cannot have been preceded by any state of nature. There never can have been any "right of nature," nor any "war of all against all." Moral obligations now exist; but since they could not have arisen out of a freedom obligation, such freedom never existed.[8] The state of nature in which men lived on a basis of equality and freedom should be rejected as dangerously erroneous doctrine.[9]

3. Having rejected the contract theory of government and the belief in a state of nature, Filmer had to find some other basis for the right to rule. Since he never questioned the current assumption that the validity of political society depended on its origin, and since he denied that men existed in a pre-political state, he of necessity was driven to conclude that government has existed as long as the human race. That is, he maintained that the true basis and origin of government lie in the political power bestowed on Adam by God at the time of creation. Adam was given the right to rule over Eve as well as

[5] *Idem*, p. 55.
[6] *Idem*, pp. 44–45.
[7] *Idem*, pp. 4–7.
[8] *Idem*, pp. 2–3.
[9] *Idem*, p. 36.

over the animals and the earth itself. Also, both from the fact of
generation and from the fact that he alone could furnish them with the
means of sustenance, he came to have complete power over his children and his children's children. "Every man that is born is so far
from being free-born, that by his very birth he becomes a subject
to him that begets him."[10] That is, "creation made man prince of
his posterity."[11] Moreover, this government which was set up from
the beginning of time has been handed on as a patrimony to Adam's
heirs. Sometimes Adam's power was divided among several heirs,
and small nations thus arose. Then again two or more nations were,
by the union of great families, merged into one large empire.[12] But
in no other way than by inheritance from Adam can a valid and
legitimate right to rule be obtained. "Adam being commanded to
multiply and people the earth, and to subdue it, and having dominion
given him over all creatures, was thereby the monarch of the whole
world; none of his posterity had any right to possess anything, but
by his grant or permission, or by succession from him."[13]

Since political organization arose from the power bestowed upon
Adam, Filmer maintained that government must of course always
be monarchical. Adam was the lord of creation; and those who in-
herit the rule from him are likewise kings. Men are endowed by
God "with a natural propensity to monarchy."[14] Monarchy excels
all other forms of government; for it possesses "the best order— the
greatest strength, the most stability, and easiest government."[15] A
democracy is most to be avoided; for no matter how virtuous a group
of men are, they cannot successfully manage either the legislative
or the executive power. "There is no tyranny to be compared to
the tyranny of a multitude."[16] Even under the worst of kings the
people will be better off than under their own management, for in
order to benefit himself, a ruler must look out for the welfare of his
subjects,[17] whereas a popular majority recognizes no interests but
its own.

Moreover, monarchy should always be absolute. "The prerogative
of a king is to be above all laws."[18] "The prince is not bound by the

[10] Filmer: *Observations on Aristotle, etc.*, p. 68.

[11] Filmer: *Patriarcha*, p. 11. Filmer here took a different position than that of either Grotius or
Hobbes. (*Cf.* Hobbes: *Philosophical Rudiments*, 9, 1–2.) He maintained that children are always
subject to the dominion of their fathers. Though the prince of a realm may release the children of
one of his subjects from obedience to their father in order to attach them directly to himself, yet the
children never have any rights inherently of their own. *Cf. Observations on Hobbes, Milton, Grotius,
and Hunton*, p. 62.

[12] Filmer: *Patriarcha*, p. 21.

[13] Filmer: *Observations on Aristotle*, Preface.

[14] Filmer: *Patriarcha*, p. 49.

[15] *Idem*, p. 53.

[16] *Idem*, p. 70. *Cf. Observations on Aristotle*, p. 59.

[17] Filmer: *Observations on Aristotle*, pp. 21, 72.

[18] Filmer: *Patriarcha*, p. 99.

laws."[19] There was no rival power appointed by God to supervise Adam's rule. Hence though a king may desire a council or parliament in order to acquaint him with the needs of the people and to give popular approval to his acts, yet he governs in his own right alone.[20] There must be some final court beyond which no further appeal can be taken; and that court has by God's ordinance been placed in the will of the king.[21] Hence rebellion against the king is always wrong. Sometimes, to be sure, God removes a wicked prince by raising up his subjects against him, but even though God may use rebels for his wise purposes, the rebels are themselves "sinful and damnable."[22] Subjects must obey every command of their king with no thought of their own wish or their own safety. While Grotius reluctantly sanctioned revolution under certain conditions of "great and certain danger," Filmer replied that no subject is competent to judge when the danger becomes sufficiently great and certain.[23] While even Hobbes exempted men from obeying commands which ordered them to take their own lives or to give up their means of livelihood, Filmer refused to tolerate such slight exemptions. In Filmer the absolutism of the monarch reaches its most extreme statement.

One interesting inconsistency in Filmer's political theory is to be found in his attitude toward usurpers. Since he made the royal prerogative a matter of inheritance from Adam, he should logically have refused to countenance the rule of usurpers altogether. But he did not do so. He probably was too much aware of the impossibility of establishing the legal rights of the kings of Europe in his day by any table of descent from Adam. So he insisted that in cases where the line of a usurper has been on the throne for so long a time that all knowledge of the rightful heir has been lost, the usurper is to be taken as the true heir and obeyed accordingly.[24] Even a new usurper who drives the just king from his throne should be obeyed whenever submission to him serves the best interests of the subjects; for by preserving their own lives the subjects may some day be able to restore their true sovereign.[25] Filmer thus justified all of the royal houses of Europe, but at the cost of violating his own patriarchal theory of government. He had, to be sure, announced a principle which, so long after Adam's death, was incapable of application and barren of value,

[19] *Idem*, p. 101.
[20] *Idem*, pp. 107–121.
[21] Filmer: *The Free-holders' Grand Inquest*, p. 40. This whole treatise was designed to show that the English House of Commons had no legislative powers, but only the right to assent to the royal will, and similarly that the House of Lords had power to give counsel, but not power to command their counsel to be accepted.
[22] Filmer: *Patriarcha*, pp. 22–23.
[23] Filmer: *Observations on Hobbes, Milton, Grotius, and Hunton*, p. 54.
[24] Filmer: *Observations on Aristotle*, p. 69.
[25] *Idem*, p. 68.

and so had to content himself with an approximation. And in his practical advice on *Directions for Obedience to Government in Dangerous and Doubtful Times*, he switched over to a mere authoritarianism and a blanket defense of the *status quo.*

4. Filmer certainly had less of a positive nature to contribute to Locke's moral and political philosophy than any other of the prominent thinkers of the seventeenth century. His influence was almost wholly negative and antagonistic. In his reliance on the Bible he marked a backward step in ethical theory. His patriarchal view was built on a Scriptural basis;[26] and its validity was a matter of the exegesis of texts. Nothing else than a dogmatic insistence on the authority of Scriptural passages could be offered for his assumptions as to Adam's monarchical power, the parents' right to complete control over their children, *etc.* Moreover, he confused philosophic principle with historic fact; and consequently, he exposed his whole system to attack on the ground that alleged facts were not historically correct.

Filmer's merit lay in his criticism of the established traditions. It is significant that he, just before the time of Locke, should have comprehended so accurately the connection between the ideas of the state of nature and of the right of revolution. He clearly showed that men living as equals, whether under the law of nature or not, could not, by any contract free or forced, be construed as signing away for all time their rights and the rights of their children. If the supreme power of decision once rested with them, that supreme power could never be arbitrarily placed beyond their control in a ruler who governed solely in his own right. Grotius who believed in a state of nature under the control of the law of nature could never consistently maintain the established power of a settled government; and Hobbes who believed in a lawless state of nature could never logically reach any legitimate principle of government at all. So Filmer, wishing to maintain political absolutism, rejected the state of nature entirely and the anarchic conception of men's natural equality. Locke of course, though recognizing the error in the reasoning of Grotius and Hobbes, was to choose the other alternative solution. But it may well have been in Filmer's writings that he discovered a conclusive argument against the outcome to which Grotius, who began with the law of nature, had by the force of tradition and the pressure of political conditions been led.

[26] *Idem*, Preface.

Book II

The Moral Philosophy of Locke

CHAPTER I

LOCKE'S THEORY OF KNOWLEDGE

1. In order to understand Locke's moral and political philosophy, it is quite necessary to keep in mind his general epistemological views. His conclusions in ethics were naturally determined to a large extent by his method of procedure, which in turn was influenced very considerably by his theory of knowledge. There can be traced in all his allusions to, and discussions of, moral and political problems the effects of the epistemological principles set forth in the *Essay*, with the same inadequacies, the same shifting of ground, and the same limitations of a rationalistic position.

Locke's disciples and critics during the last two centuries have expounded his epistemological position in a variety of quite different ways. Some of them have made him a sensationalist, and others have regarded him as an intellectualist. It is surprising that a consideration of the same *Essay* should lead to such diverse interpretations. Yet the *Essay* was, as Locke himself states, "written by incoherent parcels," [1] and its full thesis is not clearly presented. Though called an *Essay concerning Human Understanding* the first two books deal principally with ideas, the third book with words, and the fourth book with knowledge and probability—while the human understanding itself receives only incidental treatment. This apparent neglect of that faculty of the mind for which the whole treatise is named is doubtless due to the fact that Locke realized that he shared the general view of his contemporaries as to the importance of the understanding, and wished to stress what he deemed his unique contribution, namely, his theory of ideas. [2] Had he lived in a different age, when the prevailing philosophic attitude was not so rationalistic, he might have given a better balanced account of "the original, certainty, and extent of human knowledge." [3] Yet in spite of the almost exclusive emphasis upon ideas

---

[1] *Essay*, Epistle [4].

[2] *Idem*, Introduction [2].

[3] That Locke was quite aware of his slighting of the faculty of understanding in the *Essay* is evident from a later comment he made on this point. Stillingfleet had been misled by the lack of proportion in Locke's treatment of the matter in the *Essay*. So in his second letter to Stillingfleet Locke wrote: "Because treating in it [*i.e.*, in the *Essay*] of the understanding, which is nothing but the faculty of thinking, I could not well treat of that faculty of the mind, which consists in thinking, without considering the immediate objects of the mind in thinking, which I call ideas: and therefore in treating of the understanding, I guess it will not be thought strange that the greatest part of my book has been taken up in considering what these objects of the mind, in thinking, are; whence they come; what use the mind makes of them, in its several ways of thinking; and what are the outward marks whereby it signifies them to others, or records them for its own use." *Works*, Vol. IV, p. 134. Yet unfortunately

and the corresponding slighting of the understanding, there are frequent passages, both in the *Essay* and in his controversial writings, which should prevent a sensationalistic interpretation of his system of thought.

According to Locke, knowledge comes about only when the understanding or reason observes the agreement or disagreement of our ideas. In spite of ambiguities and consequent confusions which arise later in his epistemological theories, he always consistently held to this central point, that there are two distinct steps necessary to obtain knowledge—the possession of ideas and the grasp by the reason of the relations between those ideas. There is "nothing truer than that it is not the idea which makes us certain without reason, or without the understanding: but it is as true, that it is not reason, it is not the understanding, that makes us certain without ideas." [4] On the one hand, ideas, singly or in any combination, are not the completed product we call knowledge; and their relationships do not constitute knowledge until the reason observes these relationships. On the other hand, reason cannot evolve knowledge from its own activity—indeed it can not even be active without ideas as a material with which, and with which alone, it is able to work. Hence, both the possession of ideas and observation thereof by reason are essential to knowledge; and each of these two elements must in turn be briefly examined.

2. In presenting his theory of ideas Locke first raised the problem of the source or channel through which ideas can be obtained. In order to ascertain the bounds of knowledge, it is first of all necessary to "inquire into the original of those ideas, notions, or whatever else you please to call them, which a man observes and is conscious to himself he has in his mind." [5] It is rather striking that Locke sought to determine the genesis of ideas before he discussed their nature, that he endeavored to tell how we get them before he defined what they are. Much of the ambiguity which occurs in his use of the term idea later in the *Essay* is due to his failure to settle at the outset exactly what the subject matter is with which he is dealing. But Locke's problem was set him by what he considered the inadequacies of Descartes. Unwilling to accept the intrinsic clearness of ideas as the test of their validity, he had at once to find a suitable test in the consideration of their origin. So he plunged into this problem of genesis at the outset of the *Essay*, and never returned to a discussion of the nature of ideas. His critics must follow his procedure, and waive for a time the question of what is meant by ideas, in order to discover how, according to Locke, they arise.

what Locke supposed would not be thought strange has led most of his critics astray, both in his own day and ever since.

[4] *Works*, Vol. IV, p. 59.
[5] *Essay*, Introduction [3].

The first book of the *Essay* tells us how ideas do not arise; and the second book tells how they do. According to the argument of the first book, ideas are not innate—*i.e.*, they are neither present as conscious content at birth, nor are they implicitly present so as to be revealed by future mental development. The proofs for this position are that there are no universally accepted ideas or principles, speculative or practical; [6] that the persons whose minds are least affected by experience are also least likely to be aware of the alleged innate truths; [7] that the alleged innate truths are not the beginning, but the goal of the mental life, [8] and are reached, not by unfolding from within, but by reflection on the material which comes to the mind from without; [9] that widespread acceptance of certain standards is due to social tradition, education, and the force of habit; *etc.*[10] All of this discussion seems almost futile today. But Locke regarded it as necessary, in order to sweep aside various prejudices which might otherwise make men unfavorably inclined to an exposition of his positive doctrine. All sorts of dogmatism in Locke's day, theological and political, was, as has been shown, seeking sanction in God-given truths implanted in the human mind at birth. Hence if ever an empirical position was to gain a hearing, the theory of innate ideas had to be adequately refuted.

The positive statement of Locke's theory of the genesis of ideas comes in the second book. The mind is at first like a "white paper, void of all characters, without any ideas;" [11] and all the endless variety of ideas with which it comes to be furnished are derived from experience. Experience has two aspects, or is of two varieties; it includes the observation both of "external sensible objects" (*i.e.*, sensation) and of "the internal operations of our minds perceived and reflected on by ourselves" (*i.e.*, reflection). "These two are the fountains of knowledge, whence all the ideas we have, or can naturally have, do spring." [12] These initial ideas derived from experience are "simple ideas" [13] and constitute the indispensable basis of knowledge. Yet knowledge is not, for that reason, limited to the realm of the simple ideas. Simple ideas are not, in their simplicity, the only valid ideas, nor the sole material of knowledge. They are worked over, by the mental faculties of composition, of abstraction, and of comparison, into what are called "complex ideas." [14] These complex ideas are not, to be sure, immediately given in sense experience; but they are constructed out of the

[6] *Idem*, I, 2, 10-11.
[7] *Idem*, I, 1, 5.
[8] *Idem*, I, 1, 19, 25-26.
[9] *Idem*, I, 3, 23-24.
[10] *Idem*, I, 2, 22.
[11] *Idem*, II, 1, 2.
[12] *Idem*, II, 1, 2-4.
[13] *Idem*, II, 2, 1, 8, 1.
[14] *Idem*, II, 11, 6, 8, 12, 1.

simple data of experience. "The understanding or reason . . . makes or forms, out of the simple ones that come in by sensation and reflection, all the other ideas, whether general, relative, or complex, by abstracting, comparing, and compounding its positive simple ideas." [15] Hence, though "our knowledge is all founded on simple ideas," it is "not always about simple ideas." "We may know the truth of propositions which include complex ideas." [16] And the qualities of these complex ideas are often entirely different from the qualities of the simple ideas from which they are derived. But whether the mind deals with simple or complex ideas, Locke has now a genetic test for their validity which he opposes to such a test as that of the intrinsic clearness theory of Descartes. Though the mind constructs complex ideas, all the constituent parts of which they are composed are the simple ideas of experience, and elements from no other source are introduced into their structure.[17] Moreover, the mind cannot possibly frame any simple ideas for itself.[18] Hence experience is the sole basis for all the manifold ideas which the mind uses in reaching knowledge.

3. Locke divided complex ideas into three classes—substances, relations, and modes,[19] each of which calls for special comment. (a) Substances "are such combinations of simple ideas as are taken to represent distinct particular things subsisting by themselves." [20] These are the ideas which were to cause Locke most difficulty in the fourth book of the *Essay*. They precipitate at once the problem of an extra-ideational reality, to which ideas must conform. Thus they seem to assume the possibility of a knowledge which goes beyond ideas and deals directly with that extra-ideational reality. A full discussion of Locke's treatment of this problem will be given in, the next section of this chapter which deals with the nature of ideas. (b) Relation is that sort of complex idea "which consists in the consideration and comparing one idea with another." [21] These ideas of relation are very closely akin to the observation by the understanding of the agreement and disagreement of ideas. Hence the discussion of relations, though brought up by Locke in connection with ideas, may well be treated of in a later section of this chapter on the faculty of understanding. (c) The complex ideas called modes are quite different from the other two kinds. And as they are particularly important in Locke's discussion of morality, they must be more fully explained. They are those ideas "which, however compounded, contain not in them the supposition of subsisting by themselves, but are considered as dependences on, or affections

[15] *Works*, Vol. IV, p. 71.
[16] *Idem*, Vol. IV, p. 47.
[17] *Essay*, II, 22, 9.
[18] *Works*, Vol. IV, p. 71.
[19] *Essay*, II, 12, 3.
[20] *Idem*, II, 12, 6.
[21] *Idem*, II, 12, 7. *Cf.* also II, 25, 5.

of, substances." [22] They are inventions of the mind rather than attempts to copy or describe real beings. They are "made very arbitrarily, made without patterns, or reference to any real existence." [23] They do not themselves have to conform to any objective realities, but are types, brought into being by the mind, to some of which the things in the world are found to conform. Many of them are such as nothing among existing things is like, but even those of which there are instances among real beings are often framed in the minds of men before those instances are discovered or known.[24] This view, according to which ideas of *genera* and *species* are artificial creations, is what has caused Locke to be classed as a nominalist.[25] The most important aspect of his position is that propositions dealing with modes are true provided that the ideas are consistently handled. No correspondence with anything beyond the ideas themselves is required. "That which is not designed to represent anything but itself, can never be capable of a wrong representation, nor mislead us from the true apprehension of anything, by its dislikeness to it." [26] Hence, in dealing with modes, "we cannot miss of a certain and undoubted reality." Propositions about mathematics are indubitable, whether or not there are right angles and straight lines in nature. The whole development of such a branch of thought may, since it is concerned with modes, proceed freely, without reference to concrete facts, according to the rules for inner coherency. And what has been said about mathematics applies also to ethics, as will be shown in the next chapter. Truth is here to be found in internal consistency, not in any external correspondence.

4. After having dealt with Locke's views on the origin and kinds of ideas, the problem of the nature of ideas remains to be considered.

[22] *Idem*, II, 12, 4.
[23] *Idem*, III, 5, 3.
[24] *Idem*, III, 5, 5.
[25] Locke was of course opposing at this point the main doctrine of the whole school of Cambridge Platonists. Malebranche in his *Recherche de la vérité* (1674) had insisted on the non-experiential source of our ideas. He did not, to be sure, include in the term idea as much as did Locke, but only what Locke meant by mixed modes. "In perceiving anything of a sensible nature, two things occur in our perception: sensation and pure idea" (p. 121 of the English translation of 1700). That is, over and above the sensational element of an experience, there is an intellectual element. This intellectual element comes about by God's sharing with men some of the ideas in his own mind. Thus man's knowledge is a matter of "seeing all things in God." John Norris was Malebranche's most faithful English follower. In the appendix to his *Cursory Reflections upon a Book called an Essay concerning Human Understanding* (1694) Norris maintained that the ideas are produced in men by God upon the occasion of sensations, but not by the sensations themselves (p. 59). Malebranche and Norris are, for the student of Locke, the most interesting of those whom he was opposing in his doctrine of mixed modes; for they alone drew forth from him written refutations (in 1693-4, though only published posthumously). But Cudworth and the other Cambridge Platonists, however much they differed from some of Malebranche's more fantastic notions, at least agreed that there are eternal, intellectual ideas, not gained through sense experience, but apprehended intuitively by the rational faculty. Locke's extreme divergence from such a position nowhere comes out more forcefully than his statement in his *Remarks on Mr. Norris's Books*, § 20: "The immutability of essences lies in the same sounds, supposed to stand for the same ideas." Cf. *Works*, Vol. X, p. 256.
[26] *Essay*, IV, 4, 5.

For though unfortunately Locke did not deal directly with this matter himself, his critics can hardly fail to do so. It is necessary to determine from his use of the word just what he thought an idea to be. Yet it will be found that the term idea, as it appears in the *Essay* and in the letters to Stillingfleet, is responsible for a fundamental inconsistency and ambiguity which he seems completely to have overlooked. This ambiguity caused him to vacillate between two entirely different views of the nature and limits of knowledge. Each of these two views calls for separate treatment.

(*a*) According to the position set forth at the outset of the *Essay*, an idea is "whatsoever is the object of the understanding when a man thinks," or "whatever it is which the mind can be employed about in thinking." [27] Practically the same definition of the term idea is repeated later, and on the whole predominates until the fourth book. And Locke evidently supposed that what he was expressing was very simple, and would meet with no opposition.[28] He was only restating, with a somewhat new terminology, a well recognized truism which had come down from the Aristotelian logic and been reiterated throughout scholasticism. The tradition of the "Schools" taught that whatever the mind thinks of is a notion—to be an object of thought and to be a notion are two ways of stating the same accepted logical fact. Though Locke employed the word idea to convey his meaning instead of notion, he defined it at the outset as exactly equivalent to "phantasm, notion, species." [29] And when he was accused of introducing a "new way of certainty by ideas," [30] he vigorously protested. He preferred the word idea simply because "notion will not so well stand for every immediate object of the mind in thinking as idea does," but "is more peculiarly appropriated to a certain sort of those objects, which I call mixed modes." [31] He recognized, however, that terminology is an arbitrary matter, and was willing to use any word his opponents might prefer.[32] He considered that he had introduced no innovation into the real principle at stake.

[27] *Idem*, Introduction 8. *Cf.* II, 1, 1.
[28] Locke's friendly critic, John Norris, in his *Cursory Reflections upon a Book Called an Essay concerning Human Understanding* (1694) accepted these definitions as a matter of course, but went on to insist that more careful exposition of their implications was needed. He quoted Locke's words, and then commented: "Very good; so much my lexicon would have told me. But this does not satisfy. I would know what kind of things he makes these ideas to be as to their essence or nature." (p 22). Earlier in his *Reflections* (p. 3), Norris had already called attention to the point made above, namely, that Locke erred in treating the origin of ideas without discussing their nature. Thus Norris's attitude is typical of what might have been expected of the critics in Locke's own day. Locke's definition of ideas was quite traditional and commonplace when taken by itself. But that definition, when coupled with other features of Locke's work, came to contain implications which were most revolutionary. Locke thus began his *Essay* with a point on which he was in fundamental agreement with his contemporaries, and only led up to his innovations gradually.
[29] *Essay*, Introduction 8.
[30] Stillingfleet, *passim*.
[31] *Works*, Vol. IV, p. 133.
[32] *Idem*, Vol. IV, p. 144.

Yet this bit of traditional logic was joined by Locke with his theory of the origin of all ideas in sense experience. And here lies the tremendous significance of Locke for epistemological theory. The mind can think only of ideas, and at the same time ideas are the contents of sense experience. "The simple ideas we receive from sensation and reflection are the boundaries of our thoughts; beyond which the mind, whatever efforts it would make, is not able to advance one jot; nor can it make any discoveries when it would pry into the nature and hidden causes of these ideas." [33] Thus the accepted logical truism of the schools is transformed into a novel epistemological problem. Formerly any reality became a notion by being thought of; but now in Locke only those realities could be thought of which had a certain relation to the mechanism of sensation. The older theory had been free from any metaphysical presuppositions; Locke's theory seems pledged to subjectivism. The original element in Locke begins to stand out when he goes on to say that knowledge is concerned with the relations of ideas to each other, never with the relation of ideas to some extra-mental object. "We can have knowledge no further than we have ideas." [34] Whatever is not an idea is not a possible object for thought at all.

This doctrine of ideas is open to two constructions, each of which, however, leads to a contradiction. Either the term idea is so inclusive that it can be applied to any and every object, or it applies to only a certain class or type of objects. The former construction would be obtained by emphasizing those passages in which Locke echoed the traditional logic without emphasizing his treatment of the origin of ideas. But in that case, the term idea, however important for logical considerations, would have no ontological significance at all. It would mean no more than the word "thing" would mean, and might well be discarded. Locke, however, clearly intended, when he spoke of the objects of the mind as ideas, to indicate something positive about them. Ideas are one class of things set over against another class of things which are not ideas. Locke rejected the idealistic conclusion which a few years later Berkeley drew from his statements, and denied the hypothesis that all objects in the world are only ideas after all.[35] He assumed throughout his writings, in a most realistic fashion, the existence of "external objects," not themselves ideas, which operate upon our senses to produce ideas in us.[36] In the second book of the *Essay*, at the very time when he was proceeding to limit the mind to observing merely the content of sense experience, he continually spoke of the

[33] *Essay*, II, 23, 29.
[34] *Essay*, IV, 3, 1.
[35] *Cf. Works*, Vol. IX, p. 221.
[36] *Essay*, II, 1, 2, 5, 8, 7, 12.

"particular sensible objects" [37] outside the mind; and he said that "we may observe [the original or primary qualities of body] to produce simple ideas in us." [38]   Ideas may even be spoken of as "effects." [39] Then in the fourth book, he strove to prove the real existence of objects apart from the data of sense experience, *i.e.*, apart from ideas.[40]   Thus to construe Locke's doctrine as teaching that all objects are ideas is to run counter to his fundamentally realistic ontology.

The other construction to which Locke's treatment of ideas is open is that the term applies to only a certain class or type of objects.   But if human knowledge is a matter of observing the agreement or disagreement of ideas with each other, we could never know even so much as the existence of any other class of objects than ideas.   Yet, as has been shown, Locke believed that he could know that there are "external objects."   He even went further and attempted to ascertain their nature.   The constitution of matter cannot ever be fully known; but it is known to a certain extent.[41]   The primary qualities of solidity, extension, and figure belong to the real bodies; [42] and the secondary qualities, though present only in the mind, correspond to powers in the bodies to produce the ideas of the secondary qualities.[43]   Locke even believed that with acuter senses one might be able to learn why the powers in the objects produce the particular sensations we receive from them.[44]   Thus to construe Locke's doctrine as teaching that only some objects are ideas would confine knowledge within very narrow limits and contradict his numerous assertions about the existence and nature of matter.

Stillingfleet, in his criticisms of Locke, was usually not acute enough to analyze correctly Locke's epistemological position, and often missed the point.   But he does seem to have sensed the difficulty in Locke's use of the term idea.   In his reply to Locke's first letter, he is willing to accept Locke's account of the origin of ideas from sensation and reflection.[45]   But he pointed out that some of Locke's conclusions, as of the existence of God, go beyond the realm of all these ideas, and that, therefore, reason deals directly with extra-ideational objects.   He pertinently remarked that if the term idea is used broadly enough to include all these objects, it is quite futile and might better be dropped altogether.[46]   And he finally inquired of Locke: "Is not here a great

[37] *Idem*, II, 1, 3.
[38] *Idem*, II, 8, 9.
[39] *Works*, Vol. IV, p. 76.
[40] *Essay*, IV, 9–11.
[41] *Idem*, IV, 6, 11.
[42] *Idem*, II, 8, 9.
[43] *Idem*, II, 8, 10.
[44] *Idem*, II, 23, 11; IV, 6, 10. *Cf.* also *Works*, Vol. IV, pp. 77–78.
[45] *Cf.* p. 92.
[46] Pp. 92–93.

ado to make a thing plain by ideas which was plainer without them?" [47]

Locke's replies to Stillingfleet did not meet the difficulty raised. He treated the criticism, as has already been said, merely as an attack upon his terminology,[48] and failed to see that he had been charged of being guilty of a serious ambiguity. He reiterated the position taken at the outset of the *Essay*: "He that thinks must have some immediate object of his mind in thinking, *i.e.*, must have ideas." [49] Again: "My way of ideas, and of coming to certainty by them, is to employ our minds in thinking upon something; and I do not see but your lordship yourself, and everybody else, must make use of my way of ideas, unless they can find out a way that will bring them to certainty by thinking on nothing." [50] Thus whenever Locke directly faced the issue of the objects of the mind in knowledge, he insisted that they are, and must be, ideas. But he failed to see that his theory of the origin of ideas had so altered the traditional logic that his epistemological position, consistently developed, would endanger his strong prejudices in favor of a realistic ontology.

(b) Opposed to the view of ideas already explained, there continually emerged in Locke, though it was never explicitly developed, another and quite different view. Ideas are not the objects to which knowledge is directed and in which it rests, but are the instruments whereby the knowledge of non-ideational objects becomes possible. In expressing even inadvertently, this position, Locke was departing from the established logical doctrine. But such a departure was rendered inevitable by the combination of Locke's theory of the origin of ideas with his firm belief in non-mental realities. Ideas stand as a sort of screen between the mind and things; and yet their function is to disclose, not to conceal, those things. Though knowledge is still impossible apart from ideas, the mind uses those ideas simply to reveal something more ultimate. "It is evident the mind knows not things immediately, but only by the intervention of the ideas it has of them." [51] Through ideas we know something about material and spiritual substances, about the things which give rise to our ideas. And knowledge, therefore, is a matter not merely of the relation of ideas to each other, but also of the relation of ideas to things; it concerns, not merely the reveries of the mind and the consistency between modes, but also a correspondence between ideas in the mind and realities in the objective world. Knowledge deals at times with "real existence." [52] And at

---

[47] P. 96.
[48] *Works*, Vol. IV, pp. 129–134.
[49] *Idem*, Vol. IV, pp. 130–131.
[50] *Idem*, Vol. IV, p. 72.
[51] *Essay*, IV, 4, ³.
[52] *Idem*, IV, 4, ³.

these times ideas come to be called "pictures," "representations," "copies of those originals." [53]

Critics of Locke have often felt the difficulty of including "real existence" as one of the four types of agreement or disagreement observed among our ideas. They have rightly pointed out that Locke shifted his meaning. The first three types of agreement or disagreement noted are of ideas to each other; the fourth, is of ideas to things. Locke was not able to hold to his initial position that the mind knows only its ideas. For in that case he would either have been forced to give up his realistic ontology, or have laid himself open to the charge —against which he vigorously protested—that knowledge is chimerical. So he made ideas, not the final objects, but the instrumentalities of knowledge. As he said in the chapter on the reality of knowledge: "If our knowledge of our ideas terminate in them, and reach no further, where there is something further intended, our most serious thoughts will be of little more use than the reveries of a crazy brain, and the truths built thereon of no more weight than the discourses of a man who sees things clearly in a dream." [54]   He thus utterly condemned the position taken at the outset of the *Essay*. Since he would not follow that position into the idealistic conclusion which Berkeley derived from it, but maintained his belief in non-ideational substances, he had at times to repudiate the basis of much of his own work.

That Locke did not appreciate the serious ambiguity in his treatment of the term idea may have been due to his use of the word "immediate." [55]   He sometimes spoke of ideas as "the objects of the mind in knowledge," and at other times as "the immediate objects of the mind in knowledge." And though there is but a slight verbal change in the two phrases, there may yet be a great difference in the meaning conveyed by the two expressions. The former is the dominant expression in the *Essay;* but the latter is used at most significant passages, namely, where Locke's belief in independent substances is involved. Such significant passages are those in which Locke dealt with the difference between ideas in the mind and qualities in the bodies,[56] with the sorts of knowledge we can obtain,[57] and with the reality of that knowledge.[58]

The shifting of meaning in the use of the term idea [59] was not due to any development from an earlier to a more mature epistemological

[53] *Idem*, II, 31, [6].
[54] *Idem*, IV, 4, [2].
[55] *Cf.* Reid, *Essay*, VI.
[56] *Essay*, II, 8, [8].
[57] *Idem*, IV, 1, [1].
[58] *Idem*, IV, 4, [3].
[59] It is interesting to note that the ambiguity in Locke's use of the term idea was retained by Toland in that book in which he so used Locke as to draw down upon Locke as well as himself the attack of Stillingfleet. In *Christianity not Mysterious*, page 11, he wrote: "By the word idea which I make so

position in the course of Locke's literary work; for the view which is clearly the basis of his original reflections upon the human understanding not only dominated the *Essay*, but continued to be reiterated in his replies to Stillingfleet in 1697 and 1699. And when he departed from this view, it was not in controversy over the difficulties involved, nor in conscious recognition of unwelcome implications of the position, nor at times when his thought was occupied with strictly epistemological considerations. Rather the other view slipped in by unconscious transition, at unguarded moments, in passages where he was engaged upon more ontological matters. In other words, he changed back and forth between two universes of discourse, in the first of which his interest was wholly epistemological, in the second of which it was mainly ontological. And in spite of the influence of the former upon the latter, they remained somewhat apart. In his ontology he stood much closer to the Descartes whom he so much admired; [60] in his epistemology he introduced more novelties of his own. He wished to preserve the assurance of the certainty of knowledge, its indubitable character, its superiority, not only to error, but even to "belief, conjecture, guess." [61] He desired a more objective test for such an excellent possession than the Cartesian "clear and distinct" perception. So he admitted as data for knowledge only what comes from sensation and reflection, and discarded whatever is derived from any other channel. But his semi-Cartesian ontology of the existence of God, of spiritual substances, and of material substances, had been the product of a different and far less empirical epistemology.[62] And he neither fully revised the ontology in the light of his own epistemological innovations, nor developed from his own new epistemology an ontology consistent therewith. Hence, in all of his writings, there are the two irreconcilable views of the nature of ideas, the dominant one prevailing whenever he considered the problems of knowledge, the other emerging whenever he discussed the existence of things. The exact status of ideas, their essential character and nature, remains ambiguous throughout his work.

much use of here, and shall more frequently in the following discourse, I understand the immediate object of the mind when it thinks, or any thought that the mind employs about anything."

[60] It is a tradition among historians of philosophy that Locke knew little of Descartes. But it is also a grave error. Locke received from Descartes his impetus to study philosophical problems, and retained many Cartesian ideas. *Cf.* Locke: *Works*, Vol. IV, p. 48; Vol. X, pp. 77, 81. *Thoughts concerning Education*, § 193. An earlier reference by Locke to Descartes is quoted in King's *Life of Locke*, p. 122. Also there is the testimony of Lady Masham, quoted in Fox Bourne's *Life of Locke*, Vol. I, pp. 61-2.

[61] *Essay*, IV, 16, °.

[62] Locke at times showed himself much more in sympathy with the atomism of Gassendi than with the Cartesian doctrine of substance. *Cf.* especially his fragmentary work on *Elements of Natural Philosophy*. Also *cf.* those passages in his refutations of Malebranche and Norris in which he insisted on the scientific explanation of the physiology of the senses. *Works*, Vol. IX, 215-7, 221, 253-4. Vol. X, 249, 254-5. However, in the *Essay* the prevailing view is quite Cartesian. And in either case the epistemological questions involved are the same. For whether following Descartes or Gassendi, Locke was quite realistic in his ontology.

5. Knowledge, for Locke, is not a matter simply of ideas. As has been said already, it is dependent upon a second element also—observation by the understanding or reason of the agreement or disagreement of the ideas. Locke supposed that the importance of reason was so universally accepted that he need not dwell on it in his *Essay*. He resented the charge that he had invented "a new way of certainty by ideas," and insisted that his way of reaching certainty is "just such as human understanding was possessed of before I was born." [63] Reason is not just another idea, but is fundamentally different. "I know nobody that does not think that reason, or the faculty of reasoning, is distinct from the ideas it makes use of or is employed about." [64] Ideas alone would be a host of isolated atoms, which could never cast themselves into the mold of knowledge: in order to get knowledge, reason must work them over. "I never said nor thought ideas, nor anything else, could bring us to the certainty of reason, without the exercise of reason." [65]

Locke differed from most of his contemporaries, not in denying the existence of reason, but in specifying more exactly what reason is. Reason, he felt, should not be loosely treated as spinning truth out of itself, but must be explained to be that mental faculty which is suited to deal with ideas. Reason convinces us by arguments, to be sure; but "to say that the argument makes us certain, is no more than saying, the ideas made use of make us certain." [66] While many writers were carelessly speaking of propositions obtained from "true principles of reason," Locke showed more definitely that the knowledge of the propositions is obtained "from the perceivable agreement or disagreement of the ideas contained in them." [67] He was as eager as any rationalist could be to emphasize that reason furnishes us with certainty; but "the ground of this certainty lies in ideas themselves, and their agreement or disagreement, which reason neither does nor can alter, but only lays them so together as to make it perceivable, and without such a due consideration and ordering of the ideas, certainty could not be had." [68] Instead of charging Locke with denying reason, his critics should thank him for being specific in explaining what kind of a faculty it is.

Moreover, reason, unlike the ideas upon which it operates, is innate.[69] It is not acquired in the course of experience, but is one of man's "natural faculties," [70]—indeed it is "that faculty whereby man is sup-

---

[63] *Works*, Vol. IV, p. 44.
[64] *Idem*, Vol. IV, p. 65.
[65] *Idem*, Vol. IV, p. 72.
[66] *Idem*, Vol. IV, p. 60.
[67] *Idem*, Vol. IV, p. 61.
[68] *Idem*, Vol. IV, p. 59.
[69] *Essay*, I, 1, [5].
[70] *Idem*, I, 1, [1].

posed to be distinguished from beasts, and wherein it is evident he much surpasses them." [71] Just because Locke endeavored to point out the origin of our ideas, his critics have sometimes supposed that he was also talking about the origin of the understanding. They have been misled by his denial of innate ideas and emphasis upon the empirical origin of all ideas, into supposing that he rejected innate faculties or powers also. Burnet, for example, in his *Third Remarks on Locke's Essay*, wrote: "I see this word innate is still a stumbling stone; and we must ask again whether you allow any powers to be innate to mankind." Locke's reply was: "I think nobody but this author who ever read my book could doubt that I spoke only of innate ideas (for my subject was the understanding), and not of innate powers." [72] Though reason cannot begin to operate until it possesses ideas as material,[73] it does not originate with the ideas, but is independent of and prior to them. Locke refused to allow Stillingfleet to interpret him as holding that ideas are "necessary to reason." "Reason being a faculty of the mind, nothing, in my poor opinion, can properly be said to be necessary to that faculty, but what is required to its being." And nothing "can properly be said to be necessary to reason in a man, but such a constitution of body or mind, or both, as may give him the power of reasoning." [74] Locke would have been quite willing to allow the use of such a phrase as that ideas are "necessary to reasoning," *i.e.*, necessary to the exercise of reason. But though reason must wait for ideas before becoming active, it exists as a faculty prior to the advent of its materials in experience.

Thus Locke anticipated Kant to a certain extent. Sense experience and reason are both necessary for knowledge. And while reason can not from itself produce a single new simple idea, ideas can not of themselves carry on any reasoning. Locke did not, as Kant later did, elaborate upon the structure of the mind; but he maintained as fully as Kant the necessity, for knowledge, of the *a priori* factor of reason as well as the *a posteriori* factor of ideas. In expounding his doctrine of knowledge to Stillingfleet he wrote: "It may be placed in ideas and in good and sound reason too, *i.e.*, in reason rightly managing those ideas so as to produce evidence by them. So that, my lord, I must own I see not the force of the argument which says, 'not in ideas but in sound reason'; since I see no such opposition between them, but that ideas and sound reason may consist together." [75]

[71] *Idem*, IV, 17, 1.

[72] Locke never deigned to reply publicly to Burnet aside from a stinging rebuke in a postscript attached to his second letter to Stillingfleet. The quotation above is a comment which Locke wrote in the margin of his own copy of Burnet's attack (now in the Yale University Library). *Cf.* Noah Porter's article in the *New Englander*, Vol. 47, p. 45.

[73] *Essay*, II, 1, 20.

[74] *Works*, Vol. IV, pp. 11-12.

[75] *Works*, Vol. IV, p. 59.

The failure of many critics to appreciate the strong rationalistic element in Locke is probably due to two main causes. (1) Locke spoke of the mind as an "empty cabinet" or as "white paper." [76] But he used these expressions only where he was treating of the origin of ideas, and did not intend to deny that the original faculties of the soul are underived and innate. The similes he employed should not be interpreted in the light of the sensationalist psychology which claimed him as its founder. Rather one must remember that Locke retained the belief in an abiding soul substance. And whoever accepts such a soul could hardly wish to deny it some form and character of its own. (2) Locke used "perception" in two different senses. Sometimes the term means "having ideas," [77] or even, more narrowly, the receiving of ideas from the second kind of experience, reflection. [78] In this case it is only "the first step and degree towards knowledge, and the inlet of all the materials of it." [79] It is the faculty which distinguishes the animal kingdom from inanimate nature. [80] Then at other times the term perception means the observation by reason of the agreement or disagreement of ideas. [81] In this case it is the consummation of the knowledge process. It is the faculty which "sets man above the rest of sensible beings." [82] Locke was aware that he was using the word in these two senses (as well as in still a third sense which is here irrelevant), but expected no confusion to result. [83] Some of his critics have introduced the confusion. Interpreting him from the standpoint of the later sensationalist school, they suppose that perception in the second sense just mentioned is only a further instance of perception in the first sense. But what he took occasion to distinguish, they should not identify.

In addition to all the direct evidence given above of Locke's acceptance of the rationalistic position, there is an interesting piece of indirect evidence in his attack on association. The association of ideas "is as frequent a cause of mistake and error in us as perhaps anything else that can be named, and is a disease of the mind as hard to be cured as any." [84] Later psychological writers, having rejected all faculties such as the understanding, had no choice but to regard reasoning as a matter of association of ideas. Locke, however, rejected association as an "easy and unheeded miscarriage" of reasoning; and he sought to avoid all the "unnatural connections" which association set up between

[76] *Essay*, I, 1, [15], 2, [22]; II, 1, [2].
[77] *Idem*, II, 1, [9].
[78] *Idem*, II, 9, [2].
[79] *Idem*, II, 9, [15].
[80] *Idem*, II, 9, [11].
[81] *Idem*, IV, 1, [2], 3, [2]. *Cf. Works*, Vol. IV, p. 144.
[82] *Essay*, Introduction[1].
[83] *Idem*, II, 21, [5].
[84] *Conduct of the Understanding*, § 41. Also *cf. Essay*, II, 33, [1].

ideas, in favor of such real connections as the understanding directly observed. [85]

6. One final aspect of Locke's epistemology should be mentioned. Locke distinguished between knowledge and probability. On the one hand, knowledge is certain and indubitable. It partakes of the nature of universality, and is altogether free from the bias of a personal point of view. "If an intelligent being at one end of the world, and another at the other end of the world, will consider twice two and four together, he cannot but find them to be equal." [86] Knowledge thus is absolute and final. On the other hand, probability is a hazard, a guess, a matter of faith. It is so affected by a personal factor, that anything like universality in estimating chances is impossible. It leads, therefore, to a willingness to tolerate divergent opinions on many matters of even pressing human concern.

Locke considered that knowledge itself is of three degrees. (1) Intuitive knowledge is that in which "the mind perceives the agreement or disagreement of two ideas immediately by themselves, without the intervention of any other." [87] The identity of each thing with itself, the distinction between one thing and any other, many relations of our sensations, and all ultimate, abstract principles are included in this class. No proof, no intermediary connecting link or argument is necessary.[88] To get all knowledge into this form would be to attain the ideal. God's knowledge is all of this type; [89] but we human beings have only a limited amount of it. (2) Demonstrative knowledge is that in which the mind perceives the connection between two ideas "by the intervention of other ideas." [90] Knowledge of this type consists of a series of steps, each of which, however, must be intuitive. (3) Sensitive knowledge is that in which the ideas derived through our senses bear witness to "the particular existence of finite beings without us." [91] This kind of knowledge does not reach "to either of the foregoing degrees of certainty." Yet Locke would include it under the eulogistic term of knowledge instead of calling it probability. He really thus broke with what his epistemological position logically calls for, in order to keep his ontological faith in the world of external objects.

In his insistence upon the absolute certainty of knowledge, Locke showed that he shared to a certain extent the general rationalistic confidence of his age. Yet he did limit the field within which such knowledge is available. We often lack the ideas necessary for knowl-

[85] *Conduct of the Understanding*, §71.
[86] *Works*, Vol. IX, p. 250.
[87] *Essay*, IV, 2, 1.
[88] *Idem*, I, 1, 10, 18, 2, 4.
[89] *Works*, Vol. IX, p. 251.
[90] *Essay*, IV, 2, 2.
[91] *Idem*, IV, 2, 14.

edge of a subject; and even where we have ideas, we may fail to discern the connections between them.[92]   Thus Locke marks a step towards the skepticism which was beginning to fall upon philosophic thought.   Probability is necessary after all in order "to supply the defect of our knowledge."[93]   We must give our assent to many propositions, even when we are not certain of the agreement or disagreement of the ideas therein brought together.   Many times the probability is very great; at other times, it is quite slight.[94]   Yet always, in probability as in knowledge, our conclusion comes through the operation of reason upon the ideas of experience.   "Reason must be our last judge and guide in everything."[95]

[92] *Idem*, IV, 3, 1-2, 22, 12, 4.
[93] *Idem*, IV, 15, 4.
[94] *Idem*, IV, 15, 2.
[95] *Idem*, IV, 19, 14.

CHAPTER II

1. Locke's general epistemological position pledged him to a rationalistic moral philosophy. In ethics, just as in all other branches of thought, he regarded reason as the faculty through which, and through which alone, knowledge can be obtained.

But at the outset of a discussion of his ethics it is important to note just what he did, and just what he did not, mean by reason. For though there was much in his rationalistic stand which was in verbal agreement with the prevalent view in his day, he introduced, as was seen in the last chapter, a new conception of reason. His predecessors and contemporaries referred to reason in rather a loose, eulogistic sense; he treated it more strictly and exactly as a definite kind of power. They frequently viewed it as a means whereby rational beings can evolve knowledge from within themselves; he regarded it as a means whereby rational beings can judge concerning the ideas which come to them from without. They made it competent in and of itself to obtain the ultimate truth in religion and ethics; he held it to be only latent until it is furnished with materials from experience. They were pure rationalists, pointing to reason as the sole requirement for knowledge, and thus tending to make the principles discovered by reason as innate as reason itself; he was a combination of rationalist and empiricist, not only granting the necessity for knowledge of the innate faculty of reason, but also insisting that this faculty, in order to reach valid conclusions, must operate upon ideas derived from sensation and reflection. Thus though Locke accepted the widespread confidence in reason, he completely broke with the type of rationalism current before his time, and gave a new definition of reason which profoundly modified moral theory.

In this chapter, an endeavor will be made to expound Locke's view of reason as the ethical faculty. To treat reason alone without discussing the ideas to which reason must be directed is to isolate one element of Locke's philosophy in an artificial manner; but since the next two chapters will deal with the materials whence reason discovers the moral law, such isolation is not unfair nor dangerous to a well-balanced account of Locke's ethical theories. The significance of Locke's rationalism will become most clear by reviewing his attack upon innate ideas, his confidence in the mathematical demonstrability of morality, and the controversies into which he ran with his contemporaries over the exact nature of the faculty by which the principles of morality are made known.

2. In dealing with Locke's general epistemological views, only a passing reference was made to his rejection of innate ideas. Certainly there is good precedent for minimizing the first book of the *Essay* in which this denial of innate ideas appears. Locke himself barely mentioned this book in the abstract of the *Essay* [1] which he contributed in 1688 to Le Clerc's *Bibliothèque Universelle;* and Wynne, who with Locke's approval published in 1696 an abridgment of the *Essay* for use at the universities, omitted reference to the first book altogether. Yet what is trivial in sketching Locke's contribution to epistemological theory, becomes more important in dealing with his ethics. For anyone who rejected innate ideas would have to find a new basis for moral philosophy and give a new interpretation to the customary view of conscience. Hence Locke's attack on "innate practical principles" deserves careful consideration.

It is a most interesting fact that the conservatives and radicals among Locke's contemporaries resorted to very similar means of defense for their opposed theories. Both parties, orthodox and heretical, appealed to innate impressions as proof of the truth of their divergent claims. The conservative point of view is rather typically represented in John Edwards who made several scurrilous assaults upon Locke's *Reasonableness of Christianity*. He maintained that "these natural impressions in all men's minds are the foundation of religion and the standard of truth as well as of morality;" [2] and he deplored Locke's denial of the innate character of commonly accepted speculative principles because that denial led to a slighting of Christian principles too. The radical point of view is found most adequately in the writings of the deists, who, as was shown above, followed Lord Herbert in his reliance on innate truths. The only material difference in the appeal which conservatives and radicals alike made to innate truths was over the question of whose minds contained the infallible impressions. The conservatives always emphasized the wide differences between themselves and the unbelieving mass of men; the radicals always emphasized the common elements in the faith and practise of all mankind. Consequently, the conservatives found assurance of truth in the innate ideas of those only who were competent to judge (thus gaining warrant to set up extravagant claims for their own sect and to exclude all who differed from them); the radicals, however, appealed to the innate ideas of all men everywhere, reading their own favorite articles into all other faiths and all other civilizations, and

---

[1] This abstract is reprinted in King: *Life of Locke,* pp. 365 ff.
[2] *The Socinian Creed,* p. 122.

thus venturing to use even their opponents as part of the defense for their own positions. A rather mediating point of view is seen in those moderate liberals like Grotius and the other writers on natural law, who appealed to the common consent of all, and yet acknowledged that in the minds of many men the innate impressions were partly or wholly effaced. But conservatives, moderates, and radicals, however much they differed as to the number of minds in which they claimed that reliable impressions might be found, at least agreed in supposing those impressions to be innate.

Locke drew the only logical conclusion which could be drawn from these rival appeals to innate impressions by the most divergent schools of thought, namely, that all the claims were alike a matter of futile dogmatism. The belief in innate truths served only as an idle excuse for rigorous thinking; "it eased the lazy from the pains of search." [3] The advocates of innate ideas he considered as guilty of giving way to "enthusiasm" which beclouded their calm judgment. The chapter on enthusiasm towards the end of the fourth book of the *Essay* was not inserted until the fourth edition; but the dangers of enthusiasm had been noted by Locke much earlier, as entries in his journal in 1682 show. The imaginations of men's fancy "are apt to disturb and depress the rational power of the mind," [4] and lead them to entertain a proposition "with greater assurance than the proofs it is built upon will warrant." [5] Locke maintained that no form of enthusiasm is more dangerous than resorting to alleged innate ideas in lieu of genuine proof, and in opposition to that current type of enthusiasm he based his views on as careful an empirical examination of anthropological data as was possible in his day. During his early travels on the continent, he observed a great many divergences of belief and custom; [6] and he had a keen interest in the reports of those who took long journeys to the less familiar parts of the globe, as his constant references to "savages" in the first book of the *Essay* show. [7] It was probably as a result of these studies, which in method were quite a scientific advance over the procedure of other seventeenth-century writers, that Locke discarded the claims of both radicals and conservatives in their appeal to innate ideas.

Locke first took up the argument of the radicals that there are certain universally accepted truths. To this argument he replied that "there are no practical principles wherein all men agree." [8] He felt that the strength of the appeals to innate moral ideas was due to the fact

---

[3] *Essay*, I, 3, 25.

[4] King: *Life of Locke*, pp. 126–128.

[5] *Cf.* King: *IV*, 19, 1.

[6] *Cf.* King: *Op. cit.*, pp. 46–86, 109–120, 160–168.

[7] *Cf.* also Locke's letter to Thomas Cudworth, asking for information about native customs in foreign parts. Bourne: *Life of Locke*, Vol. I, p. 474.

[8] *Essay*, I, 2, 27.

that these ideas were considered in the gross, instead of separately and one by one.[9]   With a keen sense for the concrete, he insisted on examining each alleged innate idea by itself, and then could find not a single one that received an universal reception.   Those who are "but moderately conversant in the history of mankind" and look "abroad beyond the smoke of their own chimneys,"[10] can give no instance of any moral idea or principle which all men recognize and accept.   Rather there is a "great variety of opinions concerning moral rules;"[11] and whole nations slight, or even reject, the most eagerly held principles of other nations.   Instead of universal agreement, violent opposition and open conflict are everywhere to be found.   Nor will it do to argue that men give tacit consent in their minds to certain common moral principles, even when they contradict these principles in practise.   For their violation of the supposedly universal moral rules is made without any remorse, and hence without any consciousness of the rules at all.   The occasional breaking of a rule might occur even when it is known; but "the generally allowed breach of it anywhere, I say, is a proof that it is not innate."[12]   Therefore in so far as universal consent is used as a proof of innateness, the argument for innate moral ideas breaks down.

Locke next considered the claims of the conservatives that innate moral ideas are to be found in the minds of only a few.   For this narrowly dogmatic defense of orthodoxy he had even less sympathy. In the first place, there is absolutely no criterion whereby to decide which among many aspirants to recognition are the favored possessors of innate truth.   If innate impressions are to be resorted to as proof, some objective criterion must be offered to determine which of the many firmly held convictions are innate and which are fraudulent. But no such objective criterion is available.[13]   In the second place, if only a few minds possess innate impressions, the minds of children would naturally be the best minds to consult; for their original nature has been least corrupted by sin or modified by prejudice.   Yet the alleged innate ideas and principles are found only in the most sophisticated and highly trained minds.[14]   The whole appeal to innate ideas breaks down altogether, and must be rejected as an ungrounded bit of enthusiasm.

3.   Locke did not suppose at all that he had by his rejection of innate ideas weakened the rational foundation of morality.   Rather he aimed to overthrow a mistaken, and to set up a sound, type of rationalistic ethics.   Moral principles are not imprinted on the mind at birth;

[9] *Idem*, I, 3, [1].
[10] *Idem*, I, 2, [2].
[11] *Idem*, I, 2, [6].
[12] *Essay*, I, 2, [12]. *Cf.* also the *Marginalia* quoted by Noah Porter in *The New Englander* for 1887, Vol. 47, pp. 39-40.
[13] *Essay*, I, 2, [20].
[14] *Idem*, I, 1,[5],3,[2]. Also *cf.* the *Marginalia* quoted by Noah Porter in *The New Englander*, Vol. 47, p. 38.

but they are none the less true and certain. Reason can demonstrate them with mathematical accuracy. Morality can be placed "amongst the sciences capable of demonstration: wherein I doubt not but from self-evident propositions, by necessary consequences, as incontestable as those in mathematics, the measures of right and wrong might be made out, to anyone that will apply himself with the same indifferency and attention to the one as he does to the other of these sciences." [15] Locke believed in eternal and immutable truths as much as any of his predecessors; for though such truths are not to be found imprinted on the mind, they are discoverable by reason.[16] His predecessors, however much they claimed to be establishing morality on a fixed and imperishable foundation, were endangering it altogether by their dogmatism. He aimed to furnish a method and a theory of knowledge which would remedy the shortcomings of those earlier writers. For "if a right method were taken, a great part of morality might be made out with that clearness that could leave, to a considering man, no more reason to doubt, than he could have to doubt of the propositions in mathematics, which have been demonstrated to him." [17] Reason may have to wait for sense-data in order to ascertain the truth on any subject; but its findings are none the less as absolute and indubitable as when reason was supposed to evolve principles out of itself.

The science of ethics belongs, in Locke's view, to the second of the three degrees of knowledge mentioned in the last chapter. Moral principles are not a matter of intuition; rather "they require reasoning and discourse, and some exercise of the mind, to discover the certainty of their truth." Yet "this is no derogation to their truth and certainty." [18] They are on the same level as our knowledge of the existence of God. That is, they are often not apparent and self-evident when first presented to the mind; rather the ideas of which the principles are made up often require much consideration, comparison, and even the intervention of connecting links between them, before their agreement or disagreement with each other is discovered. In other words, moral principles always require proof. "There cannot any one moral rule be proposed whereof a man may not justly demand a reason." [19] All moral principles rest upon something "antecedent to them, and from which they must be deduced." What Locke considered them to rest on, and how he proved them will be discussed in the next chapter. But it is important to keep clearly in mind from the beginning that Locke considered morality to be rational, and hence to be demonstrably certain.

[15] *Essay*, IV, 3, [18]. *Cf.* also, I, 2, [1]; III, [11], [16]; IV, 4, [7], *etc.*
[16] *Idem*, IV, 11, [14].
[17] *Idem*, IV, 12, [8].
[18] *Idem*, I, 2, [1].
[19] *Idem*, I, 2, [4].

4. The significance of Locke's type of rationalism for ethical theory becomes most clear in the light of two controversies which were carried on between him and some contemporary critics. The first of these controversies arose when James Lowde published in 1694 his *Discourse concerning the Nature of Man*. In the third chapter of this book he devoted several pages to a criticism of Locke's denial of innate ideas, to which Locke replied in the *Epistle to the Reader* in the second edition of the *Essay*. Lowde made further remarks on Locke in his *Moral Essays* in 1699.[20] But the controversy was not extensive; and it was conducted in a fair and courteous spirit.

Lowde contended that the proper foundation for religion and morality lies in the nature with which God has endowed man, and hence in innate principles or original notions. He declared that these innate principles do not become explicitly known to all men, and are certainly not consciously apprehended by children and idiots. He rejected Locke's supposition that the minds of children would be the best place in which to find innate notions; for "those who make this objection, as I before intimated, will not give the defendant leave to state his own question, and explain his own sense and meaning of it; but will put such a sense upon these words, *innate* or *natural*, as if a thing could not be thus natural or innate to the soul, unless it did so immediately and necessarily stare children and fools in the face, that they must necessarily assent thereto, even before, by the common course of nature, they are capable of assenting to anything." He asserted that by innate notions he meant those supreme principles to which the minds of men may come under proper guidance to give certain assent. "Those who defend this question make these natural or innate notions more conditional things, depending upon the concurrence of several other circumstances, in order to the soul's exerting of them. . . . The truer judgment of these natural notions ought to be taken rather from the most perfect state of man, rather than as they do or do not show themselves in children and idiots." [21] Innate notions are thus the goal of the rational life of man, not its beginning. And he proceeded to adduce Locke's theory of intuitive knowledge [22] as evidence that Locke himself, in spite of his denial of innate principles really granted the point at issue.

Locke wisely recognized that the controversy between Lowde and himself was largely one of terminology. He pointed out that Lowde in some passages rejected the kind of innate ideas which he had attacked, and simply applied the word innate to those self-evident and indubitable truths which he also had maintained to be within the power

[20] I have not been able to trace this work in any libraries available to me.
[21] *Discourse concerning the Nature of Man*, pp. 78–79.
[22] *Idem*, p. 80.

of reason to discover. He declared that the "several other circumstances" which Lowde granted as necessary to successful operation of reason were to be found, as he himself had clearly shown, in the gaining of ideas from experience. He criticized the phrase "the soul's exerting them" as an unhappy expression; but he tried to make it equivalent to "beginning to know them," thus smoothing over any difference which otherwise might have remained between him and Lowde.[23]

Undoubtedly, however, Locke went too far in trying to harmonize Lowde's theory with his own. For though Lowde often granted all that Locke insisted upon, Lowde at other times held to the older position against which Locke argued. He yielded to Locke's empirical teaching when he acknowledged that the innate notions are not found out "without any assistance from the outward senses, or without the help of some previous cultivation," or when he granted that reason "requires some supervenient assistance before it arrive at a true exercise of itself." But in other passages he maintained that the soul is not wholly dependent upon sense in all of its operations, but has another and distinct source of knowledge in its native endowments. "The notions are in the same sense connatural to the soul as reason itself is. . . . Our souls have a native power of finding or framing such principles or propositions, the truth or knowledge whereof no ways depends upon the evidence of sense or observation." [24] He departed so radically from Locke as to say that even if reason requires sense experience to arouse it, it may, once it is aroused, work upon other material. In some passages he assented to all that Locke was anxious to make clear, only to contradict himself immediately. For example, he wrote: "Those who assert those natural notions do not suppose them superimposed or imprinted upon the soul, *in esse completo;* but suppose them to be native properties and qualifications of the soul, as it is such as God first designed to make it." [25] In the first phrase of this sentence he might seem in close agreement with Locke; but in the second phrase he obviously shows that after all he was not. For he there insisted that though the innate notions are not explicitly in the mind from birth, yet they are native to it; and that when reason makes the notions evident to men, reason accomplishes its task, not by observing the agreements or disagreements between ideas derived from sense, but by disclosing the full import of the natural rational endowment of the soul. Thus Locke exaggerated, probably with irenic motives, the extent of the harmony which he found between Lowde and himself. He must have appreciated that Lowde was a quite second-rate thinker, whose views were not consistent and exact,

[23] Locke, *Essay*, Epistle to the Reader. 2nd edition.
[24] Lowde, *Op. cit.*, pp. 52–53. *Cf.* also pp. 89–90.
[25] *Idem*, pp. 82–83.

and who could not be regarded as fully aware of the import of all of his own assertions. But at least the conflict between Locke and Lowde makes it evident that while Locke found the moral faculty in man's innate reason, he did not find any moral principles or maxims either explicitly or implicitly present within reason. He distinguished carefully between innate truths and truths which in the course of experience reason discovers to be self-evident and certain.

5. The second controversy which throws light on Locke's treatment of reason as the ethical faculty is that with Thomas Burnet. Burnet published his *Remarks on Locke's Essay* in 1697, to which Locke made a short and stinging reference in a postscript to his second letter to Stillingfleet. Burnet then wrote his *Second Remarks* in 1697, and his *Third Remarks* in 1699. Locke did not deign to make any public reply to these further attacks, and quite hurt Burnet's pride by his contemptuous silence. Yet Locke revealed that Burnet's criticisms rankled him somewhat by the comments which he scribbled in his own handwriting in the margin of his copy of the *Third Remarks*.[26] Burnet made several points in his three pamphlets against Locke,[27] of which two are important to consider here—his supposition that Locke denied the faculty of reason to be innate, and his theory of a special innate moral faculty in conscience.

(*a*) Burnet's mistaken supposition that Locke denied any innate faculty such as reason was due to his sensationalist interpretation of Locke's epistemology. He complained that Locke recognized no truths except those which come from experience, and yet that the data from the five senses do not furnish men with a knowledge of moral principles. "As to morality, we think the great foundation of it is the distinction of good and evil, virtue and vice, *turpis* and *honesti*, as they are usually called; and I do not find that my eyes, ears, nostrils, or any other outward senses make any distinction of these things, as they do of sounds, colors, scents, or other outward objects." [28] Of course such a criticism utterly misses the point of Locke's *Essay;* and it is not surprising that Burnet thus ruffled Locke's serenity and drew forth a harsh comment from him. Locke never supposed that a jumbling about of sense data created moral distinctions; but he did wish to confine the operations of reason to the simple ideas and the complex ideas derived therefrom. The trouble with Burnet was that he confused innate ideas with innate faculties or powers; [29] and he concluded that since Locke denied the one, he also denied the other, and was thus limited to unregulated and uncontrolled sense data. That Locke in his ethics held firmly to the epistemological theory which he

---

[26] *Cf.* Noah Porter, *The New Englander*, Vol. 47. pp. 33–49.
[27] See below, Book II, Chapter V, § 3.
[28] Burnet: *First Remarks*, pp. 4–5.
[29] Burnet: *Third Remarks. Cf.* Porter: *Marginalia Lockeana*, pp. 36–37.

laid down in the *Essay*, and required both a rational and an empirical element for the securing of knowledge, is apparent from two of the comments he made upon Burnet. In one place he wrote: "If by moral principles you mean a faculty to find out in time the moral difference of actions (besides that this is an improper way of speaking to call a power principles), I never denied such a power to be innate; but that which I denied was that any ideas or connection of ideas was innate." [30] In another place he wrote: "Prove the distinguishing sense of virtue and vice to be natural to mankind before they have learned the measures of virtue and vice from something besides the senses, and you will have proved something." [31]   Thus Locke combined an insistence upon the innate faculty of reason with an equal insistence upon the need for ideas from experience. And Burnet's criticism was an altogether unwarranted isolation of one of these two equally vital elements, and a total disregarding of the other.

(*b*) Burnet also brought the charge against Locke that he ignored "natural conscience." This criticism was closely related to the other one just discussed. Burnet supposed that since a knowledge of good and evil cannot be gained from the senses, it must be obtained from some other source which may be called conscience. Conscience is "a natural sagacity to distinguish moral good and evil;" [32] it is "an original principle, antecedently to any other collections and recollections." [33]   To be sure, the voice of conscience may be obscured and perverted; but at least it is the best guide man has, and so should be appealed to sincerely. Without such a moral guide as the voice of an innate conscience, man would never learn the distinction between good and evil at all.

Now Locke was perfectly willing to recognize conscience, even as in a certain sense innate. He had made an entry in his commonplace book, probably many years before he wrote the *Essay*, according to which he asserted that every man, however humble and uneducated, "has a conscience, and knows in those few cases which concern his own actions what is right and what is wrong." [34]   But this conscience is not a unique faculty especially constructed for knowledge of moral affairs: it is reason engaged upon ethical problems. Conscience "is nothing else but our own opinion or judgment of the moral rectitude or pravity of our own actions." [35]   Locke's objection to Burnet's criticisms was not that Burnet emphasized conscience, but that he treated conscience in a loose and uncritical fashion. Burnet called conscience "knowledge

[30] Noah Porter: *Marginalia Lockeana*, p. 38.
[31] *Idem*, p. 41.
[32] Burnet: *Third Remarks*. *Cf.* Noah Porter: *Op. cit*, p. 37.
[33] Burnet: *Third Remarks*, p. 4.
[34] King: *Life of Locke*, p. 283.
[35] *Essay*, I, 2, 8 (4th edition)

or sense or instinct." He said that "it rises as quick as any of our passions, or as laughter at the sight of a ridiculous accident or object." [36] He was thus guilty, in Locke's opinion, of two errors. In the first place, he varied in his treatment of it, identifying it sometimes with a mental faculty, but more often with the verdicts of that faculty. He made it equivalent to "the laws of nature" or "the supreme law," and then concluded that not only the moral faculty but also the moral laws were innate. Against this careless kind of argument Locke's keen mind could not but protest. Locke asked Burnet to distinguish between the moral law and that faculty by which a man judges of the conformity of his actions with that law. The faculty is innate, but the law is not. Hence only the faculty, *i.e.*, reason engaged on moral problems, can be referred to as "natural conscience." Conscience must not be supposed to create moral distinctions—it only discovers them. "Conscience is not the law of nature, but judging by that which is taken to be the law." Or, "conscience is the judge, not the law." [37] In the second place, Burnet's resort to conscience without understanding just what it is was in Locke's opinion but "the laying down a foundation for enthusiasm." [38] And such a method in ethics is most dangerous and undesirable: it is merely the attempt to erect another infallible guide without any better claims to obedience than the Roman Church.[39] Because of the association of ideas which really do not belong together, men come to believe that the things which stir their emotions deeply are of corresponding moral value. But moral laws are meant to restrain and curb men's passions. Prejudice and emotional bias should be controlled by reason. The kind of conscience which Burnet extolled would lead to ruin. "Principles of actions indeed there are lodged in men's appetites; but these are so far from being innate moral principles, that if they were left to their full swing they would carry men to the overturning of all morality." [40] The consciences of different men urge diametrically opposed actions; for the dictates of their consciences are only too often the voices of unrestrained passion. The only reliable kind of a conscience is the untrammeled voice of reason, judging according to the real connections between the objects with which it deals. Thus in place of an authority which would change from person to person according as their emotions varied, Locke set up as judge that rational faculty which alone can reach conclusions of an eternal and immutable validity.

[36] Burnet: *First Remarks*, p. 5.
[37] Noah Porter: *Op. cit.*, pp. 35-41.
[38] *Idem*, p. 38.
[39] King: *Life of Locke*, p. 103. *Cf.* Patten: *The Development of English Thought*, p. 164.
[40] Locke: *Essay*, I, 2, [13].

CHAPTER III

1. The last chapter having been devoted to discussing Locke's treatment of reason as the ethical faculty, an attempt will now be made to outline the system of ethics to which his rationalism led. For since reason was not for Locke a set of infallible principles, but only a faculty whereby the agreements and disagreements of ideas can be perceived, his system of ethics could be built up only by furnishing reason with some empirical material to work upon. The inconsistency previously noticed in Locke's use of the term idea here looms up again, and two quite different moral theories result. According to the first of these theories, the one which corresponds to his treatment of ideas as "whatsoever is the object of the understanding when a man thinks," [1] and the one which predominates throughout the *Essay* whenever the possibility of knowing moral truth is being considered, morality is concerned with "mixed modes." Mixed modes, as was shown above,[2] are those ideas which the mind of man can construct by compounding simple ideas of several kinds into one complex whole. That is, the ideas out of which moral truths are made are "voluntary collections of ideas," [3] arbitrarily brought together without reference to any objective standard. They are not only often framed prior to any experiences akin to them, but also are not even attempts to copy external objects. "In framing these ideas the mind searches not its patterns in nature, nor refers the ideas it makes to the real existences of things, but puts such together as may best serve its own purposes, without tying itself to a precise imitation of anything that really exists." [4] Moral ideas are "the creatures of the understanding rather than the works of nature." Yet they are not, therefore, to be supposed to be fantastic. Rather they are "real essences"; for though in the case of substances the nominal and real essences are quite different, yet in the case of mixed modes which are known as they are in their real being, the nominal and real essences coincide and are the same.[6] Hence moral ideas, being real essences, have attached to them class names or universal terms; and

---

[1] *Cf.* above, Book II, Chapter I, § 4 (a).
[2] Book II, Chapter I, § 3.
[3] *Essay*, III, 5, [5].
[4] *Idem*, III, 5 ,[6]. *Cf.* also III, 11, [15], [18].
[5] *Idem*, III, 5, [12].
[6] *Idem*, III, 3, [15-18].

under them many of the ideas we are continually receiving from our senses may be grouped and ordered.

Moral propositions or rules are obtained by perceiving the agreement or disagreement of the moral ideas to each other. Hence moral rules are timeless, for the mixed modes out of which they are constructed are "ingenerable and incorruptible," and have no temporal connection with the "mutations of particular substances." [7] Also they are eternal and immutable; for the modes, once fabricated, have a definitely fixed character, and so bear forever the same relations to each other. Of course, the meaning of the terms attached to the modes may change from person to person and from time to time, and thus the propositions made therefrom will be different; but such changes are purely verbal, indicating that one moral truth has been superseded in men's attention by another, not that what was once true has become false. Once a moral term is defined, many truths necessarily follow from its relations to other such terms. Hence, moral truth is the "speaking of things according to the persuasion of our own minds, though the proposition we speak agree not to the reality of things." [8] It is just because of this independence of moral ideas and propositions from any necessary conformity to objects that ethics can be demonstrated. If ethics like physics involved reference to external things, it could only result in probability. But since like mathematics it deals only with mixed modes, it can be a science. The propositions of ethics are true provided that they conform to the requirements of inner consistency. "Upon this ground it is that I am bold to think that morality is capable of demonstration, as well as mathematics; since the precise real essence of the things moral words stand for may be perfectly known, and so the congruity or incongruity of the things themselves be certainly discovered, in which consists perfect knowledge." [9] Therefore it is our own fault if we do not obtain knowledge of morality. We have only to construct our own complex ideas and to note their connections. Whoever fails to think clearly on moral matters is guilty of "a great negligence and perverseness": [10] uncertainty or obscurity is evidence of laziness. Because of the nature of the mixed modes, a whole system of morality can be constructed by careful attention to the ideas present to the mind, without any reference to realities beyond.

Locke granted, however, that even in ethics some confusion of thought is likely to result. This confusion is due largely to the difficulties of language. In the first place, moral ideas cannot be represented, as mathematical ones can, by "sensible marks" or figures. One cannot draw a diagram of justice. The only means of distinguishing

[7] *Idem*, III, 3, [19].
[8] *Idem*, IV, 5, [11]. *Cf.* also III, 11, [17].
[9] *Idem*, III, 11, [16]. *Cf.* IV, 4, [7], 12, [8]. Also *Works*, Vol. IV, pp. 405-406.
[10] *Essay*, III, 11, [15].

mixed modes in an objective fashion is to give names to them. But names are not understood in the same way by different men, or by the same man at different times. There is no archetype or standard in nature whereby men can keep their terms definitely attached to the same ideas. In the second place, moral ideas are so complex that the precise group of simple ideas involved in their structure is difficult to determine. Some persons may omit as trivial an element which others regard as most important. A complex idea may not be altered much by the omission or inclusion of a certain simple idea; and thus moral terms may never be defined exactly but may be used for several similar groups of ideas. The memory is not capable of retaining the precise combination of parts for which the many moral terms and phrases stand. The more frequently an instance of a complex idea is met with in nature, the more exact it and its designation become. But nature does not furnish us with regular and permanent examples of all our moral ideas. Consequently, even the science of ethics will only approximate perfect formulation.[11]

Locke did not give many illustrations of the concrete moral ideas and truths which could be known according to his theory of ethics. But the few specific cases he did mention are most interesting. The manufacture of the separate moral ideas is the simplest part of the task. Sacrilege and adultery, justice and gratitude are ideas which can be formed and defined without reference to any acts committed. The idea of murder is obtained by compounding the idea of man and the idea of killing; and if to this combination is also added the idea of a father, there results the idea of parricide. Similarly, the ideas of adultery and of father and daughter or of mother and son unite to form the idea of incest; and the ideas of killing and of a particular part of a weapon produce the idea of stabbing.[12] These ideas, however, are only the rudiments for a knowledge of morality. They serve as terms for propositions which reason can build up by perceiving the agreements and disagreements between them. Complete moral propositions framed from mixed modes Locke did not often adduce. But two pieces of moral truth he discussed in a passage so significant that it should be quoted in full. " 'Where there is no property there is no injustice' is a proposition as certain as any demonstration in Euclid: for the idea of property being a right to anything, and the idea to which the name 'injustice' is given being the invasion or violation of that right, it is evident that these ideas, being thus established, and these names annexed to them, I can as certainly know this proposition to be true, as that a triangle has three angles equal to two right ones. Again: 'No government allows absolute liberty'. The idea of government being

11 *Idem*, III, 9, ⁶⁻⁹, 10, ⁴; IV, 3, ¹⁹, 4, ⁹.
12 *Idem*, III, 5, ⁵⁻⁶, 12, 9, ⁷.

the establishment of society upon certain rules or laws which require conformity to them; and the idea of absolute liberty being for any one to do whatever he pleases; I am as capable of being certain of the truth of this proposition as of any in the mathematics." [13] Here Locke gave evidence of the kind of method he would pursue in ethics. The mixed modes are examined in their relations to one another. Those which are perceived to agree are equated to each other; those which are perceived to disagree are negated of each other.

2. Before proceeding to sketch other ethical theories which Locke elsewhere advanced, it may be well to note the inadequacies of this first theory—especially as Locke seems to have been aware of these inadequacies and may even have turned to the other theories in order to reach a sounder position. In the first place, the system of morality based on mixed modes can almost be called futile. Locke was wont to claim that knowledge is best advanced by finding out the relations between abstract ideas.[14] But even if much of his claim were granted, the knowledge thus obtained is not sufficient for ethics; for it lies in the realm of timeless abstractions, while conduct lies in the realm of particulars and temporal change. The truths discovered by perceiving the relations between mixed modes may be eternal and immutable, and may throw considerable light on objective moral situations; but they are not enough to serve as a guide in problems of human conduct. As Berkeley wrote in commenting on this theory in his *Commonplace Book:* "To demonstrate morality it seems one need only make a dictionary of words, and see which included which. At least, this is the greatest part and bulk of the work. Locke's instances of demonstration in morality are, according to his own rule, trifling propositions." [15]

In the second place, the system of morality built on mixed modes could not give rise to moral obligation at all. Even though government and absolute liberty are inconsistent, such a truth does not disclose which is good and which bad. From that truth it no more follows that men should relinquish part of their liberties to the government than from the mathematical theorem about the equality of the three angles of a triangle to two right angles it follows that men should spend their lives drawing triangles. However important the propositions might be which are derived from a system of abstract ideas arranged as Locke would arrange them, these propositions would be assertions of logical implication. But logical implication and moral obligation are not equivalent, even though a knowledge of the former may be indispensable to the proper fulfilment of the latter. Even if

[13] *Idem*, IV, 3, [18].
[14] *Idem*, IV, 12, [7].
[15] Berkeley: *Works*, Vol. I, p. 39. Leslie Stephen, in his *English Thought in the Seventeenth Century,* Vol. II, p. 86, quoted Berkeley and expressed his agreement with the criticism. A similar criticism upon Locke is given by Hertling: *John Locke und die Schule von Cambridge*, p. 30.

"man" were one of the abstract ideas in the system of mixed modes, no advantage would result; for to expound what ideas agree with man and what disagree is not to explain what is right and what wrong for man to do.[16] Locke occasionally laid down moral rules which are really adequate, as, for example, the teaching that "we should love our neighbors as ourselves."[17] But how by any comparison of mixed modes did "should" get into that proposition? Locke's theory might disclose static truth, but could not produce obligation. In the *Essay* he wrote: "If it be true in speculation, *i.e.*, in idea, that murder deserves death, it will also be true in reality of any action that exists conformable to that idea of murder."[18] But how could one ever discover on Locke's theory, that murder deserves death? The relations between the mixed modes are all timeless, simply revealing logical implications. Hence the propositions derived therefrom could not give information concerning what consequences should follow an event in a temporal order, *i.e.*, concerning the fitness of one idea giving place to another as its proper moral complement. The outcome of Locke's morality of mixed modes either is a futile hierarchy of abstract ideas, or else assumes, without warrant, some further criterion. Yet Locke suggested no further criterion than the agreement of ideas in those parts of his *Essay* in which he attempted to build up a system of morality upon mixed modes.

3. Locke, as was shown in an earlier chapter, did not use the word idea in a consistent way; and when he shifted the meaning of that term, he was led, not only to a different epistemological position, but to a different moral theory. According to the second epistemological view, ideas are instruments whereby the mind gains knowledge of objects which lie beyond it. Morality thus becomes a matter of the relations, not of abstract ideas, but of realities themselves. Locke seems to have felt at times the inadequacy of his ethics based on mixed modes. Just as in his logical speculations he occasionally yielded to an intense realistic bias and treated directly of the nature of external things, so in his ethics the same bias appeared, and he then discussed, not the implications of mere ideas, but the rights and duties of men. He undoubtedly never realized the shifting of which he was guilty and the ambiguity to which it led. To be sure, he in one place considered a possible objection against the former moral theory, to the effect that the names of substances as well as of mixed modes are made

---

[16] Wollaston in *The Religion of Nature Delineated* identified sin with an act which interfered with a true proposition. That is, moral wrong equals intellectual error. This theory which Wollaston developed may have been suggested to him by Locke, as he followed Locke in many respects. But how can an act interfere with or contradict a proposition? If Locke had developed this part of his ethical theory, he would either have been led to Wollaston's position, or have adopted some other criterion for moral conduct than propositions about abstract ideas.

[17] *Conduct of the Understanding*, Chapter 43.

[18] *Essay*, IV, 4, 8.

use of in formulating moral principles; and he thought that he could dispose of this objection by saying that the natures of the substances "are not so much inquired into as supposed." [19]   But the objection is not so easily met.   For even if the substances are not fully known in their real essences, yet the ideas of those substances are certainly not mixed modes.   And the truth of propositions dealing with the ideas of substances is a matter, not of mere inconsistency, but of correspondence with real existence.   Even if, as Locke supposed in the cases of God and of oneself, the existence of substances can be certainly known, the ideas of those substances are not abstractions which the mind can create arbitrarily.   Locke referred to the idea of God in one passage [20] as if it were an abstract idea; but he surely did not intend any such thing, and was only guilty of an unfortunately careless expression of his thought.   Hence, even though ethics remains a completely rationalistic system, it no longer is simply a matter of the implications of mixed modes.

Locke discussed ethical theory from the standpoint of this second type of rationalism in several passages of the *Essay* and in the *Two Treatises of Government*.   The group of passages in the *Essay* and the bulk of the *Treatises* are not, however, altogether akin; for the *Essay*, as will be shown in the next section, makes use of a further element which does not figure largely in the *Treatises*.   Hence the ethical theory underlying the political doctrines of the *Treatises* really requires separate analysis.   The *Treatises* reveal, as clearly as any of Locke's works, his supreme trust in reason.   But instead of the continual insistence on the importance of abstract ideas and on the drawing of inferences from mere definition, there is recourse to the phrase "the law of nature" and a consequent direct handling of the objective realities and situations which ideas reveal.   The law of nature is mentioned twice in the *Essay*.[21]   But it is not there utilized to any great extent; for it is not a conception which fits in properly with Locke's theory of the origin of ideas, the new and unique feature which in the *Essay* he was aiming to contribute to philosophic thought. But however inconspicuous in the *Essay*, it is the dominant conception in the *Treatises of Government*.   Like Locke's partial retention of Cartesian ontology, it is a relic of the tradition under which he had grown up and with which he considered himself to have much in common.   By means of it he took his stand with Grotius and the writers who were opposing Hobbes.   He never for a moment so forgot the epistemological theory of the *Essay* as to confuse the law of nature with an innate law; but in many respects he followed Grotius and his

[19] *Essay*, III, 11, [16].
[20] *Idem*, IV, 11, [13].
[21] *Idem*, I, 2, [6], [13].

other predecessors in that general tradition rather closely. Where he was least concerned with the theory of knowledge and the origin of ideas, his realistic ethical thought developed most clearly.[22]

Locke, of course, made the law of nature identical with the law of reason. However much he modified the traditional theory of innate ideas by the introduction of empirical elements, he never ceased to retain the strong rationalistic emphasis of his century. Though force is "the way of beasts," reason is "the rule given between man and man." [23] Mankind has always been under this rule. Adam was so created that he could "govern his actions according to the dictates of the law of reason which God had implanted in him;" and "the law that was to govern Adam was the same that was to govern all his posterity." [24] Reason alone furnishes a guide suitable to man's dignity: it is "the candle of the Lord" which puts man above the level of the brute creation. It alone can rule the stormy passions: it alone is the means of overcoming violent outbursts of the animal instincts and so of establishing "the eternal, immutable standard of right." [25] Locke must have realized the inadequacy of Hobbes's theory, according to which the law of nature which is the law of reason is relegated to an impotent and insignificant status, and the civil law is made the moral law and the source of obligation. If reason discovers a law, it is *ipso facto* the moral law, beyond which there could be nothing more ultimate. Surely the law to which man is subject "could be no otherwise than what reason should dictate: unless we should think that a reasonable creature should have an unreasonable law." [26] The law of reason gives to man that rule which is "suitable to his nature." [27] The law of reason and the law of nature are but two expressions for the same principle, and that principle is the foundation of morality.

There are passages not a few in which Locke seems to have given a somewhat metaphysical interpretation to the law of nature, not explicitly, but by suggestion. The law of nature would then still be

[22] There is some justification for an attempt to harmonize Locke's seemingly diverse ethical theories in the *Essay* and the *Treatises on Government*. In an extract from his *Journal* which is quoted in King's *Life of Locke*, pp. 121-122, Locke contrasted the demonstrable sciences of mathematics and morality with "physics, polity, and prudence." Polity then is only a matter of probability, since it deals with objects beyond our ideas. Now, undoubtedly, the bulk of the matters discussed in the *Treatises on Government* would come under the head of polity. It is my opinion, however, that Locke would have included the law of nature within the limits of the science of morality. It is not so much a part of polity, as it is the ethical presupposition on which as a foundation polity must be treated. The whole drift of Locke's writing is such as to make it seem highly probable that he regarded the law of nature as rigidly demonstrable; yet certainly it is not demonstrable in the same way in which the science of morality is supposed in the *Essay* to be demonstrable. Unfortunately, Locke never wrote out his mature ethical views. Since he did not, inaccuracies are to be expected. But I refuse to attempt a "sympathetic harmonization" of Locke, and prefer to hold that he unconsciously shifted his meaning and was guilty of inconsistency. The inconsistency in his ethics is only parallel to that already noted in his epistemology.

[23] *Of Civil Government*, 181.

[24] *Idem*, 56. *Cf.* also 6, 12.

[25] *Works*, Vol. VII, p. 133.

[26] *Idem*, Vol. VII, p. 157.

[27] *Idem*, Vol. VII, p. 11.

equivalent to the law of reason, but would also be something additional. If moral propositions are not simply made up of abstract ideas, but deal with the things for which the ideas stand, and if at the same time reason, though only a faculty which perceives the agreements and disagreements of the objects before the mind, yet attains a knowledge of those moral propositions, it follows that there must be some connection between things in nature, for reason to apprehend, a connection between things which may well be called the law of nature. For example, when Locke made the statement quoted above that the law of reason demands obedience on the ground that it is alone suitable to man's nature, he implied that harmony with the course of nature is the ultimate moral criterion, even, perhaps, that nature itself has a moral structure. Again, when in the *Treatises* he dealt with crimes like adultery, he found their wrongfulness to consist, not in their mere logical inconsistency with other modes, but in their opposition to nature. Such crimes "have their principal aggravation from this, that they cross the main intention of nature, which willeth" other courses of conduct.[28] Thus Locke contended that nature has her own "will;" and though he obviously intended the expression as figurative, he seems to have implied that nature manifests a law and calls for obedience. Harmony or correspondence with this intention or law of nature is the standard of right action, and an attempt to run counter thereto is sin. This law is prior to human reason; for human reason does not create or determine it, but discovers it. It depends upon the nature of things, and is knowable by reason only because the nature of things and the reason of man came from the same Creator.

Such a metaphysical interpretation of the law of nature as a substantial quality of the framework of the world is difficult to prove;[29] for the evidence is not definite and tangible, but comes from the general atmosphere and tone of the *Treatises of Government*. In either case, however, whether Locke did or did not read the moral law into the structure of the world, he made a serious effort to develop ethics on the rationalistic foundation. And he met now with greater success in formulating concrete principles than when he was discussing merely mixed modes. Some of the agreements and disagreements among ideas by which the relations of things are revealed will be more fully treated in later chapters.[30] But a few must be mentioned here by way of illustration of the degree of success which Locke attained. A fundamental moral principle follows from the observation by reason of the natural equality of all men. "All that share in the same com-

---

[28] *Of Government*, 59.

[29] If Locke did have such a theory in mind he would therein show the influence both of Cicero and the Roman Stoics, and of Cudworth and the Cambridge Platonists, who endeavored to push back moral distinctions into the very nature of things.

[30] *Cf.* below, Book III, Chapters I–III.

mon nature, faculties, and powers are in nature equal, and ought to partake in the same common rights and privileges." [31]   Or, as the point was later expressed: "Creatures of the same species and rank, promiscuously born to all the same advantages of nature, and the use of the same faculties, should also be equal one against another without subordination or subjection." [32]   A second fundamental principle is the right to self-preservation. "Men, being once born, have a right to their preservation, and consequently to meat and drink, and such other things as nature affords for their subsistence." [33]   And no invasions of this right by isolated individuals or by an organized state is morally valid. [34] Similarly, a host of other principles illustrating Locke's method could be given.   Men are entitled to ownership of their own persons and the products of their own labor; and thus arises the right of property (within limits later to be noticed). [35]   Also "truth and the keeping of faith belongs to men as men." [36]   Likewise, "a man should forgive, not only his children, but his enemies, upon their repentance, asking pardon, and amendment," [37] etc., etc.   Thus Locke derived from reason's perception of the agreements and disagreements of ideas the various rules which go to make up the law of nature.

4. There is, as has been said, a series of passages in the *Essay* in which ethical theory is treated in quite as objective a fashion as in the *Treatises of Government*. These passages were reserved for special discussion in this section because they contain a further element not utilized to any extent in the *Treatises*. This further element is the idea of God. Though Locke did, to be sure, mention God in several paragraphs of the *Treatises*, he did not there employ the idea as a means of proving his moral rules, but derived his conclusions rather from the perception of the agreement or disagreement of other ideas altogether. The religious foundation for ethics, however, which was vaguely suggested in the *Treatises*, comes to figure quite prominently in parts of the *Essay*. The existence of God is "so fundamental a truth, and of that consequence, that all religion and genuine morality depend thereon." [33]

The difference between the ethical theory of the *Treatises* and the group of passages from the *Essay* which are now being considered is probably to be explained as simply one between deriving a few particular moral rules and expounding a general moral theory. The epistemological method is the same. Ideas are in each case instru-

[31] *Of Government*, 67.
[32] *Civil Government*, 4. Also *cf.* 87, 95.
[33] *Idem*, 25.
[34] *Idem*, 135.
[35] *Idem*, 25 ff.
[36] *Idem*, 14.
[37] *Works*, Vol. VII, p. 133.
[33] *Essay*, IV, 10, ⁷. *Cf.* also *Works*, Vol. VII, p. 161.

ments which reveal external things, and not mixed modes arbitrarily created. But while the moral rules in the *Treatises* were propositions which did not happen to depend on the idea of God as one of their elements, yet Locke maintained in the *Essay* that no general ethical theory could be stated unless the idea of God were included as the most important constituent. Consequently it might be inferred that though some rules, as those in the *Treatises*, were attainable without a consideration of God, most moral rules would be more closely connected with religion and the nature of God.

Locke sometimes used the religious sanction for morality in a way which, as will be shown in the next chapter, involved a break with his rationalistic ethics; that is, he made moral rules follow from God's arbitrary commands with rewards and punishments attached thereto. But there was no need for departing from the rationalistic position just because the idea of God was introduced. And he often utilized the idea of God, as he used the ideas of man, labor, equality, *etc.*, simply as part of the material upon which reason is to operate Reason cannot properly understand the relationships between objects, and consequently the true nature of morality, without taking into account the greatest and most powerful being in the world. From the idea of God as from other ideas, reason discovers moral principles. In 1681 Locke wrote in his journal that whoever "has a true idea of God, of himself as his creature, or the relation he stands in to God and his fellow-creatures, and of justice, goodness, law, happiness, *etc.*, is capable of knowing moral things or of having a demonstrative certainty in them." [39]   The same view later appeared in the *Essay:* "He also that hath the idea of an intelligent, but frail and weak being, made by and depending on another, who is eternal, omnipotent, perfectly wise and good, will as certainly know that man is to honor, fear, and obey God, as that the sun shines when he sees it; for if he hath but the ideas of two such beings in his mind, and will turn his thoughts that way, and consider them, he will as certainly find that the inferior, finite, and dependent is under an obligation to obey the supreme and infinite, as he is certain to find that three, four, and seven are less than fifteen, if he will consider and compute those numbers." [40]

Thus, though morality is here conceived as involving a knowledge of God's existence and nature, yet moral laws are not anything arbitrary. Morality is not reduced to mere obedience to divine fiats, but is altogether rational. The moral laws which reason demonstrates from its ideas of God and the other realities in the world are binding, not only upon man, but also upon God. For example, in *The Reasonableness of Christianity*, ethical distinctions are prior to and independent of the

[39] *King: Life of Locke*, p. 121.
[40] *Essay*, IV, 13, ⁴. *Cf.* also IV, 3, ¹⁸.

divine will. The moral part of the Mosaic law is contrasted with the ceremonial part; and while the latter is of "a limited and only temporary obligation by virtue of God's positive injunction," the former is "of eternal obligation." [41] And though God may accept faith in Jesus as Messiah in lieu of complete conformity to "the law of works," yet he cannot justify men indiscriminately; for he would not himself be "an holy, just, and righteous God," if he abrogated a single precept of the moral law. He cannot himself overturn "the measures of right and wrong" so long as the nature of things remains unchanged; and if he tried to do so, he would "be introducing and authorizing irregularity, confusion, and disorder in the world." [42] Thus, Locke in many passages employed the idea of God as the foundation of morality without in any way departing from his thoroughly rationalistic system.

5. The second type of rationalistic ethical thought which appears in the *Treatises of Government* and in certain parts of the *Essay* is in one respect an improvement over that other theory which is built upon mixed modes. Whether based on the law of nature or more exclusively on the idea of God, it views ideas as instruments for the knowledge of external realities, and deals with the objective world of moral struggle, thus avoiding the criticism made by Berkeley to the effect that Locke's moral propositions were trifling. But in other respects this second type of theory was hardly as satisfactory as the first.

In the first place, the law of nature as developed in the *Treatises of Government* does not seem to afford an adequate criterion for a distinction between right and wrong. The agreement or disagreement of the things which ideas reveal is more difficult to ascertain than the agreement or disagreement of ideas taken as objects in themselves. Reason in the writings of Locke and the other rationalists of the seventeenth and eighteenth centuries, proved to be an effective means of destructive criticism; for it could show that there was no necessary connection between things which had been traditionally associated. But it was not so fruitful a means for constructive work. Locke's fellow-rationalists had supplemented their faith in reason by some other standard such as innate truths (*cf.* the writers on the law of nature), the will of God (*cf.* the deists), or pleasure (*cf.* Hobbes), and then used reason to estimate the correspondence of men's actions to those standards. But Locke seems to have aimed in much of his writing to build up a purely rationalistic ethics in which reason would evolve the principle of morality from non-moral elements as well as observe the correspondence of actions thereto. Such an attempt was destined to inevitable failure. In making the attempt Locke was necessarily guilty of one of two errors. In the one case, he would have

[41] *Works*, Vol. VII, p. 13.
[42] *Idem*, Vol. VII, pp. 111–112.

had to identify the moral law with the actual course of nature. Whatever is, is right. For if two things coexist or follow each other as cause and effect in temporal succession, they are *ipso facto* demonstrated to be logically compatible.[43] Thus Locke would once more, as in the case of the ethics based on mixed modes, be confusing what is with what ought to be. He would be making a jump from a statement of fact to a justification or condemnation thereof, from description to evaluation. But such an error he could hardly have made, even if he had consistently identified morality with "the intention of nature." For, as he himself held, sin is a common occurrence. The law of nature is often transgressed. The state of war is as actual a situation as peaceful society. What reason perceives to "belong" together was never equated by Locke to what is observed to take place together. In the other case, Locke would have escaped from the error of merely sanctioning whatever occurs only to lapse into dogmatism. And this error is the one of which he seems actually to have been guilty. He simply made the law of nature include the moral principles which he himself happened to profess, *i.e.*, the moral principles of the liberal Christians and Whigs of his day. Other moralists such as Hobbes had undertaken to prove quite contrary principles. And since both sets of principles are exemplified by certain facts of experience, it is difficult to see how reason could select either set without importing some moral standard beyond itself. As both truthfulness and deceit, forgiveness and revengefulness are practised by different men, neither one can be said to "agree" with man more than the other. Locke seems to have been guilty here of the "enthusiasm" against which he elsewhere protested. He who was so effective an antagonist of dogmatism at most points seems here to have fallen into the fault he criticised. Perhaps it was the phrase "the law of reason" which misled him. The very supposition of law is out of place in dealing with reason as he conceived it. Reason might render judgments on matters of fact. Its conclusions might be spoken of as "the decisions of reason" or "the verdicts of reason." But they should not be referred to as a law. By using the term law, Locke was deluded into confusing description and evaluation. But this fallacy was unavoidable to a purely rationalistic ethics. As long as he regarded reason as evolving moral distinctions through its own activity, instead of as an instrument contributing to the success of moral enterprises defined by non-rational factors, just so long he was necessarily involved in the error which has been discussed.

[43] Thus J. F. Stephen says in his *Horæ Sabbaticæ*, Vol. II, pp. 153–154, that Locke's principles properly carried out would lead to the result "that the only questions which it is possible to treat with much hope of arriving at a permanently satisfactory conclusion upon moral and political subjects are questions of fact—questions, that is, as to the consequences which do, in fact, follow from certain courses of conduct."

In the second place the idea of God does not seem to have enabled Locke to obviate the difficulties of his rationalistic ethics. For in so far as he used the idea of God as the chief idea from which reason deduces the moral law, he was thrown back upon the nature of things once more. If morality came from God's arbitrary fiat, the difficulty would vanish (only, however, to be succeeded by a greater one). But since morality is prior to God's will, something according to which even God's will is guided, the difficulty remains. The moral attributes of God could be discovered by reason only from the nature of God and the other realities in the world, *i.e.*, from the law of nature. But the dependence of morality on the law of nature has been shown to be unsatisfactory.

Burnet was aware of the difficulty in which Locke was here placed. Though Locke had proved God to be all-knowing, all-powerful, and eternal, yet such attributes were insufficient for knowledge of the moral law. As Burnet said, it is not enough "that we know the physical or metaphysical attributes of the divine nature: we must also know its moral attributes, as I may so call them, such as goodness, justice, holiness, and particularly veracity. Now these I am not able to deduce or make out from your principles." [44] Locke replied to this attack by saying that the other attributes of God can be known from the few mentioned in the *Essay;* [45] but he seems to have been replying from the point of view, not of his rationalistic ethics, but of a different system of morality based on rewards and punishments. Unless some further criterion for ethics is put forward than the agreements which reason perceives between its ideas, even including the idea of God, the moral law must be either a statement of existing fact or a dogmatic begging of the issue. Locke himself seems to have realized the inadequacy of an attempt to base ethics wholly on reason; and, as will be shown in the next chapter, he endeavored to introduce a non-rational standard. Reason would still be important for ethics; but it would no longer have to evolve the principle on which morality is based.

6. Locke's attempts to establish ethics as a science on a purely rationalistic basis was thus never carried through to a consistent and successful conclusion. His confidence that morality would be mathematically demonstrated was an accompaniment of the epistemology which led to regarding moral principles as derived from a consideration of mixed modes. But this type of ethics he failed to develop because of the ambiguity in his treatment of the nature of ideas. In the *Treatises of Government* and in much of the *Essay*, he dropped all reference to mixed modes, and resumed his naïvely realistic bias of mind. Consequently, he gained an objective emphasis which makes

[44] *First Remarks*, p. 7.
[45] Noah Porter: *Marginalia Lockeana*, pp. 36, 42.

his principles more practical and useful.   Yet he certainly opened
the door at the same time to the charge of dogmatism.   In the *Treatises*
he evolved morality from the law of nature; and in certain sections of
the *Essay* he evolved it from the idea of God.   In both cases he thus
brought in ideas of substances in a realistic way.   But in all the types
of rationalistic ethics reviewed in this chapter, he was in error in expect-
ing to end up with moral distinctions instead of starting with them.
This procedure was not, however, the only one which Locke followed.
An entirely different type of ethical theory will be reviewed in the next
chapter.

CHAPTER IV

HEDONISTIC ELEMENTS IN LOCKE'S ETHICS

1. In addition to the attempts which have been outlined to define morality in terms of the rational connections of ideas, there is also in Locke another quite different approach to the ethical problems. This approach is the hedonistic theory which is stated most fully in the latter half of the second book of the *Essay*, and appears occasionally in other parts of the *Essay* and in the *Treatises of Government*. These hedonistic elements probably came to Locke from two sources. One source was surely the work of Hobbes. The definition of good and evil in terms of pleasure and pain, the analytic discourse upon the passions in the twentieth chapter of the second book of the *Essay*, the theory of human liberty which was given in the first edition of the *Essay*, are all so akin to Hobbes that it is almost incredible to suppose that Locke could here have been independent of his great predecessor. The other source was probably the work of the deists. For like the deists Locke tended to resolve virtue into implicit obedience to the will of God, which will is binding because it is enforced by the rewards and punishments of the future life. All of the hedonistic elements in Locke can be understood easily in the light of these two sources of influence.

Locke's statement of the hedonistic position is quite simple. Sometimes he identified good and evil immediately with pleasure and pain themselves; more often he applied the terms to the objects which produce pleasures and pains in us; and occasionally, he recognized that both usages were legitimate, the former in a primary, the latter in a secondary, sense. Thus the predicates good and evil may be affirmed either of pleasures and pains directly or of their causes. A characteristic passage is the following: "Now, because pleasure and pain are produced in us by the operation of certain objects, either on our minds or on our bodies, and in different degrees, therefore, what has an aptness to produce pleasure in us is that we call good, and what is apt to produce pain in us we call evil; for no other reason but for its aptness to produce pleasure and pain in us, wherein consists our happiness and misery." [1]

There is little in this initial statement of hedonism in which Locke did not agree with Hobbes. Happiness is defined altogether in terms of pleasure. [2] The removal or lessening of pain is included within the

---

[1] *Essay*, II, 21, ⁴³. *Cf.* II, 20, ¹⁻², 21, ⁶², 28, ⁵. Also King: *Life of Locke*, p. 310.
[2] *Essay*, II, 21, ⁴³. King: *Op. cit.*, p. 116.

meaning of the term pleasure, and the loss or diminishing of pleasure is included within the term pain.[3] The distant consequences of actions are to be taken into account as well as the immediate ones; and though every pleasure is in itself good, yet, since some pleasures bear pains in their trains, men should choose those things which produce the greatest balance of pleasure in the long run. "If I prefer a short pleasure to a lasting one, it is plain I cross my own happiness."[4] Moreover, the determination of what objects are good is entirely relative to each individual's tastes. What arouses pleasure in one person may not do so in another, so that nothing can be considered as good in and of itself apart from its effects on men's minds. "The happiness of man consists in pleasure, whether of body or mind, according to every one's relish."[5] In any case the hedonistic standard is clearly emphasized. "It is a man's proper business to seek happiness and avoid misery." Men should seek to have "as much of the one and as little of the other as may be;"[6] for in pleasure and pain lies the ultimate distinction between good and evil.

Yet even at the outset Locke differed from Hobbes on one important point. Whereas Hobbes identified pleasure and pain with the harmony or conflict of the internal motions of the body, Locke regarded pleasure and pain as subjective states of mind which "join themselves to almost all our ideas," and which may be the result of thoughts within the mind as well as of impressions on the body.[7] "By pleasure and pain, delight and uneasiness, I must all along be understood (as I have above intimated) to mean not only bodily pain and pleasure, but whatsoever delight or uneasiness is felt by us, whether arising from any grateful or unacceptable sensation or reflection."[8] Thus while Hobbes's view tended to be materialistic, Locke's hedonism avoided any such implication. Locke was not concerned in the *Essay* with the physiology of sensation, as Hobbes always was; and his medical knowledge did not lead him to assign a material basis for all feelings of pleasure and pain. Pleasure does, to be sure, come from health and sensuous experiences; but it also comes from reputation, from the possession of knowledge, from doing good to others, and from the expectation of future bliss.[9] And these other sources of pleasure were not traced back by Locke to any necessary bodily conditions.

2. Locke, however, as was mentioned above, regarded Hobbes with extreme disdain. Consequently, even if he learned much from Hobbes he would hardly be found to concur in all the doctrines of the *Leviathan*.

    [3] *Essay*, II, 20, [16].
    [4] King: *Op. cit.*, p. 306.
    [5] *Idem*, p. 116.
    [6] *Idem*, p. 306.
    [7] *Essay*, II, 7, [2].
    [8] *Idem*, II, 20, [18].
    [9] King: *Op. cit.*, pp. 306–307.

He not only avoided a materialistic interpretation of pleasure, but also gave hedonism a devout and pious turn by putting behind it a theological sanction. That is, he differed from Hobbes, not in his willingness to define good in terms of pleasure, but in his view of the source whence the greatest pleasures are found to come. In other words, though he took over much from Hobbes in the way of psychological basis of ethics, he stood more with the deists in his theory of the relative values of the different pleasures which men may seek to enjoy.

Locke distinguished between what he called natural good and evil, and moral good and evil. The pleasures and pains which occur naturally in the normal course of things fall into the first class; those which are annexed as rewards and punishments to a law ordained by some law-maker fall into the second class. "The difference between moral and natural good and evil is only this: that we call that naturally good and evil which, by the natural efficiency of the thing, produces pleasure or pain in us; and that is morally good or evil which by the intervention of the will of an intelligent free agent, draws pleasure or pain from it, not by any natural consequence, but by the intervention of that power." [10] Men are justified in taking into account all sources of pleasure and pain; for all pleasure and pain, from whatever source derived, are good and evil. Yet when men are concerned with those pleasures and pains which are the "natural" results of their actions, they are merely prudent.[11] Only when they concern themselves primarily with the extra-natural results which are imposed upon them by some law-maker are they really moral.

The only law-maker whom Locke deemed as capable of making a law which could bind men's consciences is God. Men live under the law of God, and that law is the measure of their duty. The pleasures he confers and the pains he inflicts are so overwhelmingly great that in comparison with them all other pleasures and pains may be overlooked by the moralist as trivial. The divine rewards and punishments must not be confused with the natural pleasures and pains which come upon men in this life in the normal course of things. If God did not use additional quotas of pleasure and pain to enforce obedience to his decrees, his decrees would be in vain—i.e., what he commanded would have authority over men only in so far as the natural consequences of the same conduct were good. In order to get from the natural to the moral sphere, one must leave consideration of the

[10] King: *Op. cit.*, p. 311. *Cf.* also *Essay*, II, 28, ⁵⋅⁶.

[11] *Cf. Works.* Vol. X, p. 307. Also King: *Op. cit.* pp. 88, 97–98. Locke was not indifferent to the good things of this life. "The next thing to happiness in the other world is a quiet, prosperous passage through this.. . . The study of prudence then seems to me to deserve the second place in our thoughts and studies." Patten (*The Development of English Thought*, p. 160) speaks of Locke as "a puritan plus the ideal of comfort." Such a characterization is excellent. Locke did not despise worldly success and fortune. *Cf.* his *Thoughts concerning Education*, §§ 67–70, 141–146. Yet he would not hesitate for a moment to sacrifice such success and comfort for the sake of the joys of heaven.

ordinary pleasures and pains of this life in favor of the special rewards and punishments which would not follow unless the course of nature were interfered with by God's supernatural power.

The effect of a theological sanction for a hedonistic ethics is to remove the emphasis from the present life to the next. Thus immortality becomes a fundamental necessity for morality; without it only natural good, and not moral good, would be possible. Locke spoke very slightingly of the kind of morality which is based on the rewards and punishments of this life only.[12] Heaven he regarded as "our great business and interest." [13] The present life is but a probation which cannot give men any deep happiness. "This life is a scene of vanity, that soon passes away; and affords no solid satisfaction, but in the consciousness of doing well, and in the hopes of another life." [14] To be sure, Locke sometimes settled moral issues on the hedonistic basis without considering anything but the consequences for men in the present world, as in the case of some of the moral rules put forth in the *Treatises of Government*. But whenever he became more conscious of the philosophical principles of his thought, and whenever he was engaged upon a religious theme, he stressed the importance of immortality and the fate which awaited men in the future world.

3. In spite of Locke's supposition that no other law than that of God was so enforced by large quantities of pleasure and pain as to have a moral claim over men, yet he recognized it as obvious that most men actually do judge of the morality of their actions by other standards. God is not the only law-maker who as a matter of fact controls men's consciences; indeed, he is hardly the chief factor in popular opinions of right and wrong. "The laws that men generally refer their actions to, to judge of their rectitude or obliquity, seem to me to be these three: (1) the divine law, (2) the civil law, (3) the law of opinion or reputation, if I may so call it. By the relation they bear to the first of these, men judge whether their actions are sins or duties; by the second, whether they be criminal or innocent; and by the third, whether they be virtues or vices." [15] Thus three distinct standards are used, some by some men, others by others. Few men in the world may know the will of the true God; but many have an idea of a rule supposed to be derived from some divine being and enforced by future rewards and punishments. Practically all men take account to some extent of the laws of the commonwealth; for the penalties attached to offenses committed against these laws are usually quick to overtake the guilty. Far the most influential law upon men's conduct is probably the law of opinion; for while the judgments of God do not fall

[12] In a letter to Tyrrell in 1690. *Cf.* King: *Op. cit.*, p. 199.
[13] King: *Op. cit.*, p. 97.
[14] In a letter to Anthony Collins, Aug. 23, 1704. *Works*, Vol. X, p. 298. *Cf.* also King: *Op. cit.*, p. 89.
[15] *Essay*, II, 28, 7. *Cf.* II, 28, 13.

upon men until the future life, and the sentences of the state may be lax or unenforced, the verdict of public opinion is merciless and swift. Men cannot stand out against the contempt of their fellows. "He must be of a strange and unusual constitution who can content himself to live in constant disgrace and disrepute with his own particular society." [16] The law of opinion is therefore the measure which men most commonly apply to their conduct.

Locke's discussion of the laws or sanctions used by men was misunderstood by some of his contemporaries to be a statement of his theory of the real source of moral distinctions. He quite clearly did not mean anything of the kind. He was describing what as a matter of fact is the ordinary procedure of the mass of men, and had no desire to defend or encourage that procedure. When his friend Tyrrell expressed disapproval of this section of the *Essay*, he wrote a letter to obviate Tyrrell's objections. In this letter he expressed himself so clearly as to leave no room for doubt. "If you will look into the end of that chapter, you will find it is not of concernment to my purpose in that chapter, whether they be as much as true or no; but only that they be considered in the minds of men as rules to which to compare their actions, and judge of their morality. . . . I did not design to treat of the grounds of true morality, which is necessary to true and perfect happiness; it had been impertinent if I had so designed; my business was only to show whence men had moral ideas, and what they were." [17] Yet, since Locke brought up the relation of morality to the laws of God, of the state, and of popular opinion, it may be well here to add a further comment in explanation.

Locke was in complete and violent opposition to Hobbes in regard to the relation of morality to the civil law. Indeed, since he accepted much of Hobbes's general hedonistic psychology, it was probably Hobbes's resolution of morality into obedience to the commonwealth which led him to hold so bad an opinion of his predecessor. He was aware, to be sure, of the necessity for civil or legal penalties in order to control certain men whose consciences are not sensitive to higher appeals. "Fear of punishment [by the state] often does what virtue should do." [18] Yet such punishment is nothing more than an external prop to morality. Against Hobbes's view Locke insisted that "we are under obligations antecedent to all human constitutions." [19] Human laws cannot create obligations which bind the conscience: they are purely penal, and not moral. It is of course true that men are under obligation to obey the civil laws; but that obligation arises,

---

[16] *Idem*, II, 28, [12].

[17] King: *Op. cit.*, pp. 200–201.

[18] Bourne: *Life of Locke*, Vol. II, p. 322.

[19] *Essay*, IV, 12, [4]. Locke did not mention Hobbes in this passage, though the view attacked is that set forth in the *Leviathan*.

not from the civil laws, but from the law of God. The virtues which presuppose society and government (such as obedience to magistrates and honesty in recognizing others' property rights) have the same source and origin as the purely private virtues (such as love of God and chastity). In both sets of virtues "the rule and obligation is antecedent to human laws, though the matter about which that rule is may be consequent to them." [20] Indeed, it may even happen in rare cases, as will be shown in a later chapter,[21] that men may righteously resist the civil laws and the magistrates. Yet even though such resistance is usually morally wrong, the guilt is due to a higher duty and sanction than government as such can create. Civil laws should be built upon and conform to moral laws; and moral laws are prior to and more ultimate than civil laws.

Locke took a very similar view of the relation of morality to the law of opinion. He made two distinct points here—that the nature of morality does not rest on popular opinion, and that the most common test used by man wherewith to judge of morality is conformity to popular opinion. His emphasis on the latter led some of his critics to overlook the former point. He wrote in his journal as early as 1678: "The principal spring from which the actions of men take their rise, the rule they conduct them by, and the end to which they direct them, seems to be credit and reputation, and that which at any rate they avoid, is in the greatest part shame and disgrace. . . . He therefore that would govern the world well, had need consider rather what fashions he makes than what laws; and to bring anything into use he need only give it reputation." [22] The same view he repeated in the *Essay* and in later short fragments. But he never ceased to insist on the other aspect of the matter, too. The standards of public opinion are "pretended and supposed everywhere to stand for actions in their own nature right and wrong," [23] but may not really be coincident therewith. He was willing to go so far as to acknowledge "that though it [*i.e.*, reputation] be not the true principle and measure of virtue, . . . yet it is that which comes nearest to it." [24] And he pointed out that an act which might be harmless when performed apart from society, might become a vice when performed in the midst of society, because the sentiment of public opinion would result in such disesteem for the doers of the act as to weaken their moral authority.[25] Nevertheless, all the knowledge of virtues and vices gained by listening to public opinion "amount to no more than taking the definitions

[20] King: *Op. cit.*, pp. 61–62.
[21] *Cf.* below, Book III, Chapter II, § 4.
[22] King: *Op. cit.*, pp. 109–110.
[23] *Essay*, II, 28,[10].
[24] *Thoughts concerning Education*, § 61.
[25] King: *Op. cit.*, pp. 292–293.

or significations of the words of any language, either from men skilled in that language, or the common usage of the country . . . so that the ideas of virtues taken up this way teach us no more than to speak properly according to the fashion of the country we are in." [26] If virtue is taken for those actions which are commanded by popular opinion, the standard of virtue would vary from country to country, and would nowhere entirely coincide with the true principle of morality.[27]

The two contemporary critics of Locke who most misunderstood him on this matter were Norris and Lowde. They can hardly be supposed to have been familiar with all the passages quoted in the preceding paragraph. They may have been misled by the phrase "philosophical law" which in the first edition Locke had used to express what in later editions he called "the law of opinion or reputation;" for the term "philosophical law" might easily be taken to refer to what has been demonstrated as valid. Yet there is much in the part of the *Essay* they attacked which should have kept them from such total misapprehension as they had. Norris thought he was opposing Locke when he said that "praise and dispraise may be a probable sign, or secondary measure, but it can never be the primary measure or law of virtue and vice . . . for praise or dispraise does not make, but supposes the difference of virtue and vice as already settled and antecedent to it." [28] In order to correct Norris's false interpretation of his meaning, Locke not only altered the phrase "the philosophical law," but also changed the wording of a whole paragraph in the second edition of the *Essay*.[29] Lowde likewise supposed he was contending against Locke when he maintained that virtue and vice are "founded upon something more fixed and certain than the custom of countries, or the mode and fashion of those with whom we do converse;" and he expressed regret that so simple a matter was confused by "the ingenious author of the *Essay of Human Understanding*." [30] To Lowde Locke wrote an answer which appeared in the second edition of the *Essay* as part of the *Epistle to the Reader*. He there once more reiterated the statement that in the passage which Lowde attacked he was only "enumerating the rules men make use of in moral relations, whether these rules were true or false," and did not aim to construct his own system of morality.[31] The laws of opinion should be so molded as to be harmonious with the moral laws; and the moral laws are as

---

[26] *Idem*, pp. 309–310.
[27] *Cf. Essay*, I, 2, [18].
[28] Norris: *Cursory Reflections upon a book called an Essay concerning Human Understanding*, pp. 32–33.
[29] *Cf.* Fraser's edition of Locke's *Essay*, Vol. I, p. 477.
[30] Lowde: *Discourse concerning the Nature of Man*, pp. xv–xvi.
[31] *Essay*, Epistle to the Reader, [12-14].

independent of the laws of opinion as they are of the enactments of governments.[32]

Locke took a different view of the relation of the moral law to the divine law. Of course he would have denied the identity of the moral law with the many absurd and contradictory notions of God's will which men of various lands have. In the section of the *Essay* in which he discussed the laws by which men ordinarily judge their conduct, he wished to point out that most ideas of the divine law are inadequate. Men do not get a true knowledge of morality from "the Alcoran of the Mahometans and the Sanscrit of the Bramins . . . or any other supposed divine revelation whether true or false." [33] Yet when men have a true idea of God's law and compare their actions to that law, then, as Locke said, they possess "the only true touchstone of moral rectitude." [34] This standard does not vary as do the laws of opinion, civil laws, and heathen superstitions; hence it, unlike the others, does give rise to genuine distinctions between right and wrong which are of eternal and immutable validity.

4. When Locke adopted a hedonistic ethical theory in parts of his writings, he did not thereby reject reason. To be sure, reason is no longer permitted to define the nature of morality. Pleasures and pains are not mixed modes, from which reason, by perceiving their agreements or disagreements, can discover moral principles. Rather they are simple modes, indescribable, indefinable, unanalyzable; and they already, before reason begins to work upon them, are in themselves good and evil. Reason does not here evolve ethical distinctions from elements which are entirely non-ethical, as in his more purely rationalistic ethics Locke endeavored to maintain; but reason works upon material which carries within itself the nature of good and evil which is the basis of the principles of morality. Yet even if ethical distinctions are now regarded as arising from a non-rational source, reason still has a considerable function to perform—indeed it is indispensable to the successful outcome of the moral life. One only has to picture what conduct which rejects the guidance of reason would result in, in order to understand the vital importance of reason. The cause of all moral errors is neglect of the voice of reason.

According to the hedonistic standard, everything which produces pleasure is, in so far, good. Moreover, since men have variant tastes and are pleased by quite different things, what is good for each man is

---

[32] It is most interesting to note that the third Earl of Shaftesbury, whose entire education Locke supervised, had the same misunderstanding of Locke's moral principles as Norris and Lowde. In his *Characteristics* he wrote: "Virtue, according to Mr. Locke, has no other measure, law, or rule, than fashion and custom; morality, justice, equity depend only on law and will." Vol. I, p. 346. We can only conclude that Locke, in training the Earl, overemphasized prudence and the desirability of winning others' esteem.

[33] King: *Op. cit.*, p. 201.

[34] *Essay*, II, 28, 8.

an individual matter to be settled by himself. And yet, though everyone seeks his own good, nearly all men fall constantly into sin. The
reason for their sinfulness is certainly not a desire to bring evil and
pain upon themselves, but is failure to judge correctly what will really
give them pleasure. They do not look far enough into the future, but
choose on the basis of immediate goods. "Were every action of ours
concluded within itself, and drew no consequences after it, we should
undoubtedly never err in our choice of good: we should always infal-
libly prefer the best." [35] But such is not the case. What gives pleasure
in the present may be followed by pains in the future which may partly
or wholly balance the initial good. "Our voluntary actions carry not
all the happiness and misery that depend on them along with them in
their present performance, but are the precedent causes of good and
evil, which they draw after them, and bring upon us, when they themselves are past and cease to be." [36] Hence, in making any choice men
should not be tied down to a consideration of immediate advantage,
but should give due weight to remote advantages also. And the most
overwhelmingly important goods are those of the life to come. Though
the pleasures of this life are attractive to all men, they are as nothing
compared to the joys of heaven. Luxury and debauchery may give
more pleasure for a brief moment than sobriety and study; but in
their ultimate effects they give a great overbalance of pain.[37] Nothing
which this life can offer can possibly recompense one for missing the
rewards which await those obedient to God's commands in the next
world.

Because of the varied multitude of goods which are offered to men,
and the complex considerations which are involved in the making of
any choice, the passions of the moment cannot safely be trusted as a
guide. Reason alone can fairly weigh the different quantities of pleasure and pain. Reason alone can carefully compare the various allot-
ments of good and evil which diverse courses of action involve. Reason
alone can correctly measure the conformity of men's actions to the
divine law. Men are too prone to act while they are still ignorant of
the full consequences of their choices. Even where they are not ignorant, they are likely to overlook these consequences through inad-
vertence. Unfortunately, present goods and evils are usually permitted
to bear too much weight as over against absent good and evils. Men
are "deceived by the flattery of a present pleasure to lose a greater." [38]
They rest satisfied in what they have without thinking of the inevitable
outcome. The bliss of heaven is so much more than any earthly joys
can amount to, that reasonable men will endure any privations now

[35] *Essay*, II, 21, 60.
[36] *Idem*, II, 21, 61.
[37] *Idem*, II, 21, 55.
[38] King: *Op. cit.*, p. 307

for the sake of the rewards to come. Yet most men blindly seize the transient and fleeting pleasures of the moment, refusing to consider the eventual penalties, or foolishly supposing that in their cases the penalties are not inevitable. "Men abandon themselves to the most brutish, vile, irrational, exorbitant life, without any check, or the least appearance of any reflection, who, if they did but in the least consider what will certainly overtake such a course here, and what may possibly attend it hereafter, would certainly sometimes make a stand, slacken their pace, abate of that height of wickedness their actions rise to." [39] Reason, if allowed to control, would recognize the relative values of various pleasures and pains, and would guide us to choose the largest amount of good. "The cause of our judging amiss, when we compare present pleasure or pain with future, seems to me to be the weak and narrow constitution of our minds." [40] Hence, in order to judge aright, reason must prevail. Thus even in a hedonistic ethical theory, there is an important place for reason. Only where reason measures various quantities of earthly pleasure, and especially compares human actions to the law of God, can men make a successful effort to live happy, *i.e.*, moral, lives. To be rational is to be moral; to be irrational, is to be immoral.

5. The question of the part which reason plays in Locke's hedonistic theory brings up the problem of freedom or liberty. This problem Locke considered in the twenty-first chapter of the second book of the *Essay*. He offered two quite different explanations of human liberty, and realized himself the imperfections of this part of his work. As Fraser says, the chapter is one "which, notwithstanding all Locke's painful labor, is perhaps the least satisfactory in the *Essay*." [41] The first explanation which Locke gave appeared in the first edition of the *Essay*. But he remained quite discontented with this statement of the matter, and suspected a lurking fallacy in his reasoning. [42] In the second edition of the *Essay*, a second explanation was offered, though the earlier view still remained in many sections, so that two quite distinct solutions of the problem of human liberty were mixed up in confusion with each other. Each of the two explanations requires separate comment.

According to Locke's earlier view, liberty consists "in our being able to act or not to act, according as we shall choose or will." [43] Liberty is something which a person may possess, but is not an attribute of the will. Locke, like Hobbes, denied that the will is an agent which does things. The will may be referred to as a faculty; but faculties

[39] *Idem*, p. 359.
[40] *Essay*, II, 21, 66.
[41] Fraser's edition of Locke's *Essay*, Vol. I, p. 380.
[42] *Cf.* his letter to Molyneux on Jan. 20, 1693. *Works*, Vol. IX, p. 305.
[43] *Essay*, II, 21, 27.

must not be supposed "to stand for real beings in the soul that performed those actions" which go on in the mind.[44] Though Locke is nowhere as clear in his thinking on this matter as was Hobbes, he seems to have agreed with his predecessor in viewing the will as a name for certain types of activity which men manifest. The will is "a power or ability to prefer or choose."[45] But the power to choose cannot be said itself to choose; rather the person who has the power chooses. Hence, though the will cannot be spoken of as free, the person may in many instances be free. Whenever a man considers any course of conduct, he cannot help but prefer to act or to forbear acting. One or the other preference must be made; and the will is not an agent which expresses the preference, but the name for the fact that men have preferences. Hence, there is no liberty in making a preference. Liberty is a matter of being able to carry out the preference. "Freedom consists in the dependence of the existence, or not existence of any action, upon our volition of it; and not in the dependence of any action, or its contrary, on our preference."[46] In so far as a man can carry out only one of two alternative courses of action, he is bound by necessity; and even if he prefers to perform that one which alone he is able to perform, he is none the less constrained. That is, an action may be voluntary and necessary at the same time.[47] In so far as a man can carry out either of two alternative courses of action according to his preference, he is free. Freedom is the absence of external constraint and the power of self-direction, no matter which of two alternative preferences may in any given case be held. Liberty involves more than voluntary action; for it includes the power to have done the quite opposite thing if the other preference had been made.[48]

This view of liberty which Locke put forward did not, as has been said, satisfy him. Perhaps it was just because he was forced to agree so much with the despised Hobbes that he distrusted his solution of the problem. Liberty he considered indispensable to morality; for if either matter or even God controls men altogether by external power, there can be no such thing as duty or obligation.[49] And though he confessed himself unable to reconcile the divine omnipotence with human freedom, he insisted on remaining "as fully persuaded of both, as of any truths I most firmly assent to."[50] He decried Hobbes for "resolving all, even the thoughts and will of men, into an irresistible fatal necessity."[51] Yet in denying that the will is free and guides the

[44] *Idem,* II, 21, [6]. *Cf.* also II, 21, [14], [15], [17], [20].
[45] *Idem,* II, 21, [17].
[46] *Idem,* II, 21, [27]. *Cf.* also II, 21, [22-25].
[47] *Idem,* II, 21, [10-11].
[48] *Idem,* II, 21, [8], [21], [27].
[49] *Works,* Vol. X, pp. 255–256.
[50] *Idem,* Vol. IX, p. 305.
[51] *Idem* Vol. X, p. 256.

selection of preferences, he came so close to the same fatal necessity, that he tried to find some other adequate solution of the problem. He showed his discussion of liberty to "a very ingenious but professed Arminian," evidently hoping for some aid; but the Arminian made no objections.[52] After months of thought on the matter, however, he reached a new theory which he outlined in a letter to Molyneux,[53] and incorporated in the second edition of the *Essay*.

According to this later view, liberty "is a power to act, or not to act, accordingly as the mind directs." [54] The will is now carefully distinguished from desires; and though the strongest and most pressing desires usually determine the will, yet such is not always the case. For the mind possesses "a power to suspend the execution and satisfaction of any of its desires, and so all, one after another." [55] In addition to particular desires there is also a "general desire of happiness" which "operates constantly and invariably in us;" and by suspending action for a time, men can determine whether the good at which any particular desire aims is consistent with their real happiness. The will is no longer defined as a general name for having preferences, but is now regarded as the power which delays for a time and finally permits the execution of desires. It is "a power to direct the operative faculties to motion or rest in particular instances." [56] Liberty, therefore, is not simply freedom from external constraint, but is a matter of the subjection of one's passions to the guidance of reason. Locke's overwhelming confidence in, and respect for, reason was such that he could not long remain content with a view of human freedom which made choice, as it was in Hobbes, a matter of the strongest desire. Even in his earlier statement of the matter he never openly so expressed his opinion; but what he did say would, if pushed to its logical outcome, have involved the unwelcome conclusion. His more mature view escaped any such implication. Liberty gives a chance for reason to prevail. Whoever does not suspend judgment and permit reason to view various immediate pleasures in the light of one's ultimate happiness, is an immoral and base victim of passion. From failure to use this liberty to be rational "comes all that variety of mistakes, errors, and faults which we run into in the conduct of our lives, and our endeavors after happiness; whilst we precipitate the determination of our wills, and engage too soon, before due examination." [57] Thus once more Locke gives evidence that the peculiar genius of his best thought

[52] *Idem*, Vol. IX, p. 305.
[53] *Idem*, Vol. IX, pp. 325-326.
[54] *Essay*, II, 21, [73]. Also in a letter to Molyneux: *Works*, Vol. IX, p. 326.
[55] *Essay*, II, 21, [48]. *Cf.* also II, 21, [53-54].
[56] *Essay*, II, 21, [73]. Also in a letter to Molyneux: *Works*, Vol. IX, p. 326.
[57] *Essay*, II, 21, [48].

tended to rationalism, that even in the hedonistic part of his writings he did not lose his assurance in the importance of reason, that the very search for the greatest amount of pleasure must be guided in a rational way.

6. Locke's hedonistic ideas cannot be said ever to have constituted an independent and self-sufficient ethical system. They enabled him to avoid the chief difficulty of the type of ethics outlined in the last chapter, *i.e.*, the difficulty of getting from the realm of description to the realm of obligation and evaluation. In pleasure and pain he had something which he regarded as good and evil in themselves, so that it was not necessary to evolve moral distinctions from non-moral elements. The most important feature of his hedonistic thought for the future history of a British ethical philosophy was the theological sanctions. Though he seems to have started by accepting Hobbes's general psychological background for ethics, he departed from Hobbes at many points. He was too much devoted to the interests of religion to admit much of the materialistic and worldly emphasis of Hobbes. He not only insisted on pleasures of the mind as well as of the body, as if the former had no physiological basis, but also held up the rewards in heaven as so completely outweighing all other pleasures as to be alone worth considering. Hence, though he acknowledged every pleasure as a natural good, he defined moral good wholly in terms of those pleasures gained by obedience to God's will. The sanction of popular approval and of the civil law are of trifling account in comparison with the divine law. Locke considered, therefore, that even though reason does not discover the source of good and evil, reason is still necessary as a guide to the highest happiness. The unregulated passions precipitate one into a rush for immediate gratifications with no thought for the future. Reason alone can strike a suitable balance between the claims of many conflicting goods. Human freedom consists, not simply in liberty from external control, but in the ability to suspend the operation of the passions until reason has examined the particular desires for specific goods in the light of the general desire for the highest happiness. Yet if Locke had endeavored to carry out the development of ethics on this basis, he would have found a fresh difficulty facing him. For in so far as God's will is an arbitrary power, the possibility of discovering the content thereof by reason is excluded, and recourse would have to be had to revelation. Such recourse was contrary to the supposition that morality can be proved by reason as well as known by revelation. It is a curious fact that Locke and the early deists here shared an opinion which was in opposition to their liberal theological position. Neither he nor they, in so far as they rested ethics on the positive commands of God, could logically have done

other than rely on revelation to supply the contents of those commands; and yet he insisted that reason was as competent as revelation to make known the rules of morality, and they rejected revelation altogether. This difficulty may have escaped Locke's attention just because there was side by side with his hedonism the other and completely rationalistic theory.

CHAPTER V

THE RELATION BETWEEN THE RATIONALISTIC AND
THE HEDONISTIC ELEMENTS IN LOCKE

The connection between the various types of ethical theory in Locke has been a source of considerable confusion to critics and historians. How should Locke be classified? Can the purely rationalistic and hedonistic elements of his thought be harmonized and made part of one unified system? Or are they inconsistent and separate strands which he held alternately and never brought together? An attempt will be made in this chapter to examine two related problems and Burnet's criticism of Locke upon this matter.

1. The first question of importance for the historian of Locke to consider is the relation between virtue and pleasure. Undoubtedly, the relation is an intimate one. As he wrote in his *Thoughts concerning Education:* "I place virtue as the first and most necessary of those endowments that belong to a man or a gentleman. . . . Without that, I think, he will be happy neither in this nor the other world." [1] But either of two alternative interpretations is here possible. According to one alternative, virtue and vice are distinctions which rest upon the nature of things as discovered by reason; and pleasure and pain are simply the fitting consequences which God in his justice has arranged as rewards and punishments therefor. According to the other alternative, virtue and vice are constituted as such by the consequences in pleasure and pain which follow certain types of action, and can therefore be defined in terms of their consequences. In the former case, virtue is the primary conception, and pleasure is a proper culmination which fortunately happens to crown a virtuous life. In the latter case pleasure is the goal and end of conduct, and virtue is the best means thereto. Which of these alternatives did Locke accept?

Critics have been ready on both sides to interpret Locke as holding one of the alternatives to the exclusion of the other. [2] But they have

---

[1] *Thoughts concerning Education,* § 135. *Cf.* also *Essay,* I, 2, ⁶.

[2] On the one hand Curtis (*An Outline of Locke's Ethical Philosophy,* p. 137) maintains that Locke repudiated "the basing of moral distinctions on the utility of actions to produce happiness," and defined happiness in terms of virtue. So also Alexander (*Locke,* in the *Series of Philosophies Ancient and Modern,* p. 72) holds that in Locke's view "the value of moral laws is not derived from the pleasure and pain they bring by way of sanction." On the other hand, Sir James Fitzjames Stephen (*Horæ Sabbaticæ,* Vol. II, pp. 134–136) takes the view that Locke expounded "the criminal law theory of morals," and treated morality as "a system having for its object the attainment of happiness." Likewise, Sir Leslie Stephen (*English Thought in the Eighteenth Century,* Vol. II, p. 81) says that in Locke "virtue is approved because visibly conducive to happiness, and conscience is merely our opinion of the conformity of actions to certain moral rules, the utility of which has been proved by experience." The latter two critics are much

thus erred in selecting for emphasis that element of Locke's thought which is most in harmony with their own views. Locke never reduced his various ideas on ethics to a systematic statement. He was receptive to many influences, and reflected the many sources from which he derived inspiration. It would be a mistake to attempt to fit all he said into one harmonious whole. Rather it is best frankly to recognize the diverse elements as more or less unrelated aspects of his thought. At certain times he certainly tried to make ethics a purely rationalistic science, insisting that a man's will should "be always determined by that which is judged good by his understanding," that "we should take pains to suit the relish of our minds to the true intrinsic good or ill that is in things," and that "the eternal law and nature of things must not be altered to comply with his [i.e., any man's] ill-ordered choice." [3]   At other times he wrote as if virtue were to be measured by the consequences for happiness. By belittling the pleasures of the present world in favor of those in the life to come, i.e., by subordinating all other sanctions to the theological sanction, he may have deemed himself to have avoided the reproach which usually attaches to the scramble for pleasure; but he none the less adhered to the principle of hedonism. Though he maintained that God has so attached pleasures and pains to things that we will not be able to find our highest happiness in our present environment, but will be led to seek our bliss in the next world,[4] yet he valued heaven for the pleasure it affords. "Virtue, as in its last obligation it is the will of God, discovered by natural reason, and thus has the force of a law; so in the matter of it, it is nothing else but the doing of good, either to oneself or others; and the contrary hereunto, vice, is nothing else but the doing of harm." [5] Consequently, neither element of Locke's thought can be stated in terms of the other. While the rationalism of his epistemological theory led him to one point of view (or rather to a series of closely related points of view),[6] his practical British "common-sense," [7] and his simple piety, led him to quite another. So sometimes the nature of virtue is, in his ethics, independent of pleasure, even though it merits pleasure as a reward; and at other times the nature of virtue is constituted by the pleasures which it is destined to secure. The former position is

fairer to Locke than the former ones. For J. F. Stephen recognizes (p. 150) that in the *Treatises of Government* Locke followed a rationalistic method; and L. Stephen goes on to point out vacillations in Locke in which Locke became at times rationalistic. Sidgwick in his *Outlines of the History of Ethics*, pp. 175-178, gives a properly balanced account of the rationalistic and hedonistic elements in Locke, and is a happy exception to the one-sided attitude of most critics.

[3] *Essay*, II, 21,[54,57].
[4] *Idem*, II, 7, [5].
[5] King: *Op. cit.*, p 292.
[6] *Cf.* above, Book II, Chapter III.
[7] It must be remembered that Locke was interested in many of the acutely pressing problems of his day, in economics, finance, foreign trade, agricultural restoration in Ireland, *etc.* And in such problems pleasure was a much more handy standard to apply than was the perception of the agreement or disagreement of ideas.

the one which is more consistent with the bulk of his original philosophical speculations; the latter is the one which is more in keeping with his interest in economic and political affairs, his deistic tendencies, and his implicit trust in religion.

2. A question closely related to the preceding is the relation of God's will to the moral law. In both the rationalistic and hedonistic aspects of his thought Locke brought ethical distinctions ultimately back to God. Indeed, it is probable that it was just this stating of the problem of morality in religious terms which kept him from noting the discrepancies between the two points of view which he at different times maintained concerning the connection of virtue and pleasure. But the religious sanction, instead of resolving his difficulties, only made them more acute. The will of God in imposing rewards and punishments may be related to good and evil in either of two ways. In one case God is the most important of the realities from the ideas of which reason ascertains the moral law; and the will of God, directed according to the dictates of his reason, simply adds rewards or punishments to the obedience or disobedience of the moral law, in order to compel men to take their duties more seriously and to satisfy the requirements of justice. In the other case God is the chief source whence flow pleasures and pains; and his will is therefore the creator of moral distinctions, the essential fact in terms of which good and bad must be defined. The difference between these two points of view is very fundamental. According to the former, things are commanded or forbidden by God because they are right or wrong; according to the latter, they are right or wrong because God commands or forbids them. However, it seems that Locke never faced this issue squarely. If he had consistently made virtue prior to pleasure, he would also have made good and bad more ultimate than God's will; but he seems to have felt the inadequacies of a purely rationalistic ethics, as has been shown, and found it difficult to evolve moral distinctions from terms which were non-moral to begin with. If he had consistently made virtue a means to pleasure, he could have gone on to define good and bad wholly in terms of the consequences arbitrarily attached to certain courses of conduct by the power of God's will; but he was unwilling to renounce his rationalism to such an extent. And so he vacillated between two theories of the relation of God's will to the moral law, as in the case of the relation of virtue to pleasure.

The passages in which Locke used the idea of God as the basis of a rationalistic ethics have been referred to above.[8] It is only necessary here to produce the passages in which he held to the opposite view-

---

[8] *Cf.* above, Book II, Chapter III, § 4.

point.[9] He made at times a most significant division of ethical considerations into two parts. The first part is the collection of ideas such
as drunkenness, lying, modesty, frugality, which may be called "positive absolute ideas." The second part is the comparison of men's
actions to the law of God. The positive absolute ideas do not in themselves, nor in their relation to each other, determine morality. Only
the conformity of actions relatively to the divine law enables conduct
to be called "good, bad, or indifferent." [10] Morality here comes to be
a consequence of will rather than of reason alone. To oblige the conscience, as Locke wrote in his journal in 1676, is the same thing as
"to render the transgressors liable to answer at God's tribunal, and
receive punishment at his hands." [11] And in the *Essay* he maintained:
"The true ground of morality . . . can only be the will and law of a
God, who sees men in the dark, has in his hand rewards and punishments, and power enough to call to account the proudest offender." [12]
"Without a notion of a law-maker, it is impossible to have a notion of
a law, and an obligation to observe it." [13] And though reason is useful
in comparing men's conduct to the law, reason does not frame the law
also. Thus Locke at times made the will of God in imposing rewards
and punishments the origin of right and wrong.[14]

The inconsistencies in Locke's account of the relation of God's will
to the moral law nowhere come out more clearly than in his brief paper
Of Ethics in General. This paper, which is the nearest approach to a
systematic statement of his position, reveals a striking distrust of the
ability of reason to establish solely by itself an acceptable theory of
ethics. "Whoever treats of morality so as to give us only the definitions
of justice and temperance, theft and incontinency, and tells us which
are virtues, which are vices, does only settle certain complex ideas of
modes with their names to them . . . but whilst they discourse ever
so acutely of temperance or justice, but show no law of a superior that
prescribes temperance, to the observation or breach of which law there
are rewards and punishments annexed, the force of morality is lost,
and evaporates only into words, disputes, and niceties. . . . Without
showing a law that commands or forbids them, moral goodness will be

---

[9] Shaftesbury in his *Characteristics*, Vol. I, p. 346, again throws light on the views of his tutor Locke.
He says: "According to Mr. Locke, . . . God indeed is a perfect free agent in his sense; that is, free
to anything that is, however ill; for if he wills it, it will be made good; virtue may be vice, and vice
virtue in its turn, if he pleases. And thus neither right nor wrong, virtue nor vice, are anything in
themselves."

[10] *Essay*, II, 28, [15]. Also King: *Op. cit.*, p. 313.

[11] King: *Op. cit.*, p. 62.

[12] *Essay*, I, 2, [6].

[13] *Idem*, I, 3, [8]. *Cf. Works*, Vol. VII, p. 144.

[14] Thomas Fowler in his book on John Locke in the *English Men of Letters Series* (pp. 153–154) maintains that Locke, like Paley after him, made morality depend solely on the will of God. Though Fowler
exaggerates the importance of this one element in Locke's thought, yet certainly the element is con-
spicuously there, and has been too much overlooked by those critics of Locke who are themselves inclined to rationalism.

but an empty sound." Locke did not here deny that the collection of simple ideas into mixed modes was important; but he did deny that reason could by examining these modes determine which are good and which are bad. In addition to that elementary form of ethical inquiry, "there is another sort of morality or rules of our actions, which though they may in many parts be coincident and agreeable with the former, yet have a different foundation, and we come to the knowledge of them in a different way; these notions or standards of our actions, not being ideas of our own making, to which we give names, but depend upon something without us, and so not made by us, but for us. . . . To establish morality, therefore, upon its proper basis, and such foundations as may carry an obligation with them, we must first prove a law, which always supposes a law-maker: one that has a superiority and right to ordain, and also a power to reward and punish according to the tenor of the law established by him. This sovereign law-maker who has set rules and bounds to the actions of men, is God, their Maker." Therefore, the task of the moralist is to show that certain laws are what God wills for men.[15]

This passage from Locke's short paper on ethics has been quoted liberally because of its great significance. Some critics of Locke have endeavored to harmonize the two aspects of his thought by supposing that God's will declared that law which God's reason discovered as being in accordance with the nature of things.[16] But such a defense of Locke cannot be permitted. For if the will of God were controlled by moral distinctions noted by his reason, men, having the faculty of reason also, could define the moral law apart from reference to God's will. There would then be no need for the "second sort of morality," in which moral laws are treated as positive divine enactments. There would be no need to suppose a law-maker with rewards and punishments back of the law. But the fact that Locke did feel the need for such a law-maker argues against this attempted harmonization. Locke's strong hedonistic sympathies, adopted from the teaching of Hobbes and reinterpreted in the light of deistic theology, could not be assimilated into the rationalistic ethics which he attempted to build on the foundation of his epistemological theories. In addition to being a rationalist and an admirer of Grotius, Hooker, and Pufendorf, Locke was also a pious Christian. So it was easy for him to follow the deists in their resolution of moral obligation into obedience to the divine will, with the background of hedonistic assumptions. Any rationalist

---

[15] King: *Op. cit.*, pp. 309–313.

[16] *E.g.*, Curtis: *An Outline of Locke's Ethical Philosophy*, pp. 49–62. The inconsistency in Locke is, however, recognized by other critics. J. F. Stephen in his *Horæ Sabbaticæ*, Vol. II, p. 153, says: "It is poor logic to argue that Infinite Wisdom commanded a thing because it is right, and that it is right because it is commanded by Infinite Wisdom; yet this is the fallacy into which Locke falls throughout the whole of this essay" (*i.e.*, the *Treatise of Civil Government*).

could well reinforce his system of ethics by an exhortation to obey God. But Locke seems to have done so, not merely to derive from religion a further homiletical aid for a morality based on a prior principle, but to attain a principle which would be itself a philosophical foundation for morality. In so doing, he was guilty of equivocation.

3. Thomas Burnet was aware of the implications for ethical theory of those passages in the *Essay* in which Locke appealed to God's will as the criterion. In his *First Remarks* on the *Essay* he wrote: "You allow, I think, moral good and evil to be such antecedently to all human laws; but you suppose them to be such (if I understand you right) by the divine law. To know your mind farther, give me leave to ask, what is the reason or ground of the divine law? whether the arbitrary will of God, the good of men, or the intrinsic nature of the things themselves? . . . You seem to resolve all into the will and power of the law-maker. But has the will of the law-maker no rule to go by? And is not that which is a rule to his will a rule also to ours, and indeed the original rule?" [17] To this criticism which has so much justification Locke returned only an angry evasion. "Whoever sincerely acknowledges any law to be the law of God, cannot fail to acknowledge also that it has all the reason and ground that a just and wise law can or ought to have; and will easily persuade himself to forbear raising such questions and scruples about it." [18] But other critics than Burnet have insisted upon raising such questions and scruples; and since Locke refused to face the criticism frankly, the inconsistency remains in his work. Burnet returned to the same line of attack in his *Second Remarks*. He insisted that morality cannot be constituted "by the will of God only, if you take that will for an arbitrary power." And he gave three reasons for his position. First, there would be no fixed moral law, and God might be the author of what is called sin. Though Locke of course regarded God's will as unchangeable, and hence the moral law flowing therefrom as eternal and immutable, yet Burnet's point is a good one. For if God's will is arbitrary and not determined by the nature of things, there is no possible way of establishing the contention that it may not change, and thus reverse present moral laws. Secondly, if right and wrong are determined to be such by the will of God, God's holiness ceases to mean anything. Being above moral distinctions, God could have no moral attributes. Thirdly, if God's will is the creator of the moral law, it must be through his power as the rewarder and punisher of his creatures. But in that case, love of God and love of virtue would be resolved into self-love; men would obey God, not for his sake, but for their own; and morality

[17] Burnet: *First Remarks*, p. 6.
[18] Locke: *Works*, Vol. IV, p. 188.

would depend on sheer might, not on distinctions discovered by reason.[19]

To these elaborated criticisms Locke did not reply at all. He considered them as impertinent and spiteful jibes. His silence, however, seemed to some of his followers as yielding a point to Burnet. So in 1702 Mrs. Cockburn brought out her *Defense of Mr. Locke's Essay.* She endeavored to defend Locke on the ground that while moral distinctions rested on the nature of things, these distinctions could be spoken of as having the force of a law only when rewards and punishments were attached by God to men's compliance with or deviation from their natural duties.[20] Unfortunately, Locke did not himself reply to Burnet; and his letter of thanks to Mrs. Cockburn [21] cannot be regarded as assent to her answer to Burnet. Hence it seems only fair to conclude that while on other matters mentioned in an earlier chapter Burnet's lesser mind misunderstood and distorted Locke's meaning, he here sensed an important difficulty which Locke would not properly consider.

[19] Burnet: *Second Remarks,* pp. 21–25.

[20] Cockburn: *Defense of Mr. Locke's Essay,* p. 14. This view was suggested by Culverwel and Pufendorf also, who divided law into precept and sanction, and thus held that law, though discovered by reason, is not binding until enjoined by God. *Cf.* above, Book I, Chapter I, § 2.

[21] *Works* Vol. X, pp. 314–315.

CHAPTER VI

THE SPRINGS OF ACTION IN LOCKE'S ETHICS

1. A moralist should not be content merely with defining the nature of good and evil, the source of moral distinctions, the criterion of moral judgment. From these more general problems he should proceed to investigate the possibilities of attaining a higher standard of morality in personal and social affairs. He should examine the springs of action in human nature, and thus determine what motive power animates men in the struggles of life. Then upon this knowledge of psychological matters, he should seek to build up a theory of moral education, a description of the technique requisite to train men to overcome temptations to evil and to acquire virtuous habits. Not until the bearings of a philosopher's general position upon educational issues are observed, does the significance of his thought become entirely clear.

Locke is a notable instance of a moralist who did discuss the implications of his ethical views for the practical problems of moral education. He was concerned in all of his speculations, as was shown above, by a desire to promote morality and religion. He was both engaged upon matters of economic and political reform, in which he had many opportunities to observe men's motives, and was also greatly interested to arouse in men a solicitude concerning their ultimate destinies. Consequently, it is not surprising to find him puzzling over the question of what are the springs of action. This question was a difficult one for him to answer; for a different solution of it would have been required in order to sustain the validity of each of the ethical theories which he at various times put forward. If he was to continue to defend his purely rationalistic ethics, he would have had to maintain that the dictates of reason control conduct. If he was to adopt a thoroughly consistent hedonism, he would have had to allow pleasures and pains to determine men's actions. The former of these alternatives he accepted in his short essay on the *Conduct of the Understanding*, and the latter in the first edition of the *Essay*. But he was satisfied with neither of these solutions. He was finally driven in the second edition of the *Essay* [1] to a mediating position, akin to the new theory

---

[1] The second edition of the *Essay* was of course written at an earlier date than the *Conduct of the Understanding*. Nevertheless, the view expounded in the second edition of the *Essay* does seem to be a compromise between the rationalistic and hedonistic elements in his thinking. The pure rationalism of the later work simply proves the point made in an earlier chapter; namely, that Locke did not develop from an earlier to a more mature type of ethical theory, but held inconsistent and unharmonious theories throughout the years in which he was writing his various works.

of human liberty which he was there expounding. This view was a compromise, and was the nearest approach which Locke ever made to a synthesis of the varied elements which usually remained unconnected and apart in his thought.

Then in addition to Locke's different discussions of the springs of action, he gave an important further evidence of his position in the *Thoughts concerning Education*, the first important English treatment of educational theory. Nowhere in his writings does the significance of his attitude to moral problems stand out more clearly. What he there said will thus serve as an excellent conclusion to the review of Locke's ethics which has been made in the last four chapters. The theory of the *Thoughts concerning Education*, though not entirely consistent, is on the whole more nearly so than anything else Locke ever wrote. The work was put together, on the basis of notes written nearly a decade earlier, during the same months in which he was revising the *Essay* preparatory to the second edition; and it very probably was the influence which helped him to find the particular solution of his former difficulties to which he finally gave expression in the second edition of the *Essay*.

2. The most deeply held of Locke's philosophical convictions may be said to have been his confidence in reason. However much he may at times have departed from the rationalistic camp, he always returned with undiminished assurance to the original emphasis. Yet in no one of his works except the short essay on the *Conduct of the Understanding*, written in 1697, did he consistently state, without the admixture of some hedonistic elements, his belief in the power of reason to control conduct. In even the most rationalistic parts of the *Essay* he seems to have acknowledged that occasionally a passion might be so strong as to sweep a man precipitately to do what in calmer moments he would have refrained from. But in the *Conduct of the Understanding* he recognized no such possibility. "The will itself, how absolute and uncontrollable soever it may be thought, never fails in its obedience to the dictates of the understanding." [2] A man is governed, not by pleasure and pain, but by ideas and knowledge. Whatever acts he performs follow from some reason which he has for the acts. All his other faculties submit to the guidance of the understanding. "The understanding, with such light as it has, well or ill informed, constantly leads; and by that light, true or false, all his operative faculties are directed." The springs of action are "the ideas and images in men's minds." Thus Locke here admitted the possibility of no vice except that of error in judgment. And if he had developed this view into a theory of moral education, he would have had to maintain that moral education was a matter solely of the training of the reason, *i.e.*, was identical with intellectual education. Sin would come from faulty

---

[2] *Conduct of the Understanding*, 1.

ideas or ignorance; virtue would come from true ideas or knowledge. The moralist would have nothing to do except to discover the proper method for the conduct of the understanding.

Locke did not carry out this extreme rationalistic view of the springs of action in any other part of his writings. His rationalism was usually of a different type—that reason should, but unfortunately does not always, control conduct. His denunciation of "enthusiasm" and most of the *Essay* were written from this more moderate point of view. But before discussing this theory, it may be well to turn to the statement of the extreme hedonistic position.

3. In the first edition of the *Essay*, where Locke seems to have been still largely under the influence of Hobbes, the springs of action are set forth as wholly a matter of the greatest pleasure. The will or volition, as was shown in an earlier chapter, is not a faculty apart from the desires which thrusts itself into the situation in a somewhat miraculous manner and decides which desire shall be allowed to regulate conduct; but rather will is a general name for the fact that there are desires, preferences, or choices. Thus the important question for the moralist is as to what determines the preferences. Locke's answer to this question was that preferences are always determined by pleasure. "The preferring the doing of anything to the not doing of it . . . is nothing but the being pleased more with the one than the other." [3] A man cannot help being pleasantly affected by some objects and painfully affected by others; nor can he help his preferring of the pleasures to the pains. Also when two or more rival pleasures are offered to a person at once, he cannot do other than choose the greater; for a greater pleasure often excels a smaller pleasure as much as the smaller pleasure excels a pain. Hence, the will is determined to be what in every particular case it happens to be "by something without itself." [4] Indeed, if the ideas men derive from sensation and reflection did not have pleasures and pains joined to them, there would be no motive for their choosing one course of action rather than another, so that they would be idle and inactive, passing their days as in a dream. In that case "we should neither stir our bodies, nor employ our minds, but let our thoughts (if I may so call it) run adrift, without any direction or design, and suffer the ideas of our minds, like unregarded shadows, to make their appearances there, as it happened, without attending to them." [5] Consequently, the importance of pleasure and pain as the motives in action cannot be overestimated. All the emotions can be defined in terms of those two simple ideas. "Pleasure and pain, and that which causes them, good and evil, are the hinges on which our passions turn." [6]

[3] *Essay*, First Edition, II, 21, [28]. *Cf.* Fraser's edition, Vol. I, p. 375.
[4] *Essay*, First edition, II, 21, [29]. *Cf.* Fraser's edition, Vol. I, p. 375.
[5] *Essay*, II, 7, [2].
[6] *Idem*, II, 20, [3]. *Cf.* King: *Op. cit.*, p. 308.

Even in the first edition of the *Essay*, however, Locke disclosed his dissatisfaction with the view he was expounding. It seemed to drive him to the conclusion that moral education was impossible, since action follows the greatest balance of pleasure, and men are not free to choose what objects they will find their pleasures in; and it seemed to leave no opportunity for reason at all. He was almost apologetic in his statement of this extreme hedonistic view. He wished to escape the conclusion that men were mere creatures swayed by the strongest pleasure. And so he devoted three paragraphs [7] to the point that it is not an imperfection in man to be determined by the greatest good (good here being used in the hedonistic sense). Men would be slaves if they were determined by anything other than the greatest good. God's will chooses the supreme happiness, and men are most like him when they do likewise. "It is as much a perfection that the power of preferring should be determined by the will." Men surely do not desire "to be at liberty to play the fool." Only madmen are free in the sense of being able to choose the worse alternative or of having no preference between pleasure and pain; and in contrast with madmen, "an understanding free agent naturally follows that which causes pleasure to it and flies that which causes pain, *i.e.*, naturally seeks happiness and shuns misery." [8] Nevertheless, in spite of this seeming defense, Locke seems to have remained discontented with his theory. He dreaded what he viewed as the fatalism of Hobbes; and he was apprehensive lest he was putting men too much under the control of the mechanical play of a balance of pleasures, and was thus leaving no room for the guiding activity of reason.

4. Locke's more mature views were set forth in the second edition of the *Essay*. He had continually gone over the chapter in which he discussed the springs of action, as he wrote in a letter to Molyneux, [9] and finally discovered what he believed to have been his error. The error, he maintained, was his having incorrectly used the word "thing" when he should have used the word "action," [10] by which verbal mistake he led his own thought astray. In the first edition he had improperly argued that a man could not be indifferent toward an object, but must desire or not desire it. He now insisted that many objects, even objects which a man recognizes as certain to give him pleasure if he should attain them, may nevertheless be indifferent. Many absent goods may not arouse any desires at all; when a man is easy and content as he is, further goods may have no appeal. Even if the further goods do

[7] *Essay*, First edition, II, 21, 30-32. *Cf.* Fraser's edition, Vol. I, pp. 376-377.
[8] King: *Op. cit.*, p. 310.
[9] *Works*, Vol. IX, p. 317.
[10] The passage in the first edition in which this error appeared reads as follows: "Is then a man indifferent to be pleased, or not pleased, more with one thing than another? Is it in his choice, whether he will or will not be better pleased with one thing than another? And to this I think every one's experience is ready to make answer, No." *Cf.* Fraser's edition of the *Essay*, Vol. I, p. 375.

stir up some desire, such desire may be so slight as to be negligible in its effect on conduct.[11]   What a man cannot help preferring or not preferring, being pleased or not pleased with, is a proposed or contemplated action.   But since proffered pleasures do not necessarily give rise to desires, *i.e.*, do not necessarily arouse the operative faculties, a man may have several goods before his mind and may exercise his reason upon their relative merits without being at once driven, in an almost mechanical way, to seek the one which seems at first to be the greatest.   There is thus a gap between having things present to the mind and being impelled to seek or to avoid them.

The gap between having things present to the mind and being impelled to seek or to avoid them can be filled of course only by that which is the spring of action.   This Locke now conceived to be uneasiness— which is the same thing as pain, torment, anguish, misery, or desire.[12] "The chief, if not only spur to human industry and action is uneasiness." [13]   Only a present pain, therefore, whether of body or of mind, at once gives rise to an activity which seeks to get rid of the pain.   A present pleasure, so far from stirring to activity, calms the mind, causing contentment with the existing situation; and a contemplated future pleasure or pain has no direct effect upon the operative faculties, unless it first produces a present pain.   An absent good may be so much better than the present is without it that a keen desire for it, *i.e.*, a pain, may appear; and an absent pain may be so terrible that a present pain may arise and an immediate action result to avoid the impending catastrophe.   Yet it may be said that pain or uneasiness, and never pleasure, is the spur to action; for while most pains lead to action, only those pleasures indirectly do so which first produce pain as an intermediary connecting link between the idea of them as absent and the enjoyment of them as present.

Locke realized that in rejecting his earlier opinion that the will is determined by the greatest pleasure, he was departing from an "established and settled" theory which had behind it "the general consent of mankind." [14]   But he thereby greatly strengthened his position.   For the earlier opinion made an absent, and as yet unattained, pleasure the cause of men's activity.   Such a theory is untenable.   "It is against the nature of things that what is absent should operate where it is not." [15]   The attainment of pleasure or escape from pain is still the end at which activity aims.   But in the earlier view Locke confused this end of action with the efficient cause or spring of action.   In his more mature view he made the proper distinction.   That pleasure which,

[11] *Essay*, II, 20, [6].
[12] *Idem*, II, 7, [2], 20, [15], 21, [32].
[13] *Idem*, II, 20, [6].
[14] *Idem*, II, 21, [35].
[15] *Idem*, II, 21, [37].

just because absent, is the goal of an action, cannot be the existing agent which leads to the action. Unless the idea of the pleasure as absent arouses uneasiness, it will not produce action at all. Hence, while Locke remained a hedonist in his statement of the end of action, he was not bound down to any mechanical balance of pleasures in his statement of the causes which give rise to action.

The bearing upon educational theory of the view that uneasiness is the spring of human action is considerable. Though Locke granted that occasionally a particular pain or uneasiness was so violent as to lead at once to action, yet he insisted that usually such was not the case. "The ordinary and successive uneasinesses . . . determine the will, but with a power of suspension." And in this period of suspension there is an opportunity for the free play of reason. It is not clear whether, according to Locke, the directing work of reason enters into the situation before the various possible absent pleasures arouse feelings of uneasiness, or whether reason restrains the feelings of uneasiness from operating even after the feelings are actually present. The latter alternative seems to be favored by Locke's language, though the former could be more easily maintained. But in either case, since the will is no longer identified with the desires, but is a power in the mind to suspend or release the operation of the desires, reason has an opportunity to prevail. Reason can so picture to the mind the allurements of an absent good, as to give rise to an uneasiness which will be more powerful than the other uneasinesses which previously were present. Even though the strongest uneasiness may at length prevail, action will be deliberative, and not impulsive. That is, the uneasiness which after reason has been at work is keenest will be so because it is reasonable for it to be so, not merely because it is connected with some violent passion. Thus not only pleasures and pains, but reason also, are important factors in regulating conduct; and all these factors must be taken into account in a theory of moral education.

5. Locke's *Thoughts concerning Education* is probably to be rated as the most consistently developed of any of his writings. It is in fairly complete harmony with the view just outlined in which uneasiness is the spring of human action. It sums up the main features of his thought in a striking way, and reveals which of the aspects of his various ethical theories really were the most firm and central convictions. Three points in particular call for special notice.

(*a*) Locke approached the problem of education from an angle which would doubtless have surprised some of the critics who misunderstood his attack in the *Essay* on innate ideas. He deemed it necessary for those who desire to train children to know the exact nature of the material upon which they have to work. As even in the first book of the *Essay* he granted that "there are natural tendencies imprinted on the minds of men" which can be summed up as "a desire of happiness and an aversion to misery,"[16] so he made a similar analysis of men's original, or innate, endowment in the *Thoughts concerning Education*. He spoke of "the natural make" of men's minds, "the unalterable frame of their constitution," "native propensities," "prevalences of constitution."[17] These natural aptitudes were stamped upon men's minds by God, and hence, though they "may perhaps be a little mended," they "can hardly be totally altered and transformed into the contrary,"[18] *i.e.*, though they "are not to be cured by rules, . . . with art they may be much mended, and turned to good purposes."[19]   Men do steadily pursue pleasure and always will; and the problem of education is, not to stamp out the pursuit of pleasure, but to rationalize it.[20]

(*b*) The educator, therefore, must use pleasures and pains as the means of furnishing the proper motive power in children.   The pleasures and pains he may use are of several kinds.   In the first place, he should make the most of the natural pleasures and pains which the children happen to feel.   He should not allow the studies of lessons which they are to learn to "be made a burden to them or imposed on them as a task."[21]   He should preferably not force lessons on them when they are indisposed, but should base his instruction upon "the favorable seasons of aptitude or inclination."[22]   In the second place, the educator should also use artificially imposed pleasures and pains, *i.e.*, rewards and punishments.   He should not resort to beating or physical chastisement except in very rare cases of otherwise incurable stubbornness, nor should he employ as rewards such things as sugarplums, finery, or money; for such pleasures and pains are not the accustomed consequences of actions in ordinary living, and hence are not effective in establishing habits which may be permanent.[23]   Nevertheless, some form of rewards and punishments is necessary.   "Reward and punishment are the only motives to a rational creature; these are the spur and reins whereby all mankind are set on work."[24]   Some pleasures and pains "must be proposed to children if we intend to work upon them."[25]   The proper ones to use are esteem and disgrace; for "a love of credit and an apprehension of shame" are not only "the most powerful incentives to the mind," but are permanent influences which will continue to advance the interests of virtue throughout men's lives.[26]   The sooner children are made responsive to social opinion, the better for the formation of their habits of moral response.   In the third place, the educator should endeavor to implant in children the notion of God as the source of "all manner of good to those that love and obey

[16] *Idem*, I, 2, 3.
[17] *Thoughts concerning Education*, §§ 101–102.
[18] *Idem*, § 66.
[19] *Idem*, § 102.
[20] *Idem*, § 143.
[21] *Idem*, § 73.
[22] *Idem*, § 74.
[23] *Idem*, §§ 47–52, 82–84.
[24] *Idem*, § 54.
[25] *Idem*, § 55.
[26] *Idem*, § 56.

him." [27]   Sensibility to common praise and blame is only "the proper stock whereon afterwards to graff the true principles of morality and religion." [28] The standards of popular opinion are at best only an approximation to genuine morality. Conduct becomes really moral only when it is coupled with and based upon the law of God.

(c) An educator has other means at his disposal, however, than the imposing of pleasures and pains. Indeed, he must have some further means if he is to make the law of God effective in its control of men; for the rewards and punishments attached to that law are wholly future. The teacher must aim to develop in children the power of self-direction, of examination, of proffered pleasures, of suspension of action pending the decision of reason. Locke occasionally wrote in a manner which recalls his purely rationalistic ethical system; [29] but he usually aimed to put reason in control, not as itself the moral standard, but as a means to securing the greatest pleasure. "The principle of all virtue and excellency lies in a power of denying ourselves the satisfaction of our own desires, where reason does not authorize them." [30] There is no moral fault so serious as the inability to restrain the importunity of a present pain for the sake of a greater pleasure which reason perceives to be in store. Haste and impetuosity are the gravest sources of vice. Deliberation in advance of action is the surest guarantee of virtue. Hence an educator should teach children the art of the mastery of their desires, "the custom of having their inclinations in subjection." [31] The supposition that children cannot be reasoned with is quite mistaken. They may not grasp intricate arguments at an early age; but they can perceive the agreement or disagreement between the ideas essential to morality. They like to be "treated as rational creatures," being proud of the compliment thus paid to them.[32] Indeed of almost any boy it is true that "the sooner you treat him as a man, the sooner he will begin to be one." [33] Thus in educational theory and practise the development of a habit of listening to the voice of reason is the most essential point.

6. In summary it may be said that there is suggested at least somewhere in Locke's writings a theory of the springs of action to correspond to each phase of his ethical views. The theory of the *Conduct of the Understanding* to the effect that ideas are the springs of action corresponds to the rationalistic ethics which finds the origin of moral distinctions in the perception by reason of the agreements or disagree-

[27] *Idem*, § 136.
[28] *Idem*, § 200.
[29] *Cf. Idem*, §§ 31, 33. He here advised one "to deny himself his desires, cross his own inclinations, and purely follow what reason directs as best, though the appetite lean the other way." But even here he did not deny that what reason directs as best is only a greater future pleasure than the one on which the present inclination is bent.
[30] *Idem*, § 38. *Cf.* also § 45.
[31] *Idem*, § 107.
[32] *Idem*, § 81.
[33] *Idem*, § 95.

ments of ideas, whether those ideas are mixed modes or are the instruments through which the mind discovers the nature of external things. Similarly the theory of the first edition of the *Essay* to the effect that the will is determined by the strongest preference which takes possession of the mind fits in with the first and cruder statement of hedonism in which Locke still stood near to Hobbes. And finally the theory of the second edition of the *Essay* to the effect that uneasiness gives rise to action under the usual guidance of reason corresponds to the final form of hedonism in which virtue lies in the rational search for the highest happiness. Though the last of these three theories was not chronologically the culmination of Locke's thought, it was the statement of the matter which was the closest approximation to a synthesis of the various ideas which he held most firmly. It emphasized the importance of reason, and yet at the same time recognized the rights of pleasure and pain to determine the nature of morality.

With this third theory the principles of the *Thoughts concerning Education* are in harmony. Locke in this treatise placed morality in a life devoted to a satisfaction of those desires only which reason authorizes one to follow. He recognized the natural aptitudes of men, and did not advocate their total suppression. "Our first actions" he regarded as "being guided more by self-love than reason or reflection;" [34] and he granted that some pains, as of hunger or sickness, cannot be restrained by reason alone without some other help.[35] But in so far as self-love or other passions prevail, there is likelihood of moral wrong. Sometimes a man may sin even when he knows he is doing so; for a knowledge of the moral law does not necessarily lead to obedience thereto. The virtuous life, however, requires that reason shall prevail in all things. The passions determine various ends or goals of action, but reason alone can limit action to those particular ends which are in accordance with the divine law. Reason is not here viewed, as in the *Conduct of the Understanding*, as a faculty which guides action directly through its own power; but it is rather viewed, as in a brief fragment on judgment,[36] as operating through the other faculties. Reason mixes itself with the passions in such a way as to show the relative value of the objects towards which they are directed, and thus often succeeds in transforming the passions themselves. In the end it is always the passions, alike in virtuous as in vicious conduct, which are the springs of action; but whereas in vicious conduct the passions control the man, in virtuous conduct the man may be said to control the passions.[37]

[34] *Idem,* § 110.
[35] *Idem,* § 107.
[36] King: *Op. cit.,* pp. 299–300.
[37] Sidgwick in his *Outlines of the History of Ethics,* p. 176, sums the matter up admirably: "Locke rejects the view that the mere apprehension by the reason of the obligatoriness of certain rules is, or ought to be, a sufficient motive to their performance, apart from the foreseen consequences to the individual of observing or neglecting them."

Book III
The Social and Political Philosophy of Locke

CHAPTER I

LOCKE'S THEORY OF THE STATE OF NATURE

1. Locke's social and political philosophy rested mainly upon that aspect of his thought which has been called rationalistic rather than hedonistic. He seldom suggested the calculation of relative amounts of pleasure to be gained from various alternative courses of conduct, but usually drew his proofs from the perception by reason of the agreements or disagreements between ideas. Of the various types of rationalistic ethics outlined above,[1] he exhibited in the *Treatises of Government* neither that which is built upon mixed modes, nor that which follows from a consideration of the being of God, but rather that which depends upon the law of nature. Therefore, his political theories deal quite objectively through ideas with the realities of the external world, and yet do not fall back upon the religious emphasis which usually prevailed in his discussion of the more personal moral rules. Probably the comparative absence of hedonistic allusions in the *Treatises of Government* is due to the fact that he deduced his views on social matters from other ideas than that of God. Whenever he related the moral law to God, he seems to have at once thought of future rewards and punishments as the factor of determining importance; only when he confined his attention to the realities of this world alone, and so came across no rewards and punishments of overwhelming value, did he examine the affairs of this present life more dispassionately on their own merits.

2. As a result of his rationalistic mode of procedure, Locke was led, like all the other rationalists of his century, to base his political philosophy upon a theory of the origin of government, *i.e.*, upon a consideration of man's primitive condition and of the steps by which man supposedly established civil society. "To understand political power right, and derive it from its original, we must consider what state all men are naturally in." [2] The proper regulation of men's present organized relations to each other depends upon the kind of a state of nature in which they lived prior to the formation of governments, and upon the particular terms of the contract by which they agreed to leave the state of nature and to enter into political society. Three features of Locke's theory of the state of nature stand out with particular prominence.

[1] *Cf.* above, Book II, Chapter III.
[2] *Cf. Civil Government*, § 4.

(a) The first of these prominent features is the existence of what he called "natural rights." Since the state of nature is a state of "men living together according to reason, without a common superior on earth with authority to judge between them,"[3] it follows that all men are equal and independent. Everyone, therefore, being on a par with everyone else, has certain definite rights. These rights are not bestowed by any superior power (for there is no such power), but are a natural possession. They are discovered by reason in observing the natural relations between men. The fundamental right is perhaps the right to life or self-preservation, connected with which there is also the right to food, drink, and the other essentials of human existence. Then since no one person is superior to another, everyone has a right to do as he pleases provided he does not transgress the equal rights of his fellows. Likewise, as will be seen more fully in the next section, he is entitled to his own labor and the fruit of his labor, i.e., to his property. These various rights may be summed up as the rights to life, liberty, and property, though Locke did not always use the same formula in stating the point. Men do, because of their natural equality have "a perfect freedom to order their actions and dispose of their possessions and persons, as they think fit, within the bounds of the law of nature."[4]

(b) The second prominent feature of the state of nature is its social character. Though Locke followed Hobbes in giving each man his own peculiar rights as if each man were an atom-like entity by himself, yet he also asserted the fundamentally social nature of mankind. There is no contract necessary to make men social. Indeed, contracts could not be made unless men were social in advance of their entering into agreements with each other. From the very beginning of his existence man was "such a creature that in his own judgment it was not good for him to be alone," but was "under strong obligations of necessity, convenience, and inclination" to enter into society, which society often "came short of political society."[5] Man could neither by his own efforts provide for his own safety and essential needs, nor in himself satisfy his cravings for fellowship with others. The primitive state of nature is characterized by social relationships.

(c) The third prominent feature of the state of nature is that it is subject to the law of nature. Locke here stood with Grotius and his school against Hobbes. The law of nature is morally binding upon men in pre-political as much as in political society. Locke could hardly have taken any other position; for as was shown above,[6] the law of nature follows from a perception by reason of the relations of men to

---

[3] *Idem*, § 19.
[4] *Idem*, § 4.
[5] *Idem*, § 77. *Cf.* § 15. Also *Essay*, III, 1,[1].
[6] *Cf.* above, Book II, Chapter III, § 3. Also, Chapter IV, § 3.

each other, and men stand in many relations to each other prior to the formation of any political organization. Even in the state of nature men ought to recognize each other's rights. They do not always act according to their moral obligations; but they cannot fail to realize the fact that those obligations exist. Hence, the state of nature is not a war of all against all, a lawless struggle for private advantage. Even though there is no effective power to restrain unjust aggression and to compel fair play, yet, since men are equal, "no one ought to harm another in his life, health, liberty, and possessions." [7]

In consequence of this position that the law of nature is binding in the state of nature, Locke maintained that contracts, which Hobbes had declared to be futile and meaningless, were morally effective and obligatory. "The promises and bargains for truck, *etc.*, between the two men in the desert island mentioned by Garcilasso de la Vega in his history of Peru, or between a Swiss and an Indian in the woods of America, are binding to them, though they are perfectly in a state of nature in reference to one another." [8] The agreements between rulers of independent nations are similarly binding, even though there is no form of international control to compel their execution. The very contract upon which political society itself rests would not hold unless all contracts made in the state of nature had moral validity.

3. Locke next proceeded to describe some of the institutions which existed in the state of nature before the origin of political organizations. He wished to establish the moral order upon the law of nature and natural rights rather than upon civil laws. He had an ulterior motive in maintaining the priority of an organized social life to the establishment of government; for he wished to furnish a suitable basis for his contention later on in favor of "the right of revolution." [9] While Hobbes had viewed the dissolution of any government as the total destruction of all social obligations and moral law, Locke insisted that it involved the release from only certain political relationships and left all remaining relationships intact. Three of the pre-political institutions in Locke's theory are especially important.

(*a*) The first of the institutions which Locke deduced directly from the law of nature and natural rights is property. Every man has "in himself the great foundation of property;" [10] that is, property, though protected and regulated by statute laws, rests upon something more ultimate, something in the very nature of things. As a man's labor belongs to himself alone, unless he chooses to give it to others, so do the products of his labor. In opposition to Filmer, Locke claimed that the earth and all its abundance of fruits had not been given to Adam

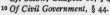

[7] *Of Civil Government*, § 6. *Cf.* §§ 37, 95. Also, *Of Government*, § 67.
[8] *Of Civil Government*, § 14.
[9] *Cf.* below, Chapter II, § 4.
[10] *Of Civil Government*, § 44.

alone,[11] but belong to all men equally. In advance of labor upon them, the good things of nature are the possession of the whole community of mankind, and can be freely partaken of by each person according to his needs. "The earth and all that is therein is given to men for the support and comfort of their being . . . and nobody has originally a private dominion, exclusive of the rest of mankind in any of them, as they are thus in their natural state." [12] But as soon as a man mixes his labor, which belongs to himself alone, with any of the goods in the world which are freely offered to all, private property comes into being. By picking up acorns or apples, by digging for ore, by harnessing a horse, by catching fish, or by plowing a portion of the earth, a man becomes owner of what, before he put his labor into it, was no more his than another's. Until he so removes articles out of the storehouse of nature into his own possession, "the common is of no use." [13] But since he has a right to self-preservation and self-development, he is entitled to establish his private claims upon whatever he needs or desires. And anyone who is unwilling to labor deserves to be deprived of his share of the common stock of things. "The condition of human life, which requires labor and materials to work on, necessarily introduces private possessions." [14]

In earlier times when the abundance of land and resources was great and the number of persons in the world was few, the institution of property introduced no hardships; for the measure of things which one man by his labor could subdue is small, and there was plenty for all. But as population increased, there was no longer enough to go around, so in order to avoid excessive claims to private ownership by one person, some limit had to be set. Locke accordingly took the position that a man is entitled to only so much of the earth's goods as he can use. No one is justified in wasting or destroying things; hence, whatever, even though shut up in an enclosure as private property, is rotting or perishing, and whatever land lies continually idle, may be taken as freely by some one else as if it were still a part of the undivided stock of common possessions. "The same law of nature that does by this means [i.e., by the exercise of labor] give us property, does also bound that property, too." Whatever more than a man is able to use before it spoils or is wasted is "more than his share and belongs to others." [15] Locke here seems to have checked up the doctrine of property to which he was logically led on rationalistic grounds by an appeal to questions of utility.

[11] Cf. Of Government, § 29: "Whatever God gave by the words of this grant (Gen. I:28) it was not to Adam in particular, exclusive of all other men; whatever dominion he had thereby it was not a private dominion, but a dominion in common with the rest of mankind."
[12] Of Civil Government, § 26.
[13] Idem, § 28.
[14] Idem, § 35.
[15] Idem, § 31.

(*b*) Upon the institution of property, Locke based the closely allied institution of money. Money does not derive its value from statute laws, but from the agreement of men in a pre-political state. It happens that many of the things useful to man's life are perishable, and that others can be safely stored for an indefinite period. Now as a man can frequently produce more of one of the perishable articles than he can himself conveniently use, the necessity of exchange with others arises. He can then store up, as the surplus profit of his labor, some kind of goods which does not spoil, to be utilized in time of need. Such hoarding is, in Locke's judgment, entirely justifiable; for "the exceeding of the bounds of his just property" does not lie "in the largeness of his possession, but the perishing of anything uselessly in it." [16] Accumulation of goods in some permanently available form is what is meant by the institution of money. Money is "some lasting thing that men might keep without spoiling, and that by mutual consent men would take in exchange for the truly useful, but perishable, supports of life." [17] It is of course the cause of "a disproportionate and unequal possession of the earth," [18] in that it permits a man to hold potentially far more of the stock of common goods than he can possibly ever use himself. Locke was affiliated, it must be remembered, with the aristocratic and governing class in England, and had an interest in the security of property values. Hence, he here consistently followed out the implications of his rationalistic premises. Though, as was seen in discussing the limits of property rights, he checked up the outcome of his rationalism at one point by a reference to a utilitarian standard, yet in judging concerning the amassing of large fortunes, he did not stop to question the desirability thereof. He found such fortunes to be consistent with his views upon the origin of property rights, and he did not go on to test his conclusion in the light of any consideration as to its effects upon the welfare of society.

(*c*) The most important probably of the pre-political institutions which nevertheless rest on a moral basis is the family. The institution of the family is an inevitable outcome of man's social nature. "The first society was between man and wife, which gave beginning to that between parents and children." [19] The family rests upon a voluntary contract which is morally binding even in advance of the existence of political power to enforce it. This contract involves a right in one another's bodies, a sharing of interests, mutual support and assistance, and proper care for the children which result from the union. The contract must therefore be regarded as binding for as long a period as is necessary for the fulfilment of the objects for which the contract

[16] *Idem*, § 46.
[17] *Idem*, § 47.
[18] *Idem*, § 50.
[19] *Idem*, § 77.

was entered upon and hence will hold over a considerable number of years.

In considering the moral problem of family relationships, the important point to determine is the extent of the power of its different members over one another. Locke here came into direct and conscious opposition to Filmer, who, upon his theory of the fall and certain texts in Genesis, made wives and children entirely subject to the dominion of their husbands and fathers. In the first of his two *Treatises of Government* Locke attacked Filmer's exegesis of Scripture and exposed in wearisome detail the absurdities in Filmer's statement of the patriarchal theory; in the second he made his own positive contribution towards a solution of the problem. He regarded the relation between husband and wife as one partly of control and partly of freedom. On matters of common interest and concern the husband, as "the abler and the stronger," naturally has the right to decide whenever the wills of himself and his wife conflict. But the husband has no more power than was bestowed upon him by the marriage contract; and on all other points, the wife retains "full and free possession of what by contract is her peculiar right," even to the extent, under some circumstances of leaving her husband altogether.[20] The wife as well as the husband, has control over their children, so that the power which Filmer incorrectly spoke of as "paternal" should be called "parental." Similarly Locke regarded the relation between parents and children as one partly of power to control and partly of obligation to serve. He carefully distinguished, as Filmer did not, between the power which parents under the law of nature possess over their children and an absolute political power. Parental power, unlike political power, is strictly limited to that early period of the children's lives when they are not capable of self-direction. Since children are not born into the state of equality with all men into which they later grow, they must for a time be controlled by their parents. Equality presupposes rationality, and hence is only gradually acquired in the course of years. The natural freedom of mankind and the subjection of children to parents are therefore consistent; the latter implies no denial of the former. Moreover, the right of parents to control their children is accompanied by an obligation to serve the needs of the children, *i.e.*, by a right of the children to receive certain care. All parents are "by the law of nature under an obligation to preserve, nourish, and educate the children they had begotten."[21] There are thus rights upon both sides; and if the parents do not recognize and accede to the rights of the children, they lose their own rights over their children. Indeed, if the parents should neglect their children and some stranger should assume the burden of

---

[20] *Idem*, § 82. *Cf. Of Government*, § 48.
[21] *Of Civil Government*, § 56. *Cf.* § 170. Also, *Of Government*, §§ 89–90.

caring for them, the stranger, and not the parents, would be entitled to control and guide them. Parental power, therefore, follows, not from the act of generation, as Filmer had supposed, but from the fulfilment of the obligation to "preserve, nourish, and educate" the children. The institution of the family is based upon the law of nature, not upon civil law; and the relationships between its members must be determined from the nature of the contract upon which it was based or from the nature of the persons involved, and not from positive enactments. Filmer's theory erred both in confusing conjugal and parental (or paternal) with political power, and consequently in exaggerating the extent of that power.

4. But though the state of nature was for Locke a social state in which moral obligations are already present, and not a state of war of all against all in which ethical distinctions do not figure, nevertheless it was not an ideally perfect state.[22] Men in the state of nature possess a certain liberty, but they frequently turn this liberty into uncontrolled license. The freedom of nature "is to be under no other restraint but the law of nature."[23] That law of nature, however, allows no exceptions; and as soon as a man violates it, he thereby destroys the peaceful quality which the state of nature might otherwise possess and introduces the state of war. Locke, to be sure, spoke of "the plain difference between the state of nature and the state of war,"[24] as if he regarded the latter as something unnatural. But it would have been fairer to his own theory if he had contrasted the state of peace with the state of war, and had included both of these states within the state of nature. The difference between the state of peace and the state of war would then be that in the former the law of nature was obeyed and in the latter it was violated. As long as all men respect others' rights, no disturbance results; the state of nature is "a state of peace, goodwill, mutual assistance, and preservation." As soon as anyone violates another's rights, disturbance begins; the state of nature becomes "a state of enmity, malice, violence, and mutual destruction."[25] As Locke maintained in his *Thoughts concerning Education* that children love dominion, "the first original of most vicious habits,"[26] so in the *Treatises of Government* he recognized the inordinate ambition and envy in men's

[22] Sir Leslie Stephen certainly erred when he said in his *English Thought in the Eighteenth Century*, Vol. II, p. 137: "Locke's state of nature is almost the ideal state; he speaks of the 'golden age' in an apparently historical sense, and regards government as introduced by the 'ambition and luxury of future ages'." Stephen quite clearly misread § 111 of Locke's *Treatise of Civil Government*. Locke there spoke of the golden age, not as a pre-political state of society, but as a civil state in which there were better governors and less vicious subjects. And he condemned the ambition and luxury of future ages, not for having made the introduction of government necessary, but for having perverted an excellent government into a poor one. Other passages in the *Treatise* also make Locke's position so plain that any misinterpretation by so admirable an historian as Sir Leslie Stephen seems very strange.

[23] *Of Civil Government*, § 22.

[24] *Idem*, § 19.

[25] *Idem*, § 19.

[26] *Thoughts on Education*, § 103. *Cf.* also, §§ 104-105.

make-up, and realized the inevitable consequences thereof on society. The "pravity of mankind" is such that the state of nature is unbearable.[27]

Since in the state of nature there is not any neutral or official power to enforce the law of nature, whoever is assailed must defend his own rights. The possession of the rights to life, liberty, and property carries with it the further right to defend these rights. "The execution of the law of nature is in that state put into every man's hands."[28] Any transgressor may be punished to that extent which is necessary for reparation or for restraint, even, if necessary, by his reduction to slavery. "The use of force without authority always puts him that uses it into a state of war as the aggressor, and renders him liable to be treated accordingly."[29] But all such punishment by the use of force will be sure to meet with resistance, *i.e.*, will lead to war. Thus, though a man exercises only that right of self-defense to which he is entitled by the law of nature, he may, and usually will, be involved in an endless struggle. Sometimes, to be sure, a swift act of avenging justice may give place once more to a peaceful state of nature. But more often a man, once plunged into the state of war, will continue in that state for most of his life. Except by incessant precaution he will have no security, no peace, no prosperity. Except by a strong defense he will be unable to maintain his just rights.

5. The state of war may sometimes lead to the existence of slavery. Locke was anxious to restrict the institution of slavery within the narrowest possible limits.[30] He denied that men can voluntarily enter into a contract to establish the relation of master and slave. Though a man has a right to life, he has not a right over his life; and hence, he cannot surrender this right to another. "No man can by agreement pass over to another that which he hath not in himself, a power over his own life."[31] Every man, being equal to his fellows, is free to do as he wishes, subject to the law of nature; and voluntarily to annul his freedom by conferring upon his fellows an arbitrary sway over him is to violate his natural equality and the law of nature derived therefrom. He may sell the products of his labor, he may sell even his labor; but he cannot sell himself. Nevertheless, though slavery cannot arise from the right of contract, Locke was driven to conclude that it may arise from the state of war. If a man breaks the law of nature by attacking others, he forfeits his own rights, and may be killed as a penalty for his wrongdoing. But his conqueror, instead of taking his life, may

[27] *Cf. Works*, Vol. VI, p. 42.
[28] *Of Civil Government*, § 7.
[29] *Idem*, § 155.
[30] Locke had the ulterior motive here of providing an argument for his denial later on of the possibility of setting up such an absolute monarchy as Hobbes advocated. No ruler could, on Locke's premises, acquire complete control over the lives and possessions of all his subjects.
[31] *Of Civil Government*, § 24.

prefer to use his services as a slave.[32] He may still, if he finds his lot intolerable and prefers death to servitude, draw death upon himself by resistance to his conqueror's will. But since most men will choose slavery to death, slavery will frequently exist. Locke did not, however, extend the right of a master to rule his slaves to an absolute political power. The conqueror who gains a right over another man's life does not thereby gain power over that man's property (beyond the degree necessary to restore the actual harm done to him), nor over that man's children.[33] Yet, though slavery is restricted to narrow limits, it must be granted as just in so far as it follows in a state of war from the defense of a man's rights invaded by another unjustly.

6. Because the state of nature, by frequently turning into the state of war, is an unsatisfactory condition of human existence, men devised a way of escape for themselves through the formation of political society. If all men had been honest and just to others, there would have been no need for any other law than the law of nature, no need for specially designated persons to enforce the mutual respecting of rights by the various members of the community, no need for government at all. But such was not the case. Hence, men became willing to give up part of their natural freedom, and "to join in society with others, who are already united, or have a mind to unite, for the mutual preservation of their lives, liberties, and estates."[34] Only by an agreement to live under a common authority to whom, instead of to the chance of arms, they may appeal, can men settle their disputes in orderly and peaceful fashion. Only by the imposition of penalties for certain crimes can the law of nature be properly enforced. Only by a contract "to enter into one community and make one body politic"[35] can the state of war be avoided. Thus it is true that "civil government is the proper remedy for the inconveniences of the state of nature."[36]

Locke's social theory according to which the state of political society is preferred to a state of nature was to a very great extent a reflection of his own experiences during the days of the Commonwealth and the Restoration in England. In a short political treatise written in 1660 he said: "I no sooner perceived myself in the world, but I found myself in a storm, which has lasted almost hitherto." As a result of those years of turmoil he came to conclude that "a general freedom is but a general bondage," that liberty from civil control "would prove only a liberty for contention, censure, and persecution." Therefore, he looked for-

[32] Idem, § 23.
[33] Idem, §§ 180–185.
[34] Idem, § 123.
[35] Idem, § 14.
[36] Idem, § 13.

ward to the restoration of ordered rule under Charles II with eager
anticipation. He could not "but entertain the approaches of a calm
with the greatest joy and satisfaction;" for "all the freedom I can wish
my country and myself is to enjoy the protection of those laws which
the prudence and providence of our ancestors established, and the
happy return of his Majesty has restored." [37]   To be sure, he soon came
to change his views concerning the desirability of Charles II as a
king; but he did not ever cease to appraise civil society as superior to
the state of nature.

7. Locke's theory of the state of nature is perhaps the most satisfactory of any of those advanced in the seventeenth century. Even
if Locke's critics to-day do not agree with the supposition of a primitive
state of nature which was formally ended by a definite contract, they
should recognize the superior merit of Locke's ideas over those of his
predecessors. Locke avoided the extremes to which most of the earlier
writers went. On the one hand, he refused to follow the deists in their
superficial optimism. He, unlike them, had no case which he wished
to make out against the priests and leaders of organized religion. So
he was not led astray into falsely idealizing the past and assuming the
natural goodness of all men. On the other hand, he did not build
up his political views on that aspect of his ethical thought which he
took over from Hobbes; and so he did not have to assert the utter
selfishness of all men unless restrained by superior force. Rather he
built up his political views mainly on his rationalistic ethics, in which
a rational consideration of various goods rather than a scramble for
private pleasure is the spring of action. Thus his theory of the state
of nature is neither that of the undisturbed golden age nor that of the
war of all against all. He followed Hooker, Grotius, and especially
Pufendorf, more closely than any of his other predecessors. He believed
in a state of nature in which reason and, hence, the law of nature were
morally binding, and yet in which, at the same time, there were the
seeds of countless quarrels and conflicts in the imperfect character of
human nature. He agreed with Filmer's criticism of Hobbes, that
unless all contracts were binding in the state of nature, the social contract on which the state rested could never be framed at all. But he
did not, however, accept Grotius's opinions completely; for he recognized the justice of Filmer's criticism of Grotius, that if the people had
the power to make the social contract, they had also the power to
abrogate it. Hence, his state of nature, though closely akin to that
of Grotius, was more significant for political theory. It not only was
something which had once existed long ago in the past, but also is
the background of all political societies into which those societies may
at any moment be again resolved.

[37] King: *Op. cit.*, pp. 7–8.

Some critics of Locke in recent discussions [38] have tried to maintain that his idea of the state of nature was not an account of how as a matter of historic fact political society came into being, but a deliberate abstraction of certain elements now present in social organization in order to examine them in isolation by themselves. Pufendorf was the only important political philosopher in the seventeenth century who denied that the state of nature was an historical era, and even he granted that it frequently prevailed between some groups of men. Locke, however, was on this point influenced, not so much by Pufendorf, as by Grotius, Hobbes, and others who held the more naïve view. He clearly believed that the state of nature was an actual period which preceded in time the state of civil society. He pointed to the state of nature, not only in the relations between independent rulers of various nations, and in the hypothetical cases (mentioned above) [39] where two men meet on a desert island, or a Swiss and an Indian meet in the woods of America, but also in the beginnings of Venice and Rome, in several communities in the Americas, in the colony of "those who went away from Sparta with Palantus," and in the early history of the Jewish people.[40] And if other illustrations of the state of nature cannot be given, the reason is that "government is everywhere antecedent to records," [41] so that knowledge of the facts is deficient.

The chief weakness in Locke's theory of the state of nature is closely akin to one of the main faults in the epistemological theory of the *Essay*. As he made the simple ideas which are the product of analysis both chronologically and logically prior to the complex ideas which are supposed to be constructed out of them, so he made the individual persons taken apart from their political relations the original and independent units out of which the civil state is later composed.[42] His contract theory of the origin of civil society is not quite as individualistic in its complications as is Hobbes's; for he insisted that many social institutions have a natural origin in the pre-political state. Yet he certainly tended dangerously near to an atomic view of society. Moreover, he assumed that men in primitive times were impelled by the same motives, and manifested the same character, as men of his own generation. He regarded them as possessing in their pre-political

[38] *Cf.* Sir Frederick Pollock in an article on "Locke's Theory of the State" in the *Proceedings of the British Academy*, 1903-1904, p. 241: "This state [*i.e.*, the state of nature], for Locke as for the schoolman, is rather a perfectly conscious abstraction than an attempt to construct the actual origin of society. The question is what a man's rights would be in the absence of any positive institutions . . . This amounts to saying that the problem is not to account for the existence of society, but to ascertain its best or normal mode of existence." When Pollock in this passage speaks of "the actual origin of society" or "the existence of society," it is of political society that he is thinking. Of course, society in the broader sense of a community of persons had no origin for Locke, but has existed as long as persons have existed.

[39] *Cf.* above, § 2.
[40] *Of Civil Government*, §§ 102-103.
[41] *Idem*, § 101.
[42] *Cf.* Alexander: *Locke*, p. 81. Alexander, however, writes as if the pre-political state which Locke described were also pre-social.

state characteristics which are the product of training in political activity.[43] He viewed political organization as due to one momentous change, engineered by men who, before as after this change, exhibited the same nature and qualities. He had no conception of a gradual growth from relatively simple to relatively complex forms of social organization, each stage of which prepared the way for the next by altering men's desires, motives, ideals, and moral sentiments. Yet, in spite of this weakness, Locke's theory, by avoiding the extremes of some of his predecessors, marked an advance in social philosophy. His account of the origin of men's various rights, especially that of property, may be faulty; but at least he recognized the important fact that mankind has from the very earliest times possessed social instincts and a social nature. He contrasted political life, not with an anti-social life (as Hobbes did), but with a social life in which the social welfare was very imperfectly attained. Thus he prepared the way for a more adequate philosophy of human progress.

[43] Cf. Seaton: *The Theory of Toleration under the later Stuarts*, p. 266: "Nothing short of an almost total lack of the historic sense could allow to pass unchallenged the absurdity of primitive man appreciating the advantages of society before it existed, and drawing up a contract for its constitution."

CHAPTER II

LOCKE'S THEORY OF POLITICAL SOCIETY

1. In Locke's social philosophy the sole alternative to the state of nature is the state of political society. The essential difference between these two states is that men in the latter have surrendered part of the freedom and some of the rights which they possessed in the former, and have in return gained peace and security. The state of nature does not prove to be a satisfactory condition of life because it lacks: (1) "an established, settled, known law, received and allowed by common consent to be the standard of right and wrong and the common measure to decide all controversies between them;" (2) "a known and indifferent judge, with authority to determine all differences according to the established law;" and (3) a "power to back and support the sentence when right, and to give it due execution."[1] In order that a political society may establish organizations to supply these three lacks, its members must hand over to its exclusive use the right to exercise certain functions which formerly belonged to them as separate individuals. They need not, and indeed never do, give up all of their natural rights, but only so many thereof as are requisite for the constitution of an adequately powerful government. They must wholly renounce their right to punish by the use of force others who attack them (except in rare cases where the appeal to law is impossible); for the retention of that right, even to a slight extent, would make ridiculous the pretentions of a government to be an impartial and mediating tribunal in the quarrels among its subjects. "There and there only is political society, where every one of the members hath quitted this natural power [of punishing offenders], resigned it up into the hands of the community in all cases that exclude him not from appealing for protection to the law established by it."[2] Their other rights men may, however, retain, at least within certain limits which the statute laws of the government will set; for these rights will often be of assistance to their possessors without in any way infringing upon the welfare of others or without disturbing the public order.[3] Men will of course be more constrained in their activities under a political society than if they remained in a state of nature. Yet, such constraint does not so much restrict as preserve their real freedom. For "law in its true

[1] *Of Civil Government*, §§ 124-126. *Cf.* also, §§ 3, 88.
[2] *Idem*, § 87.
[3] *Idem*, §§ 128-130.

notion is not so much the limitation, as the direction, of a free and intelligent agent to his proper interest." [4]   Though men have not in political society the right of private judgment on many matters, they are provided by the community with the protection which in a state of nature they had to provide for themselves; and they consequently have more liberty to exercise the remaining rights left to them after the political society was formed.

In the state of political society the community of course possesses the power to supply the three things which the state of nature lacks; *i.e.*, it possesses the three corresponding functions of the legislative,[5] the judicial, and the executive.   It is vested with three rights—the right of defining in statute laws the various articles of the law of nature and of attaching suitable punishments to their infraction; the right of intervening in all quarrels and of determining the relative merits of the contending parties; and finally the right of employing force so as to keep internal order in the community and to protect the community from the assaults of other groups without.[6]   These three rights it must exercise in such a way that all the members of the political society will know where and in whom the rights reside.   It must publicly declare and make easily known to all its citizens the civil laws with their appropriate penalties, and also the officers competent to judge and execute those laws; for otherwise men would find that "their peace, quiet, and property will still be at the same uncertainty, as it was in the state of nature." [7]   Yet once due publicity has been given to the laws and proper announcement has been made of the designated officials, the government is justified in proceeding to carry on the legislative, judicial, and executive rights which were surrendered to it.

Locke consistently maintained that the state of political society is superior to the state of nature.   Men lose little, and gain much, as the result of forming a commonwealth.   "The commonwealth seems to me to be a society of men constituted only for the procuring, preserving, and advancing their own civil interests." [8]   In other words, "the end of government is the good of mankind." [9]   Unless men were sure that they would benefit by the agreement to enter the political society, they

---

[4] *Idem*, § 57.

[5] What Locke called "the legislative" must not be confused with a legislature.   Only in certain forms of government will the law-making power be vested in a legislature.

[6] In another passage, §§ 145–147, Locke divided what is here referred to as the executive power into two parts—the administration of the internal affairs of a nation, and the management of foreign affairs. He then restricted the term executive power to the former of these two functions, and spoke of the latter as the federative power.   He would place the executive under the complete, and somewhat detailed, control of the legislative; but he would leave the federative more to its own initiative.   Foreign affairs so constantly take on new and unexpected aspects that the legislative can hardly make standing and fixed laws for their guidance.

[7] *Of Civil Government*, § 136.

[8] *Works*, Vol. VI, p. 10.

[9] *Of Civil Government*, § 229.

would not consent to abandon their freedom in the state of nature.[10] But they do divest themselves of their full liberty and restrict their rights by the political contract, because only in that way can they gain "their comfortable, safe, and peaceable living one amongst another, in a secure enjoyment of their properties, and a greater security against any that are not of it." [11]

Sometimes Locke seems to have viewed the advantages which men derive from government in a very narrow way: that is, he wrote as if he regarded the end for which political societies were established to be "the preservation of property." [12] Certainly he supposed that it was the wanton invasion of each other's property rights more than anything else which brought about strife in the state of nature; and he maintained that when government was once more established it should not attempt to take over the functions of other organizations, such as the family, the church, etc. He belonged to the *laissez faire* school of economic thought; and he considered that men's material prosperity as well as their less tangible ideal interests could best be secured without much governmental action. Nevertheless he protested in several passages against too narrow an interpretation of property.[13] "By property I must be understood here, as in other places, to mean that property which men have in their persons as well as goods." [14] Again he defined a man's property as "his life, liberty, and estate." [15] And he explained the civil interests which constitute the end of the commonwealth as including "life, liberty, health, and indolency of body, and the possession of outward things, such as money, lands, houses, furniture, and the like." [16] Perhaps it would be fair to say that Locke's emphasis on the protection of property as the chief end of government and as the function which government must exercise most vigilantly was due to his belief that men do not offend against the law of nature and attack others' rights so flagrantly in any other respect as in the case of property. Even though he was a conservative in his attitude to wealth, he would hardly have consented, in spite of some misleading paragraphs of the *Treatises*, to limit the advantages derived from political society exclusively to undisturbed enjoyment of one's material

[10] Locke did not distinguish between the common good and the good of each separate person, but assumed always that the former included the latter. In the same paragraph he wrote that "no rational creature can be supposed to change his condition with an intention to be worse," and also that the political contract establishes a government which is "directed to no other end but the peace, safety, and public good of the people" (§ 131). Locke does not give any indication of having ever realized that there is any problem in this identification of private and public interests.

[11] *Of Civil Government*, § 95.

[12] *Idem*, §§ 94, 124.

[13] Leslie Stephen in his *English Thought in the Eighteenth Century*, Vol. II, p. 142, concluded that for Locke the political contract was entered upon primarily to obtain a sanction for an unequal distribution of property. Surely this is an exaggeration and perversion of Locke's position.

[14] *Of Civil Government*, § 173.

[15] *Idem*, § 87.

[16] *Works*, Vol. VI, p. 10.

possessions. He did undoubtedly regard government in a negative rather than in a positive way, as something to restrain men from certain kinds of wrongdoing, rather than as an agent to secure all sorts of public goods. But he wished it to do more than protect property in the narrow sense; he wished it also to guard human life, to see to it that all men were enabled to retain their natural freedom (within boundaries to be defined by law), and thus to thwart any unwholesome assaults upon men's activities.

2. There is no point which Locke insisted upon more constantly and more forcefully than that all legitimate governments rest upon the consent of the governed. "No government can have a right to obedience from a people who have not freely consented to it." Unless men voluntarily agree to join the political society by which they are governed, they "are not in the state of freemen, but are direct slaves under the force of war."[17] Locke agreed with Hooker against Grotius and Pufendorf that a contract freely entered upon is the only basis for a just government. A war, even a just war, though it gives the victor an absolute power over the lives of those who wrongfully attacked him, does not give him a title to their possessions, and hence, cannot be a proper foundation for government. Either, therefore, the rulers must be chosen by the people, and the form of government likewise determined by the people; or the rulers are not legitimate rulers, and the government can justly be overthrown whenever the people feel themselves strong enough to do so.

Locke realized, nevertheless, that after men enter into political societies, they cannot always have all their preferences recognized. Though no man can be forced to leave the state of nature and to abandon any of his natural rights, it will often happen that, having chosen to do so, he will find himself subjected to a government which is not in every respect to his liking. The reason for this is that all the men who unite in a particular political society do not have on all matters the same opinions and desires, and hence that the majority must exercise power over the minority. If a group of men is to act as a group at all, it cannot wait for unanimous consent, but "should move that way whither the greater force carries it, which is the consent of the majority." The majority has "by the law of nature and reason the power of the whole."[18] Unless the majority is entitled to govern the whole body politic, no government would be possible in any satisfactory sense. Men would be withdrawing constantly from the political society they had recently joined, and would thus be reëstablishing the state of nature and depriving themselves and their fellows of the very advantages which the political contract aimed to secure. Hence, a

---

[17] *Of Civil Government*, § 192. *Cf.* § 106.
[18] *Idem*, §§ 96, 132.

political society must regard its contractual basis as permanently binding, provided that a majority of its members do not dissolve it formally. "He that has once by actual agreement and any express declaration given his consent to be of any commonwealth is perpetually and indispensably obliged to be and remain unalterably a subject to it, and can never be again in the liberty of the state of nature, unless, by any calamity, the government he was under comes to be dissolved, or else by some public act cuts him off from being any longer a member of it." [19] A man is better off under a government in which the majority rules contrary to his wishes than he is in the state of nature; and hence, he would be foolish to refuse to join a political society out of a fear that his wishes would not always prevail in determining the policies of his group.

Locke, of course, was forced to consider the fact that most men now grow up to be citizens of some already existing state, and are not partners to the original contract by which the state was set up. But the problem thus raised did not trouble him. Unlike Filmer, he insisted that children who have reached maturity and the ability to reason are free of parental control, and may, if they choose, consider themselves in the state of nature toward all their fellowmen, even toward their parents. They may then select which political society they prefer to belong to, and which government they will obey; they may even decide to found a new political society, if they can find any part of the earth as yet unpossessed. In other words, "a child is born a subject of no country or government." [20] Now if children, as is most natural and customary, simply enter into the political life of the group to which their parents belong without a statement either of acceptance or of rejection of membership in that group, they may be regarded as having given a tacit assent to the same contract which their fathers or remoter ancestors formulated long before. This tacitly given assent may later be tacitly withdrawn. But only if they openly and expressly assert their freedom from their fathers' group or their allegiance to some other group, may they legitimately withhold loyalty to the government under the jurisdiction of which they were born. While they remain within the dominions of the fathers' political group, they are bound, like any visitor from foreign parts, to obey the laws of that community. Moreover, while they are the owners of any land under a government, they are subject to the laws thereof. Parents may indeed bring pressure to bear on their children, by conditioning the granting of an inheritance upon the acceptance by their children of their political society; and also the political society itself, since it cannot permit its territory to be dismembered, may similarly condition

[19] *Idem,* § 121.
[20] *Idem,* § 118.

the privilege of receiving any tract of land as an inheritance upon an agreement by the new owner to make the same contract as that made by the former owners, *i.e.*, upon an assent to the original contract itself on which the whole political society rests.   Yet, though much pressure may in one form or another be brought to bear on successive generations, and though most children tacitly agree to enter into the political group to which their forefathers belonged, each man is free to determine his own political allegiance.   Locke thus consistently and thoroughly carried out his position that the only legitimate basis for government is the consent of the governed.[21]

3. Locke did not entirely identify political society and government. Though he in no place mentioned explicitly a twofold contract as necessary for the setting up of a government, he sometimes wrote as if he were assuming that such a twofold contract were the natural procedure.[22]   That is, he seems to have held that men first agreed to enter into a political society, and then later determined the form of government by which they would be regulated.   No political society can possibly exist unless government is instituted; and yet the association of a group of men as a political unit is primary and fundamental, and the erection of the governmental system is only a necessary consequence.   Hence, Locke distinguished between the existence of the commonwealth, by which he meant any political society of any kind, and the actual government which the people of the commonwealth might choose.

Locke followed Hobbes and others of his predecessors in the view that a government may be of one of three possible forms—democracy, oligarchy, or monarchy.[23]   The determining factor which distinguishes these three types is whether the legislative, *i.e.*, the power of making laws, is placed in the hands of all the citizens, of a select few, or of only one; for the legislative "is the supreme power in every commonwealth,"[24] and controls the executive and judicial officers.   On many other points Locke differed from Hobbes.   He maintained against Hobbes that, since government rests on the free government of the governed, a group of persons may, in forming a political society, choose to establish a particular government for a temporary as well as for a permanent period.[25]   If they establish it for only a temporary period,

---

[21] *Idem*, §§ 73–76, 116–122, 192.

[22] *E.g.*, *cf. Of Civil Government*, § 132, where Locke expressed himself thus: "The majority having, as has been showed, upon men's first uniting into society, the whole power of the community in them, may employ all that power. .   .   ." Here the uniting into society, by which is clearly meant political society, precedes the organization of government.

[23] *Of Civil Government*, § 132.

[24] *Works*, Vol. VI, p. 42.

[25] There is no inconsistency between this position and the previous contention that when a man once joins a political society he is perpetually bound to remain in it.   Locke did not declare, however, whether the termination of a temporary government also terminated the political society, or whether the political society remains intact even when it abolishes one government in order to set up another.

then at the expiration of that period they may resume once more all the powers of the political society and dispose of those powers again as they see fit. Furthermore, he maintained against Hobbes that democracy, and not monarchy, was the best form of government. He granted that monarchy was probably the earliest kind of political organization. For it is more akin than oligarchy or democracy to the pre-political institution of the family to which men are all naturally accustomed, and which men would therefore be likely to imitate when they emerge from the state of nature into political society. Either the father of a numerous family or some other good man who had the confidence of the people of his community would naturally be entrusted with the right to exercise all the powers of government; and as long as he and other similar monarchs after him (whether his descendants or not) used these powers conferred upon them for the benefit of all the people, this most simple form of government would continue.[26] But the fact that monarchy was the earliest and original type of political organization does not lead to the conclusion that it is also the best. Rather history teaches that eventually a monarchy becomes unacceptable to any group of people. A line of kings always degenerates, and men of a lower stamp get control of the government, men who ignore the terms of the political contract on which their power rests. And when such decadence occurs, the people are entitled to erect checks upon the royal power, or even to change the form of government entirely. An aristocracy also is not permanently satisfactory; for an oligarchic body which held office for life and renewed itself by an hereditary principle would be tempted, just as a monarch, to rule for selfish advantage rather than for the common good of all. The only adequate and safe form of government is a democracy in which the legislative power is vested in an assembly, the members of which hold office for a definitely limited term and are subject to being dismissed and succeeded by others.[27] Only when the legislative power is in the hands of delegates whom the people can control, did Locke feel that the government would be genuinely concerned to secure the public welfare.[28]

Locke, however, had no desire to establish a democracy in any extreme form. Though he asserted the desirability of vesting the legis-

[26] *Of Civil Government*, §§ 94, 105, 107.

[27] *Idem*, §§ 138, 143.

[28] Hobbes's confidence in absolute monarchy and Locke's vesting of the legislative in a popular assembly is paralleled by an opposition between their conceptions of the nature of a civil law. Hobbes maintained that a "law, to speak properly and accurately, is the speech of him who by right commands something to others to be done or omitted" (*Philosophical Rudiments of Government*, 3, **3**. *Cf.* also *Leviathan*, Chapter 15). Locke, however, wrote: "A civil law is nothing but the agreement of a society of men either by themselves, or one or more authorized by them; determining the rights, and appointing rewards and punishments to certain actions of all within that society" (King: *Op. cit.*, p. 117). For Hobbes, a law was an injunction imposed by a superior; for Locke, it was a self-determination of those concerned.

lative, the most important political power, in a popular assembly, he did not intend to abolish the kingship. He realized that as a matter of fact, mixed forms of government do exist and are compatible with public order and security. He did, to be sure, deny that the king should have the legislative power; and thus he favored a government which, according to his own definition, could not be called a monarchy. But he assumed throughout the *Treatises of Government* that there would continue to be a king who would exercise executive power. In spite of his unpleasant experiences under Charles II and James II, he never rejected monarchical institutions altogether. He had been most adversely impressed by the course of events under Cromwell, and had been repelled by the republican theories of such men as Milton and Harrington. Consequently, he came to hold and set forth in his *Treatises of Government* a theory of limited monarchy in which parliament holds the legislative and the king holds the executive power of the Commonwealth. The kingship, he seems to have assumed, would continue to be hereditary. But the inheritance of the royal power is not to be regarded as a natural right which the children of the monarchs possess.[29] Rather each ruler in turn derives his power, not by descent from his father, but by grant from the people, *i.e.*, by the same method by which the first king gained his authority. And thus each ruler may retain his power only as long as he abides by his agreement to administer the government with wisdom and justice. If a king is at any time deposed the people cannot be said to be setting up the principle of popular control against "the divine right of kings" or "patriarchal power"; for they only resume rights which they had on certain terms transferred to another. Yet, though Locke subjected the kings to the orders and guidance of parliament and thus of the people, he desired to retain the traditional form of government in England.[30]

Locke did not consistently carry out in his *Treatises of Government* his theory that the parliament as the legislative power was superior and the king as the executive power was subordinate. The reason for his lack of precision and definite statement on this matter was probably

---

[29] *Of Government*, §§ 93–94.

[30] To what extent Locke would wish to give political power to all classes of the population is uncertain. Even the republicans like Milton and Harrington opposed universal suffrage, and would grant the ballot only to the competent or to the land-owning classes. Locke's patron, the first Earl of Shaftesbury, proposed to restrict political rights to those who hold "lands and tenements" to the value of forty pounds per annum, and regarded the majority of the people as "generally of a mean and abject fortune in the world, and thereby subject not only to disorders and quarrels, but to be misguided also by their ignorance, and total want of that discerning faculty which electors in such weighty concerns ought to have" (*Some Observations concerning the Regulations of Elections to Parliament*, pp. 11–13). The *Fundamental Constitutions of Carolina* were none too generous either to the average men (*Cf.* §§ 70–71). Whether Locke followed these predecessors and associates is difficult to determine. His discussion of majority rule and the consent of the governed seems to point to a more broadly democratic view; but if the general assumptions of his generation are considered, his failure to state explicitly that he favored universally shared political power can almost be interpreted as satisfaction with the quite limited democracy of the English constitution in his day.

that he was primarily concerned with writing an apologetic for the form of government which came into being under King William III. He did not construct a complete system of government such as Bentham put forth in his *Constitutional Code*, but discussed the questions which happened to be pressing issues in his own day. His work was not so much an inquiry into the relative merits of various forms of government for political societies in general as a defense of the English constitution as it stood in 1689. And just as the English constitution was not a logical structure in which the functions of the various departments were precisely defined, but an historical compromise in which various unwritten precedents and extra-legal conventions were followed as well as statute laws; so Locke's theories present an inconsistent attitude on many points. On the one hand, he clearly demanded that the legislative should be supreme over the other branches of the government and should have the right to direct those other branches. The legislative may hold the executive responsible for proper conduct in the administration of the laws, and may depose and punish any official who is found guilty of corruption or inefficiency.[31] He even wrote in a short discourse on *Old England's Legal Constitution* in 1695 that "it is the duty of a prince to consent to such laws, and reform such abuses, as are made known to him by parliament, rejoice to be called home from an error, and demonstrate by his works and actions that nothing is more dear to him than the safety and love of his people." [32] The executive has "no will, no power, but that of the law;" and if he attempts to rule in his own right, he "is but a single private person without power and without will, that has no right to obedience." [33] On the other hand, Locke in many ways made the executive supreme over the legislative power. He recognized that the executive in a government may have, as in England, a share in the legislative power. The executive may have the right to withhold his consent from laws passed by parliament, may exercise original legislative power at times when parliament is not in session, may even act contrary to the established laws on the basis of his own arbitrary authority if cases of great and pressing emergency should arise, *i.e.*, the executive possesses what Locke called prerogative which he may use at his own discretion. Moreover, the executive may assemble, or refuse to assemble, the parliament, and may also dismiss the parliament. And whereas the parliament is unable to reform abuses in the method of its own election, such, for example, as the selection of members from formerly prosperous, but now deserted, boroughs, the executive is able to interfere in the matter, to regulate the basis of

[31] *Of Civil Government*, §§ 143, 149, 153.
[32] Bourne: *Life of Locke*, Vol. II, p. 319.
[33] *Of Civil Government*, § 151. *Cf.* § 152.

membership, and thus to determine somewhat the complexion, of the
parliament. Hence, to a certain extent the executive has power over the
legislative branch of the government.[34] Locke did not finally settle
this issue of supremacy between the king and the parliament. For
though he certainly in any important struggle for power would stand
on the side of the parliament, he followed in his theories the inconsistencies and curious compromises of England's constitution; and
he realized that in his own day there was grave need of the kind of
parliamentary reform which only interference by the king could
effectively and speedily accomplish.

4. Locke's indefiniteness as to the relations of the branches of a
government to each other is not so much of a difficulty in his theory
as the same indefiniteness would have been in the case of the work of
Hobbes or Filmer. Hobbes and Filmer, being anxious to deny the
right of revolution, were compelled to set up some source of power
which would be absolute and incontrovertible under all circumstances;
for if there were no such supreme authority, there would be no moral
law and no social order at all. But Locke was always able to fall back
upon the law of nature and natural rights as a final refuge in case the
mechanism of his political system did not work successfully; for the
law of nature was for him binding in the political as well as in the pre-
political state, and natural rights were for him, not the ruin, but the
basis, of the moral law. Behind political society there stands throughout Locke's thought a more ultimate standard of right and wrong.
Political society does not create, but is judged by, this standard. The
positive laws of a commonwealth must, in order to carry weight, be
"conformable to the laws of nature." [35] A government is not free to do
as it pleases; for "the obligations of the law of nature cease not in
society," but rather "the law of nature stands as an eternal rule to all
men, legislators as well as others." [36] Even monarchs are subject to
the same standard, and cannot claim any special privilege for themselves; they stand on the same moral level as all other men, and
"nobody, no power, can exempt them from the obligations of that
eternal law." [37] Therefore, the indefiniteness of Locke's arrangement
of political powers among the branches of a government is not fatal
to his principles; for in every case the officials are subject to judgment
by the people who joined to make the political contract.

Locke, in other words, stood, as Hobbes and Filmer did not, for
the right of revolution. He had taken a view very similar to that of
Hobbes earlier in his life; for in an entry in his journal in 1676 he set
forth the position that since the end of civil society is peace, no opposi-

[34] *Idem*, §§ 139, 151, 154, 157-158, 159-160.
[35] *Of Government*, § 92. *Cf. Of Civil Government*, § 12.
[36] *Of Civil Government*, § 135.
[37] *Idem*, § 195.

tion of a violent kind is to be tolerated, that every citizen should obey the magistrates or submit passively to the penalties for disobedience, that no dictate of conscience can justify rebellion.[38] But though he may have been following Hobbes for a time on account of his eagerness to see the uncertainties and perils of the period of the civil wars ended by a stable and permanent government, the tyrannies of Charles II and James II, and the adversities suffered by his patron the first Earl of Shaftesbury, led him to change his views. And of course in the *Treatises of Government,* which were written to justify the Revolution of 1688, he could not do other than stand for the right of revolution.

The conditions upon which revolution is morally permissible Locke explained in some detail. Resistance to a prince is the natural right of his subjects whenever the prince exceeds the power conferred upon him by the political contract. If the prince sets up his own arbitrary will in place of the established laws, if he hinders the legislative body from assembling in its due time, if he attempts to convene a parliament composed of his own tools, if he betrays his own subjects to a foreign power, if he seeks to confiscate the property of his subjects—if in any way he violates the trust imposed in him, he thereby dissolves the government according to which he was appointed to rule, and so ceases to be prince any longer. The "using of force upon the people without authority, and contrary to the trust put in him that does so, is a state of war with the people." In a state of war all men have equal rights, and no person can claim peculiar respect or special privileges. A king who has exceeded his proper powers no longer is king, and cannot expect to be treated with the reverence which as king his person received. "In all states and conditions the true remedy of force without authority is to oppose force to it." [39] Locke here recognized a distinction, as Hobbes and Filmer had not, between having the power to rule and having the right to rule—a distinction which, as he pointed out, alone enabled one to know lawful princes from pirates.[40] Some rulers may as a matter of fact rule by the mere might of the sword; but they may lawfully be overthrown as soon as their subjects gather sufficient force to meet them in an open contest. "Whosoever uses force without right, as everyone does in society who does it without law, puts himself into a state of war with those against whom he so uses it; and in that state all former ties are cancelled, all other rights cease, and everyone has a right to defend himself, and to resist the aggressor." [41] Thus revolution against a high-handed tyrant is justified on the ground that the tyrant has violated the political contract on which his power rests.

[38] King: *Op. cit.,* pp. 62–63.
[39] *Of Civil Government,* § 155. *Cf.* §§ 202, 214–217, 222.
[40] *Of Government,* § 81.
[41] *Of Civil Government,* § 232.

Locke mentioned two special cases in which revolution against a ruler is permissible, which cases are especially interesting because he thereby attacked the very central position of Hobbes and Filmer. His two predecessors had insisted that the power of the government must be absolute; and also they had maintained that an usurper who once establishes his rule should be obeyed just as the legitimate ruler. Locke, however, denied the right of rule to either absolute monarchs or to usurpers. In the first place he refused to regard absolute monarchy as really a government. "Absolute monarchy which by some men is counted the only government in the world is indeed inconsistent with civil society, and so can be no form of civil government at all." [42] Locke had two reasons for this position. The first reason was that since men have not a power over their own lives, they cannot give such power to another; that even if a prince conquered a group of people in a just war, he would not thereby acquire a title over their possessions or over their children; that, consequently, there is no possible way in which the title of absolute monarch could arise. [43] The second reason was that since there is no neutral judge to decide between an absolute monarch and his people, absolute monarchy is no other than the state of war, an unjust assertion of arbitrary power which justifies the people in taking things into their own hands and retaliating with revolution. In the second place, Locke likewise contended that an usurper may properly be resisted. Even though an usurper does not attempt to assume more power than the people had agreed to surrender to the lawful sovereign, he can claim no allegiance. For in making a political contract a group of persons has the right, not only to determine the form of government they desire to live under, but also to designate the particular rulers to whom they are willing to entrust the powers of that government. An usurper cannot annul part of this contract and preserve the remaining features. He, by his very act of usurpation, destroys the contract entirely. Hence he stands in the relation of an unjust oppressor to his subjects, and may be resisted whenever the people venture to risk the fortune of open war. [44] In both of these cases Locke repudiated the political philosophy of Hobbes and Filmer. He refused to recognize the *de facto* possession of power as constituting a moral right to rule, and insisted upon judging all monarchs by the terms of the freely made contract upon which government rests.

Moreover, just as Locke granted the right of revolution against an unjust prince, so he granted the right of revolution against an unjust government of any kind. [45] The legislative as well as the executive branch of the government may be the part of the government which

[42] *Idem*, § 90.
[43] *Idem*, §§ 177, 179.
[44] *Idem*, §§ 197-198.
[45] *Idem*, § 201.

exceeds its powers and rules for private advantage; and in that case it may be overthrown. Locke did, indeed, speak of the legislative branch as "the supreme power of the commonwealth;"[46] but this supremacy should not be interpreted as affecting his previous assertion that government rests on the consent of the governed. In the same paragraph in which he referred to the legislative as the supreme power in the community, he also explained that this supreme power is "only a fiduciary power to act for certain ends," and that "there remains still in the people a supreme power to remove or alter the legislative, when they find the legislative act contrary to the trust imposed in them."[47] The inconsistency between these two statements is purely verbal.[48] By supreme power Locke explicitly stated that he did not mean arbitrary power nor absolute power. Rather he meant power to act in certain specified ways and to regulate the other branches of the government accordingly, power to execute without restraint the functions bestowed in the political contract. The legislative cannot be altered nor deposed from office by the people as long as it fulfils the specifications of the contract. The people as much as the legislative are morally bound to abide by the contract, and cannot, with changing whims, annul one contract in order to make another. Hence, while the legislative rules within its rights, it retains supreme power and the people are not entitled to resume the rights which they agreed to surrender. Nevertheless, the legislative is supreme just because, and provided that, it has behind it the authority of the people. A law enacted by the legislative would have no force without the sanction of "that which is absolutely necessary to its being a law, the consent of the society."[49] If the legislative should grasp at arbitrary power, if it should invade the property rights of the people, if it should delegate its power to others, if it should refuse to proclaim fixed, settled laws which everyone can inform himself about—then it *ipso facto* ceases to be the legislative and becomes an open foe of the people, it declares a state of war, it loses entirely the power which previously under the terms of the political contract had been supreme. The people are by the wrongdoing of the legislative freed from their obligations under the contract, may revolt, and may establish, at their pleasure, a new form of government.

The underlying rationalism in Locke's theory is most conspicuous in the limitations which he set to the right of revolution. The people are not justified in overturning a government whenever they can

---

[46] *Idem*, § 134.

[47] *Idem*, § 149.

[48] H. Barker in his article on Locke in Hasting's *Encyclopædia of Religion and Ethics*, Vol. VIII, p. 118, regards this inconsistency as fundamental and real. He fails to note that the supremacy of the legislative is complete under one condition and disappears entirely under another condition. *Cf.* Locke: *Of Civil Government*, § 243.

[49] *Of Civil Government*, § 134.

thereby serve their own interests (as Bentham and the utilitarians were wont to maintain). They as much as the governing authorities are under obligation to fulfil the contract which they freely made in establishing a political society. The ethical principle upon which the right of revolution rests is derived, not from a consideration of consequences of a desirable or undesirable kind, but from a consideration of the legal clauses of an agreement between a people and their rulers. Reason judges the morality of social movements by their agreement or disagreement with a standard determined upon in the past. So Locke limited the right of revolution to certain specified cases. A people may revolt only when they have been assailed by an "unjust and unlawful force;" when they have no opportunity to appeal to a neutral tribunal according to the processes of law, or find no such tribunal in existence; and when a majority of them agree to coöperate in the revolution.[50] A small group of people, a minority of the people, are never warranted in disturbing the peace of the community by resistance to the government. As long as the majority of the people feel no inconvenience and are not aroused by the inconvenience which a few of their number may happen to feel, so long the government may claim to be acting within its rights. The people may well prefer that a few men suffer dangers from the rulers of the state than that the peace of the entire group be disturbed. Since the majority of the people made the political contract, the majority must also be obtained to consent to the abrogation of the contract. Only within these narrow legal limits is there a right to revolution.

5. The dissolution of government did not lead for Locke, as it did for Hobbes, to the dissolution of society. Locke did not always state clearly just what the dissolution of a government involved. Sometimes he seems to have supposed that it meant only the overthrow of a certain form of government, but left the people in a political union with each other, and so required them to remain together in the formation of a new system of government.[51] At other times, and more usually, he seems to have held that the dissolution of government meant the entire break-up of political society. Every member of the dissolved government would then "return to the state he was in before with a liberty to shift for himself and provide for his own safety, as he thinks fit, in some other society."[52] In other words, the people who had been held together by a government "become a confused multitude without order or connection,"[53] and are at liberty to look out for their own welfare in any way they see fit. But in either case, whether the dissolution of government relieves people from only a

[50] *Idem*, §§ 204–208.
[51] He was here arguing on the basis of a twofold contract, as mentioned above in § 3 of this chapter.
[52] *Of Civil Government*, § 211.
[53] *Idem*, § 219.

part or from all of their political obligations, society is not destroyed. Since Locke did not regard a contract as necessary to bind a host of isolated, atom-like individuals into social relations with each other, but regarded some form of social relationships as inherent in the constitution of human nature, he was able to hold that the annulment of the political contract did not disrupt society altogether. The return to the state of nature might result in a certain amount of disorder and confusion, but it would in no way involve an abrogation of social duties and of the moral law. It would restore men to the complete freedom and to all of the natural rights which they originally enjoyed. But because it would also deprive them of all political protection, it would simply be a period of transition to be terminated by a new political contract.

6. The main fault in Locke's social and political philosophy is probably the method which he followed. His rationalism tended, as indeed rationalism always tends, to become legalism. As a rationalist he could logically take account of the consequences of certain courses of action just as much as he could as a hedonist. And sometimes he did so. For example, he sanctioned the control which parents may exercise over their children on the ground that otherwise the children would perish; [54] he forbade a general who shoots deserters or a conqueror who enslaves captives to confiscate the property of the victims, on the ground that such confiscation would cause privation to the children of the victims; [55] he denied that men have a property-right in goods which spoil in their possession while others are subject to want; [56] above all, he favored the entrance of men into political societies on the ground that they thus gain the advantage of peace and security. In these and other such cases he based his moral principles on the good results following therefrom, and justified his social institutions by their utility in effecting desirable ends (though the good results and the utility were not measured in terms of pleasure). But more often he failed to consider consequences at all, and came to his decisions by examining the original nature of men and the alleged political contract. He believed in the equal rights of men because he perceived by reason the natural equality of all mankind; he permitted slavery because he felt it to be a just punishment to balance the offense of attacking others; he approved of the institution of money because he recognized its proper connection with the products of human toil; he granted the right of revolution because he insisted on the carrying out of the terms of the agreement between rulers and ruled; and he limited the right of revolution because he was as unwilling that the people should violate their promise

[54] *Idem,* §§ 55 ff.
[55] *Idem,* §§ 138, 180–182.
[56] *Idem,* § 31.

as that the monarch should do so. In general it might be said that Locke looked to the future in appraising the foundation of political society, and then, once political society was established, looked back to the past. Genesis is more important than outcome in the framing of most of his political and social principles. Therefore his rationalism is very weak. Though he fortunately read into the nature of man and the terms of the political contract all the elements needed in order to draw therefrom his liberal principles, yet he must have reached his ideas of the nature of man and the terms of the political contract by considering the consequences and implications of his principles. What he ostensibly deduced as the logical outcome of certain alleged agreements of ideas, he must have first come to accept on grounds of utility —otherwise he would be guilty of unwarranted dogmatism. He reached the absolute principles which served as his major premises from an empirical estimate of the results of certain courses of conduct; but he failed to realize their empirical derivation, and remained restless until he thought that he found them in the nature of things.[57] Such procedure is most unsatisfactory, both because it combines a fictitious reconstruction of the past with a legalistic dependence thereon, and because it rests content with insufficient empirical investigations instead of pressing on to a more complete and adequate survey of political data.

Another and hardly less serious fault in Locke's theory of political society is his failure to grapple with the problem of sovereignty. Hobbes had raised this problem in a violent fashion; but Locke returned to the pre-Hobbian, medieval attitude. He did, to be sure, reject any government which does not rest on the consent of the governed; but he nowhere expounded a doctrine of popular sovereignty. He dreaded the absolutism of the *Leviathan*, and seems to have supposed that in rejecting that absolutism he had to reject the doctrine of sovereignty altogether. He tried to make the law of nature, rather than any political person or body, supreme—a position which he, with his nominalistic logical views, could not maintain with as much effectiveness as did the scholastic realists of the Middle Ages. As a practical statesman he stood with the parliamentary forces in their programme of reform; but he left much power to the monarch, and he deposited still more power in the people. Of course mixed governments frequently thrive; but even in mixed governments there must be some center which in case of conflict has the ultimate power. Hobbes might be said to have abolished right in order to emphasize

---

[57] *Cf.* Leslie Stephen's *English Thought in the Eighteenth Century*, p. 138: "Vigorously as Locke can put the utilitarian argument, we become sensible that it somehow fails to give him complete satisfaction. He wants some binding element to supplement the mere shifting considerations of expediency. We constantly meet with rights of an indefeasible nature, which have somehow obtained an authority independent of the source from which they are derived."

the fact of might; Locke might almost be said to be desirous of denying the existence of might altogether in order to restore right to its lofty position. Hobbes subjected the moral to the legal; Locke would almost make the moral operate without legal instrumentalities. Locke was so intent on explaining what ought to be that he did not enough consider what is. He evidently thought he could avoid the problem of sovereignty by dividing up political functions among the various parts of the body politic.[58]

In spite of his insistence on the right of revolution Locke can hardly be spoken of as a revolutionist. His interest was obviously to provide for a stable government. But his experience under the later Stuart kings convinced him that such stability must be sought and obtained by limiting the rights of governments rather than by limiting the rights of the people. Whereas Hobbes sought peace by restraint upon the people, Locke sought it by restraint upon the rulers. He realized both that no denial of rights to the people would be effective in keeping them in subjection to oppressive tyranny, and also that the misrule of vain monarchs was the ultimate cause of the political unrest in the England of his day. His recognition of the rights of revolution was, therefore, not so much an exhortation to the people to rise against their government, as a warning to the monarchs and parliaments to recognize the wise limitations of their dominion. As T. H. Green expressed it: "What he was really concerned about was to dispute 'the right divine to govern wrong'."[59] He had no more fondness for turbulence and violence than Hobbes; but whereas Hobbes showed himself a Tory and a conservative in his theory of how to maintain peace, he showed himself a Whig and a liberal.[60] When he insisted on the right of revolution he at once added that his theory would not promote, but lessen, the probabilities of popular uprisings. For on the one hand, princes might be prevailed upon by a knowledge of the true political principles to be more considerate of their subjects' rights. And on the other hand, the people are not naturally inclined to resort to force against their superiors. The people "are not so easily got out of their old forms as some are apt to suggest."[61] Most revolutions are to be blamed upon the insolence and arbitrary actions of rulers

[58] Cf. Figgis: The Divine Right of Kings, p. 242. Figgis goes so far as to interpret Locke's Treatise of Civil Government as primarily an attack on the idea of sovereignty rather than a defense of democratic over against monarchical principles. Undoubtedly Figgis interprets correctly the implications of Locke's position. But does he not forget the practical purpose which Locke confesses he had in mind?

[59] T. H. Green: Works, Vol. II, p. 385.

[60] It may seem strange to speak of Hobbes as conservative and Locke as more liberal. Yet, though Hobbes was on the whole the more radical thinker, he was on certain points almost reactionary, e.g., in his making men's consciences and even their reason subservient to the authority of the state. Locke, on the other hand, if he did not carry his rationalism out to violent extremes, at least carried it into every department of thought. Hobbes consequently went further along some lines, but Locke went further along others. Cf. A. W. Benn: The History of English Rationalism in the Nineteenth Century, Vol. I, p. 114.

[61] Of Civil Government, § 223. Cf. § 230.

rather than upon any wantonness of the people. Therefore, a frank acknowledgment by rulers of the people's right to revolution is likely to diminish rather than increase the causes which produce the necessity for the exercise of that right.

The non-revolutionary motive behind Locke's discussion of the right of revolution is further exhibited by his reliance on his rationalistic rather than his hedonistic moral principles in his discussion of the matter. If he had been willing to justify revolutions by the hedonistic standard, he would have had to grant that revolutions were morally warranted whenever they promoted the happiness of the people. And as many people might deem that sweeping political changes would be favorable to their happiness, frequent occasions for outbreaks might arise. But since he based the right of revolution on the violation of the political contract, the occasions for the exercise of that right are few. If the people change their ideas of what they want from their government, they nevertheless have to abide by the contract they made. They are never entitled to begin a revolt unless their rulers have first revolted against them. Moreover, a few persons cannot ethically inaugurate a rebellion until they have won the support of a majority of their fellow-citizens. And as the views of the majority would in most cases be practically impossible to ascertain, there are strong obstacles in the way of revolution. Locke's legalistic rationalism and repugnance to popular uprisings are further seen to be closely connected in his position that though the enactments of a prince who exceeds his just power are not properly laws at all, yet all genuine laws are to be implicitly and unquestioningly obeyed.[62] Thus, while he was eager to justify the bloodless Revolution of 1688, he had slight sympathy with revolutions in general. In spite of his own years of exile, he had the common British preference for working out political changes by slow constitutional reforms rather than by more sudden, but also more violent, uprisings.

Locke's theory of political society is decidedly weak. He made improvements, to be sure, in the theories of Grotius and Pufendorf. He stood with Hooker against them in denying that government can justly take its origin from a war of conquest. He recognized the justice of Filmer's criticism of Grotius to the effect that a contract freely made by the people might also be abrogated again; and so he, the first among the political philosophers of the century, gave a place in his theory, however half-heartedly, to the right of revolution. He distinguished, as none of his predecessors had done, between two distinct positions: that some form of government is essential for social welfare, and that a particular government must therefore not be disturbed. And while he affirmed the former of these two positions, he

[62] Cf. Figgis: Op. cit., p. 226.

denied that the latter was a logical consequence thereof. Nevertheless, in spite of these improvements in the theory of political society, Locke's position remains weak. His reconstruction of history is probably even more untrue to the facts than the patriarchal theory of Filmer. His attempt to secure social solidity by the idea of "tacit consent" is almost ridiculous. He struggled to deduce from a fictitious contract facts with which he should have started. And since he made political rights and duties dependent upon the exact legal terms of that contract, his conclusions are as fallible as his knowledge of those terms is inadequate. He endeavored to deduce from a consideration of life in the state of nature what kind of an agreement men could be supposed to have made. But such a procedure is hardly satisfactory. The type of rationalism for which Locke stood thus seems unable to serve as a basis for a political philosophy which can meet all the objections which can be brought against it.

CHAPTER III

LOCKE'S THEORIES OF TOLERATION AND PUNISHMENT

1. There was no problem of social philosophy which absorbed so much of Locke's time and thought as that of the toleration of religious sects, and consequently of the proper relations of church and state. From his young manhood to the closing years of his life he was engaged in writing out his liberal views, though not all he wrote appeared in print during his lifetime. As early as 1667 he composed *An Essay concerning Toleration* which, however, was first published more than two centuries later in Bourne's *Life of Locke*. About the year 1682 he was aroused by Stillingfleet's book on *The Unreasonableness of Separation* to reply in *A Defence of Nonconformity*, a short work which first came out in King's *Life of Locke*. His four *Letters on Toleration*, which have been included in all of the editions of his collected works, were products of his mature years. The first and most important of these four letters appeared in Latin [1] in 1689, and was immediately translated and published in English. The next two were replies in 1690 and 1692 to criticisms brought against the first letter by Jonas Proast, of Queen's College, Oxford, and are long and at times drearily controversial. The fourth letter is an unfinished rejoinder to a renewed attack from Proast, interrupted by Locke's death, and contained in his posthumous works which were published in 1706. Thus, from his earliest years to the end of his life he was interested in toleration.

Locke's influence in advancing the cause of toleration was probably considerable. The issue had been widely discussed before his day, and many prominent men, such as John Owen of Christ Church College, Oxford, John Milton, Jeremy Taylor, and Archbishop Tillotson, had given their support to the liberal side. Locke's task was not so much to get the idea of toleration into the minds of the people of his generation as to assist those who sought to put a widely accepted idea into practise and into legal enactment. As the friend and secretary of the first Earl of Shaftesbury, Locke had a share in drawing up *The Fundamental Constitutions of Carolina*, and in securing for that new land a large measure of the toleration he desired for his own countrymen.[2] Also he was the confidential adviser of many of those who,

---

[1] Unlike most of his predecessors in philosophy Locke wrote almost exclusively in his native tongue. This letter was composed in Latin because Limborch to whom it was addressed could not read English.

[2] Locke's influence seems to be conspicuous in the best provisions of this constitution. In spite of the political conservatism of many articles, the articles on religion are noticeably liberal. *Cf.* §§ 95, 97, 100, 101, 106.

under King William III, passed the Toleration Act of 1689. And if he felt that the act did not grant all the freedom which was to be desired,[3] he at least welcomed the considerable advance it marked over previous acts of exclusion and uniformity.

(a) Locke's views in favor of toleration were based upon his theory of the origin of the state and the church. As to political society he consistently maintained the position of the *Treatises of Government* that the commonwealth is "only made to preserve men in this world from the fraud and violence of one another;" and he concluded that "what was the end of the erecting of government ought to be the measure of its proceeding."[4] As to religious society or the church, he held that it is "a voluntary society of men, joining themselves together of their own accord, in order to the public worshiping of God, in such a manner as they judge acceptable to him, and effectual to the salvation of their souls."[5] The two organizations differ so completely in their contractual basis that their functions will be correspondingly distinct. On the one hand, the state should leave to the church all matters of religious belief, ceremonial observance and ecclesiastical polity and should simply regulate those human relationships which involve the civil rights which government is designed to further. "The business of laws is not to provide for the truth of opinions, but for the safety and security of the commonwealth, and of every particular man's goods and person."[6] Since no one entered into political society to secure the salvation of his soul, government is not justified in seeking to obtain salvation for him. The magistrates are entitled to act only according to the terms of the political contract; and in making that contract, every man reserved to himself the right of determining what private measures he will adopt to save his soul. On the other hand, the church should leave to the state all exercise of force. Every church may make its own laws for the conduct of its own society and may exhort and admonish its members to obey them, may even expel from its membership any recalcitrant persons who refuse to obey. But "the exercise of church power . . . does properly extend no further than excommunication."[7] No private person, and no group of private persons such as constitute a church, ought at any time to transgress the equally valid rights of other men, in an attempt to compel those others by force to believe or act in conformity with their own convictions. The power and authority of the clergy "ought to be confined within the bounds of the church, nor can it in any manner be extended to civil affairs; because the church itself

[3] *Cf.* a letter to Limborch, June 6, 1689. *Works*, Vol. X, p. 23.
[4] Bourne: *Op. cit.*, Vol. I, p. 174.
[5] *Works*, Vol. VI, p. 13.
[6] *Works*, Vol. VI, p. 40.
[7] King: *Op. cit.*, p. 305. *Cf.* Locke: *Works*, Vol. VI, p. 16.

is a thing absolutely separate and distinct from the commonwealth." [8]
To the state alone men relinquished the right to use force in the attainment of their other rights; hence, the church must exercise other
agencies in advancing its own interests. As the state should not encroach on the rights of the church, so the church should not encroach
on the rights of the state. In general, the functions of church and state
will in no way conflict. [9]

(b) Locke carried to an extreme his opposition to governmental control of religious affairs. The positions which men accept on religious
grounds may be divided into four groups—speculative opinions or
matters of faith and creeds; practical opinions which concern society
and the believer's relations to his fellows; ceremonial practises on
points which are in themselves indifferent; and moral practises on
points which involve virtues and vices. [10] What the attitude of the
state should be to each of these four groups Locke considered separately.

In the first place, speculative opinions are of no concern to the state;
for they in no way affect men's exercise of their civil rights. They
should, therefore, neither be commanded nor be forbidden, but should
all alike be tolerated. Many individuals may consider their creed to
be indispensable to salvation. But they must remember that "the
care of each man's salvation belongs only to himself," [11] that the perdi-
tion of others is not their concern, and hence that the power of the
magistrate is not to be employed for the enforcement of credal articles.
It is interesting to note, moreover, that though Locke's primary argument for the separation of civil and religious concerns in matters of
speculative opinions was the rationalistic claim of the distinct functions of state and church, yet undoubtedly his pronounced skepticism [12]
concerning alleged knowledge of extra-mental realities also strongly
reinforced his readiness to tolerate diverse beliefs. Many religious
convictions are a matter of faith, not of knowledge, and so cannot be
established by any certain proof. God and immortality can indeed
be demonstrated, but most other theological dogmas cannot. The
limits of human understanding do not comprise such doctrines as go
to make up the rival faiths of most Christian sects. Hence, since

[8] *Works*, Vol. VI, p. 21.

[9] Locke here reveals the connection which through his father he had with the Independent or Crom-
wellian party, and the influence which that connection had upon his social views. He even at this point
broke with his predecessor, the "judicious Hooker." Hooker regarded the church as a body politic which
differed from other bodies politic only by having the true religion, and therefore put the state in care of
religious interests. "The Church of Jesus Christ is every such politic society of men, as doth in religion
hold that truth which is proper to Christianity. As a politic society it doth maintain religion; as a
church, that religion which God hath revealed by Jesus Christ." *Cf. Of the Laws of Ecclesiastical Polity*,
VIII, 1, 2.

[10] Locke at no one place made exactly this classification. But each group is treated in one part or
another of his various works on toleration.

[11] *Works*, Vol. VI, p. 41.

[12] *Cf. Essay*: Introduction, 5-6. *Cf.* also *Thoughts concerning Education*, § 136.

neither the truth nor the falsity of these doctrines can be clearly determined, the need for toleration is obvious.[13]

In the second place, practical opinions which concern society and the believer's relations to his fellows are a matter in which the state is often justified in interfering. Such opinions are to be tolerated "only so far as they do not tend to the disturbance of the state, or do not cause greater inconveniences than advantages to the community."[14] The cases in which toleration should not be extended are four:[15] (1) "No opinions contrary to human society or to those moral rules which are necessary to the preservation of civil society are to be tolerated by the magistrate." Such opinions are, however, very rare; for the welfare of the individual would be lost with the overthrow of society. (2) Opinions by which men arrogate special privileges and exemptions to themselves or to their own ecclesiastical group are likewise dangerous and deserving of state opposition. Such opinions are, for example, those according to which men claim that they do not need to keep faith with heretics, *i.e.*, with those outside of their own sect; that they owe no allegiance to an heretical or excommunicate prince; that they alone are entitled to dominion over the rest of mankind; or that they would not, if they were in a position of power, tolerate their fellows. (3) Recognition of some foreign potentate or ecclesiastic as possessing jurisdiction over the members of a religious sect who live under another government is destructive of that other government, and so must be suppressed. Locke here instanced only the case of a Mahometan who while living in a Christian country rendered supreme obedience to the Ottoman emperor; but he clearly had in mind Roman Catholics who, since they were frequently scheming at that time to deliver England once more into the power of the Pope, were disloyal to the state and false to the fundamental principle of political society.[16] (4) Atheism is such an anti-social position that it cannot be tolerated by any government; it is "a crime which, for its madness as well as guilt, ought to shut a man out of all sober and civil society."[17] Locke was here viewing morality from the theological standpoint; and though he was still quite within the limits of his most rationalistic ethical theory, he was making all moral principles dependent upon the

[13] This skepticism is closely related to the contention set forth in *The Reasonableness of Christianity* to the effect that in order to become a Christian, a man needs only to accept Jesus as messiah. That one article of faith Locke believed to be established on the basis of Scripture; other articles he regarded as more or less dubious interpretations of difficult texts.

[14] Bourne: *Life of Locke*, Vol. I, p. 178.

[15] *Works*, Vol. VI, pp. 45–47.

[16] For some reason Roman Catholics were not excluded, by the terms of *The Fundamental Constitutions of Carolina*, from settling in that new land. Ruffini, in his volume on *Religious Liberty*, p. 282, suggested that the absence of such an excluding article is perhaps to be explained by the fact that, when the constitution was drawn up in 1669, Locke and his co-workers had not yet experienced oppression and exile at the hands of the English papists.

[17] *Works*, Vol. VII, p. 162. *Cf.* Grotius: *Concerning the Rights of War and Peace*, II, 20, [46], and Pufendorf: *The Whole Duty of Man*, I, 4, [2].

existence of God.[18] "The taking away of God, though but even in thought, dissolves all." [19] These four types of practical opinions are, because of their anti-social consequences, subject to interference and control by the officers of the commonwealth. Those who hold them are the legitimate objects of special legislation and judgment. Practical opinions on other subjects should, however, be tolerated.

In the third place, ceremonial practises on points which are in themselves indifferent are no concern of the state at all. They are but "the outward form and rites of worship,"[20] and may be chosen or rejected according to the consciences and free preferences of the worshipers. They are but the symbols of things divine, and so can neither be forbidden nor commanded by the civil powers.

In the fourth place, moral practises on points which involve virtues and vices will often warrant state interference; for they may be found subversive of the welfare, even of the very existence, of society. No government could tolerate the sacrifice of infants, promiscuous uncleanness, or "any other such heinous enormities." [21] Whatever is unlawful in the ordinary course of life is also unlawful in a religious assembly. Religion cannot be used as an excuse or shelter whereby to secure permission to commit crimes. Locke did not, however, think that the state should endeavor to suppress all sins; for it may well be that some sins do not concern men's civil rights. Sins whereby a man harms only himself, may go on unchecked by the state; for civil laws, though they guard men from the fraud and violence of each other, do not guard them from the negligence or viciousness of themselves. Even when the civil laws enjoin or prohibit an act, they do so, not because the act is in itself virtuous or vicious, but because it is necessary to, or destructive of, the social peace and order.[22] Those moral practises alone may be controlled by the state which involve the rights which men established political society to protect.

(c) Locke recognized the fact that there was always the possibility of conflict between an individual's conscience and the legitimate exercise of governmental authority. If the state is administered wisely, such conflicts will not be numerous; but in any case they are likely to occur occasionally. When they do occur, the individual is warranted neither in disobeying his conscience nor in resisting the state. Locke's other worldly point of view in ethics led him to place loyalty to duty on religious grounds ahead of mere obligation to an earthly society such as the state; yet also his social theory of the quite limited right of revolution led him to deny the moral propriety of open oppo-

18 *Cf.* above. Book II, Chapter III, § 4.
19 *Works*, Vol. VI, p. 47.
20 *Idem*, Vol. VI, p. 29.
21 *Idem*, Vol. VI, p. 33.
22 Bourne: *Op. cit.*, Vol. I, p. 182. Also *cf.* Locke: *Works*, Vol. VI, pp. 23–24.

sition or rebellion by a few persons against the magistrates. The conscientious individual is thus confined to the necessity of passively accepting the punishment assigned for violation of the civil laws. He thereby both satisfies his conscience, and refrains from undermining the basis on which the political society rests. It is as entirely lawful for him to submit to the penalties as to carry out the instructions of the civil laws, and it is much more in line with his understanding of his higher duty in the light of the claims of the future life.[23] Locke thus reached a compromise between the rival duties of preparing for heaven and of remaining true to the political contract with one's fellow men.

(d) The significance of Locke's theory of toleration comes out clearly in the controversy which he had with Proast. Proast attacked Locke's theory mainly on three grounds. In the first place, he advocated the use of moderate penalties in order to bring men to consider the arguments in favor of the true religion. He granted both that the extreme penalties such as Locke held up to condemnation were wrong, and that force can never take the place of a genuine conviction of mind. But he assumed always that "no man can fail of finding the way of salvation, who seeks it as he ought;"[24] and therefore, though force cannot be substituted for reason, it may be useful in making men consider what reason has to say. Since men would frequently not pay any attention to the arguments for the true religion unless compelled to do so, force may "indirectly and at a distance"[25] bring men to accept the truth. In the second place, Proast maintained that force is to be used solely to promote the true religion, and never to promote a false religion.[26] He accused Locke of putting all religions, true and false, on the same footing: "It seems in your opinion, whatsoever is supposed the truth, is the truth . . . which evidently makes all religions alike to those who suppose them true."[27] And he insisted that if the plan of giving coercive power to only those magistrates who accept the true religion were adopted, "all false religions would soon vanish, and the true become once more the only religion in the world."[28] In the third place, Proast attacked Locke's theory of the function of a commonwealth. He charged Locke with begging the whole question in arbitrarily asserting that in the original political contract the rights of the state were restricted to keeping peace and order in the affairs of this

[23] *Works*, Vol. VI, pp. 43–44.

[24] Proast: *The Argument of the Letter concerning Toleration briefly considered and answered*, p. 7. Cf. *A Second Letter to the Author of the Three Letters for Toleration*, pp. 5–6.

[25] Proast: *The Argument of the Letter concerning Toleration briefly considered and answered*, p. 5.

[26] Richard Willis, in the *Occasional Paper*, No. VIII, p. 2, made this same point. He insisted on the right of magistrates "to use their authority and power in favor of God's church and to the advantage of true religion."

[27] Proast: *A Third Letter concerning Toleration*, p. 28.

[28] *Idem*, pp. 51–52.

world. He wished to determine the proper limits of state action, not by any alleged historical contract which could be supposed to be most anything one wanted it to be, but by the utility of exercising certain kinds of power. "Commonwealths are instituted for the attaining of all the benefits which political government can yield; and therefore, if the spiritual and eternal interests of men may any way be procured or advanced by political government, the procuring and advancing of those interests must in all reason be reckoned among the ends of civil societies, and so, consequently, fall within the compass of the magistrate's jurisdiction." [29] The state is justified in performing any functions which it is able to carry on successfully.

Locke replied fully to each of these three criticisms from Proast. In answer to the first criticism, he pointed out that it would be impossible to execute the scheme of imposing moderate penalties to make men consider. Proast's assumption that the truth is apparent to any one who will properly examine it would justify the application of more and more extreme punishments, until all men agreed and joined the one and only church in a given society. For if men did not agree, they could be regarded as not having fairly considered the arguments brought to their attention. Any degree of persecution would thus be justified. "Your principles, whatever your words deny, will carry you to those degrees of severity, which in profession you condemn." [30] Moreover, the penalties would have to be continued on indefinitely, as long as men remained unconvinced. And, finally, there is no means of determining which men have properly considered the reasons for their faith, and which have not, except by some external and unfair criterion, such, for example, as membership in the established church. Arbitrarily to select all dissenters to make them consider amounts to no more than punishing them because they are dissenters.[31] Many dissenters may have considered the grounds of their religious beliefs more carefully than most members of the established church; indeed, the mere fact that they stand out against the established church is good reason to suppose that they have given more serious thought to religion than those who flock into the accepted ecclesiastical organ- ization.[32] Thus, both because penalties, once introduced, cannot be kept moderate, and because there is no just way of deciding which men have carefully considered their religious faith, Proast's scheme is im- practicable.

[29] Proast: *The Argument of the Letter concerning Toleration briefly considered and answered*, pp. 18–19. *Cf.* also *A Third Letter concerning Toleration*, pp. 57–58.

[30] Locke: *Works*, Vol. VI, p. 281.

[31] Proast was forced by Locke to come out and confess that his scheme amounted to an attack on dissenters. In *A Third Letter concerning Toleration*, p. 24, he wrote: "Dissenters can never be supposed to consider those reasons and arguments as they ought, whilst they persist in rejecting that religion, or (in your language) whilst they continue dissenters; for if they did so consider them, they would not continue dissenters."

[32] Locke: *Works*, Vol. VI, pp. 74–75.

In answer to Proast's second criticism, Locke pointed out that Proast could not assume his own religion to be true and all others false without also granting that other persons may do the same. Every prince deems himself possessed of the true religion; every church deems itself orthodox.[33] And if one prince or state may use punishments to compel men to consider, all may do so. To deny to others what one demands for himself is to prejudge the case, to beg the whole question, to take for granted the very issue at stake. Until a given religion is proved true to all rulers, one ruler cannot claim any exclusive right to use force in promoting his religion; and after a given religion is proved true to all rulers, force would not be required. Since out of the competing religions in the world only one can be true, the use of force by the state in the interests of the established churches would do much more harm than good. Proast's recognition of the right of the believer in the true religion to use force would be claimed by every ruler to apply to his own case.

In answer to the third criticism, Locke made two points. The first point was that the use of force would, even if justified by the contract on which the state rests, not be useful. The power of a government consists "in outward force," and religion consists "in the inward persuasion of the mind."[34] Outward force may produce external conformity, but only at the risk of inner hypocrisy. Moreover, force means oppression, and oppression leads to disorder and rebellion. Even the dangerous practical opinions and immoral acts which the state must suppress are to be dealt with as generously as possible. Those who hold the opinions or commit the acts should be restrained, without, however, being compelled to renounce their position, much less to declare assent to a contrary position.[35] Toleration will make dissenters friendly to the state. Whenever dissenters give trouble to their rulers, it is because harsh treatment has made them hostile. "There is one thing only which gathers people into seditious commotions, and that is oppression."[36] Severity and force, so far from being the only way of governing and of getting rid of factions, are often the cause which produces disturbing elements within the state.[37] Seldom is force really useful in regulating religious matters. The second point which Locke made in answer to Proast's third criticism was only a reiteration that after all, even if force were useful for promoting true religion, "it does not from hence follow that it is lawful and may be used."[38] Locke would probably have found it very difficult to maintain the right of toleration for all religious

---

[33] *Idem,* pp. 5, 19, 35, 220, 556.
[34] *Idem,* p. 11.
[35] Bourne: *Op. cit.,* Vol. I, p. 170.
[36] Locke: *Works,* Vol VI, p. 50.
[37] Bourne: *Op. cit.,* Vol. I, p. 194.
[38] Locke: *Works,* Vol. VI, p. 80.

bodies on the basis of his rationalistic or legalistic ethical thought if he had not also happened to find such a decision harmonious with his judgment as to the most useful course of action to pursue. Yet he seems always to have failed to be convinced by a merely utilitarian argument for any moral position; and so he erected what he deemed best from a hedonistic standpoint into a sort of structural and basic principle whence the same conclusion could be deductively derived. Hence, he returned, as his final argument against Proast, to the terms of the political contract. In an early paper he had defined the end of religious societies to be the attainment of happiness in the future life, and the end of political societies to be "a free and peaceable enjoyment of all the good things of this life;" [39] and he concluded that since the state is concerned wholly with temporal prosperity, it may not use its power to promote religious affairs. To this point he clung consistently, and reiterated it over and over again as his final answer to such charges as Proast made.[40] Only a rationalistic principle was ultimately satisfactory to him.

2. Locke's idea of the proper form of ecclesiastical organization was that which broad-churchmen within the Church of England have always held. That is, he wished so to reduce the doctrinal requirements for membership in the church as to permit many different factions to be included harmoniously within a comprehensive church. He would not, to be sure, consent to limit the extent of toleration simply to granting easy terms of admission to one church, but insisted on full indulgence "to all who, in spite of the broadening of the national church, are still unwilling or unable to become members of it." [41] He would not be satisfied with "declarations of indulgence nor acts of comprehension such as have been practised or projected amongst us," but demanded "absolute liberty, just and true liberty, equal and impartial liberty." [42]   Nevertheless, he was also interested in comprehension for the Church of England, too. His skepticism, as revealed in his desire to reduce credal requirements to a minimum, may have been the driving motive here. At any rate he maintained that "for the most part the matters of controversy and distinction between sects are no parts, or very inconsiderable ones and appendices, of true religion," and that the multiplication of incomprehensible doctrines only drives men to atheism.[43] If dissenters wish to remain by themselves, they are entitled to do so; and the various sects within a state should in that case be as friendly to each other as individual persons

[39] King: *Op. cit.*, p. 300.
[40] *Cf.* Locke: *Works*, Vol. VI, p. 212.
[41] Letter to Limborch, March 12, 1689. *Works*, Vol. X, p. 22. Translation quoted from Bourne's *Life of Locke*, Vol. II, pp. 150-151.
[42] *Works*, Vol. VI, p. 4.
[43] Bourne: *Op. cit.*, Vol. I, p. 194.

are. But it would be even better to have the church so broad and inclusive that the necessity for dissenting bodies would be considerably
lessened.

3. Akin to Locke's theory of toleration in its liberal and generous
character is his theory of punishment. His views on punishment are
found in frequent, though scattered, references in the *Treatises of
Government*, and more fully, in connection with his definition of personal identity, in the chapter on 'Identity and Diversity' in the second
book of the *Essay*. This chapter was not in the first edition, but appeared in the second edition in answer to a suggestion from Molyneux
that some discussion of the *'principium individuationis'* be inserted in
the *Essay*.[44]

(*a*) Locke's theory of personal identity is closely related to his sub-
jectivistic doctrine of ideas, according to which the mind cannot
directly apprehend external objects, but is confined to a consideration
of its own ideas. He distinguished sharply between identity of substance, identity of man, and identity of person,[45] and regarded the
latter alone as having significance for moral philosophy. The identity
of a substance is to be ascertained in terms of its existence at a given
time and place.[46] The identity of a man consists in "the participation
of the same continued life, by constantly fleeting particles of matter,
in succession vitally united to the same organized body." [47] The
identity of a person, however, is a matter of conscious connection by
memory between different experiences. "As far as this consciousness
can be extended backwards to any past action or thought, so far reaches
the identity of that person." [48] Only where there is consciousness, and
where the being who has this consciousness can consider itself the same
being who was previously conscious at different times and places, is
there personal identity.

Locke granted that probably one consciousness is in every case
"annexed to, and the affection of, one individual immaterial substance." [49] But such one-one correspondence between a substance and
a consciousness he did not deem as demonstrably certain, nor as
necessary to his theory. One and the same thinking substance may be
accompanied by two or more persons,[50] or the same person may be
attached to two or more substances, material or spiritual.[51] That
is, identity of substance, however probable on *a priori* grounds, is not

44 Correspondence between Locke and Molyneux. *Cf.* Locke: *Works*, Vol. IX, pp. 310, 326, 327, 350.
45 *Essay*, II, 27, 8.
46 *Idem*, II, 27,1.
47 *Idem*, II, 27, 7.
48 *Idem*, II, 27, 11. (Because of an error in Fraser's notation of the sections in this chapter, it should
be stated that this reference is to the earlier of the two paragraphs numbered 11.)
49 *Idem*, II, 27, 25.
50 *Idem*, II, 27, 14-15.
51 *Idem*, II, 27, 11, 13.

essential to identity of consciousness.[52] A person simply "owns all the actions of that thing as its own, as far as consciousness reaches, and no further."[53] Whatever a person cannot recollect, even if performed by the same substance to which he is now attached, does not belong to him; and whatever he can recollect, even if performed by a different substance than that to which he is now attached, does belong to him. Person, and self, and consciousness are, for Locke, synonymous terms.

(b) Locke's purpose in defining person as he did was to obtain a suitable moral basis for his theory of punishment. The term person, unlike the term substance or even the term man, has no special metaphysical bearing. Rather "it is a forensic term, appropriating actions and their merit."[54] A person does not particularly care what pleasures or pains are assigned to the substance to which he is attached, unless he is conscious of those pleasures and pains; but he does greatly care what pleasures and pains are assigned to himself. Hence, rewards and penalties must be distributed on the basis of the identity of the persons, not the substances, who performed the acts. "In this personal identity is founded all the right and justice of reward and punishment; happiness and misery being that for which every one is concerned for himself, and not mattering what becomes of any substance, not joined to, or affected with that consciousness."[55]

(c) In Locke's social philosophy, it is, as has been stated above, the state, and the state alone, which is entitled to impose punishments. The purpose of punishment, as Locke showed in his *Treatises of Government*, is threefold: "to make it [*i.e.*, any misdeed or breach of the law] an ill bargain to the offender, give him cause to repent, and terrify others from doing the like."[56] That is, the commonwealth aims to restrain both the individual who is tempted to a crime and all others who might follow his example, and, if he nevertheless, yields to the temptation, to bring him to a better view of social obligation. Punishment, for Locke, is never vindictive nor vengeful; rather, it is corrective and educative. Though Locke held that the punishment should always be carefully proportioned to the enormity of the offense, his motive in seeking a due balance was, not to return like for like, but to find a degree of pain adequate to counteract men's evil tendencies and so to keep them from the offense. The commonwealth does not desire to avenge itself on anyone, but desires to find an efficient means of securing public order and security.

---

[52] Locke seems to have assumed as his reason for this position that the person is not immediately conscious of the substance to which he is attached. The proof of self-existence in IV, 9 ³ would then not be, as in Descartes, a proof of the existence of a spiritual substance. Locke thus marks a transition step towards Hume's rejection of the soul substance.

[53] *Essay*, II, 27, ¹⁷.

[54] *Idem*, II, 27, ²⁶.

[55] *Idem*, II, 27, ¹⁸.

[56] *Of Civil Government*, § 12

(*d*) Locke granted, however, one point which is a slight inconsistency in his theory. A man who commits a wrong when he is drunk may be punished therefor, even though he is not, when sober, aware of having done it.[57] The person who does something in his sleep or in a delirious illness is not answerable for his act; but a drunken man cannot plead the same extenuation. Locke thus seems to have violated his principle that consciousness is the only proper basis of punishment. But he justified this position, not on the ground that drunkenness is a crime and therefore cannot be alleged as an excuse for another crime,[58] but rather on the ground that want of consciousness cannot be proven in favor of the man who was drunk. Persons may feign lack of consciousness of acts committed in past states, in order to escape punishment. So the officers of the commonwealth must be on their guard against deceit and trickery, and should presume that offenders are conscious of their past misdeeds except in the cases where walking in the sleep, temporary derangement due to fever, or some such valid excuse can be clearly and definitely established.

(*e*) Locke's view of the nature of the punishments which God will inflict in the future life is a consistent outcome of his general position. He rejected the Calvinistic position that God punished men for his own glory, and maintained that God punished them solely "for their good and benefit" and "for the preservation of his creatures in the order and beauty of the state that he has placed each of them in." [59] God will judge men more justly than civil magistrates possibly can. For whereas civil magistrates must assume men to be conscious of their past acts unless lack of consciousness is established, God will know the secrets of all hearts, and so need make no dangerous assumptions. He will not attach to men the consciousness of things which they never did,[60] nor punish them for what is no longer part of their personality. His punishments will always be educative. He will, therefore, never use everlasting torments. Those souls on whom the infliction of pain is unable to bring about the needed reform and purification, he will simply deprive of immortality altogether.[61] Unlimited misery is worse than annihilation;[62] hence, where pain cannot serve as educative purpose, it will not be used, and release from existence will be substituted as the more merciful procedure. Thus, though Locke was not a universalist in hoping for the eventual salvation of all men, he at least rejected the crudely unethical aspects of the doctrine of everlasting damnation.

[57] *Essay*, II, 27, 22.
[58] *Cf.* Correspondence between Locke and Molyneux. Locke: *Works*, Vol. IX, pp. 329, 331, 333, 336.
[59] King: *Op. cit.*, p. 123.
[60] *Essay*, II, 27, 13.
[61] *Works*, Vol. VII, p. 10.
[62] King: *Op. cit.*, p. 124.

4. Locke's theories of toleration and punishment have the faults which any social philosophy based on a thoroughgoing rationalism is likely to have. His social theories, like his political theories, are ostensibly deduced as logical implications of certain alleged agreements of ideas, whereas the alleged agreements of ideas would be a bit of unwarranted dogmatism unless they were built upon a previous empirical estimate of the consequences of certain practical courses of conduct. For example, his contention that church and state are independent societies with distinct and separate functions, though the basis of his proof for toleration, was derived from a consideration of what it was advisable for church and state in the England of his day to attempt to do, and then from a reading of this consideration into historical contracts which were supposed to have been the origin of church and state. Of course, he thereby offended not only against sound philosophical procedure, but also against historical fact; for in primitive times the political organization of social groups was very intimately concerned with religious rites and ceremonies. The separation of church and state which has been attained in modern times is not to be made the norm for all levels of human civilization and all periods of social development. Just as Locke's opponents in advocating continued control of religious affairs by the government erred in supposing that what has long been must forever be, so Locke erred in supposing that what should come to be has always, except in cases of corruption, been the established rule.[63] Locke may be quite correct in his contention that government should now be non-theocratic and secular, and consequently that all religious bodies should be, within limits of social welfare, tolerated. But he was not content, as was shown, above, to prove that force in matters of religion was not useful nor desirable in the light of its effects; he had a prejudice which made him intellectually restless until he had deduced the same conclusion from the nature of things. Similarly he did not justify his theory that punishment should be disciplinary and educative by the practical consequences of such a procedure, but attempted to derive the theory from a discovery by reason of the agreements between the ideas of punishment and personality and consciousness. Locke's work thus has the defect which is the inevitable accompaniment of his method. By basing his social philosophy upon his rationalistic instead of his hedonistic ethics, he became guilty of constantly insisting upon the historical and logical priority of that which is subsequent and derived.

[63] Cf. Seaton: *The Theory of Toleration under the later Stuarts*, p. 267. Also Graham: *English Political Philosophy from Hobbes to Maine*, p. 82.

BIBLIOGRAPHY

Editions used of Locke's writings:

The Works of John Locke, Eleventh Edition, 10 vol. London, 1812.

Essay concerning Human Understanding, edited by A. C. Fraser. 2 vol. Oxford, 1894.

Of the Conduct of the Understanding, edited by Thomas Fowler. Clarendon Press Series. Fifth edition. Oxford, 1901.

Some Thoughts concerning Education, edited by R. H. Quick. Pitt Press Series. Cambridge, 1913. (reprinted.)

Lettres Inédites de John Locke, à ses amis Nicholas Thoynard, Philippe van Limborch, et Edward Clarke. The Hague, 1912.

Correspondence of Locke and Limborch. Translated from the Latin by J. T. Rutt. *Monthly Respository of Theology and General Literature,* vols. 13 and 14. 1818–1819.

Original Letters of Locke; Algernon Sidney; and Anthony Lord Shaftesbury. Edited by T. Forster. London, 1830.

Marginalia Locke-ana. Edited by Noah Porter. *New Englander and Yale Review,* vol. 47. July, 1887.

Primary sources for the predecessors and contemporaries of Locke:

Assheton, W.: *An Admonition to a Deist, occasioned by some passages in discourse with the same person.* London, 1685.

Blount, Charles: *Anima Mundi: or an historical narration of the opinions of the ancients concerning man's soul after this life: according to unenlightened nature.* London, 1679.

  Great is Diana of the Ephesians: or the original of idolatry, together with the politic institution of the gentiles' sacrifices. London, 1695.

  The Oracles of Reason, London, 1693.

Burnet, Thomas: *Remarks upon an Essay concerning Human Understanding, in a letter addressed to the author.* London, 1697.

  Second Remarks upon an Essay concerning Human Understanding, in a letter addressed to the author. Being a vindication of the first remarks, against the answer of Mr. Locke, at the end of his reply to the Lord Bishop of Worcester. London, 1697.

  Third Remarks upon an Essay concerning Human Understanding, in a letter addressed to the author. London, 1699.

Cudworth, Ralph: *A Treatise concerning Eternal and Immutable Morality.* London, 1845.

Culverwel, Nathanael: *Of the Light of Nature.* Edinburgh, 1857.

Cumberland, Richard: *A Philosophical Enquiry into the Laws of Nature: wherein the essence, the principal heads, the order, the publication, and the obligation of these laws are deduced from the nature of things; wherein also the principles of Mr. Hobbes's philosophy, both in a state of nature and of civil society, are examined into and confuted.* Translated from the Latin by John Towers. Dublin, 1750.

Deckburn, Mrs. Catherine Trotter: *A Defence of Mr. Locke's Essay concerning Human Understanding, wherein its principles with reference to morality, revealed religion, and the immortality of the soul, are considered and justified; in answer to some remarks on that Essay.* London, 1702.

Edwards, John: *Socinianism Unmasked: a discourse showing the unreasonableness of a late writer's opinion concerning the necessity of only one article of Christian faith, and of his other assertions in his late book entitled The Reasonableness of Christianity as delivered in the Scriptures, and in his Vindication of it.* London, 1696.
  The Socinian Creed: or a brief account of the professed tenets and doctrines of the foreign and English Socinians: wherein is showed the tendency of them to irreligion and atheism, with proper antidotes against them. London, 1697.

Filmer, Sir Robert: *Patriarcha: or the Natural Power of Kings.* London, 1680.
  The Free-holders' Grand Inquest, touching our sovereign Lord the King and his Parliament: to which are added observations upon forms of government, together with directions for obedience to governors in dangerous and doubtful times. London, 1679.

Grotius, Hugo: *Concerning the Rights of War and Peace.* Translated from the Latin by Wm. Evats. London, 1682.

Herbert, Edward, 1st Lord of Cherbury: *De Veritate, prout distinquitur a revelatione, a verisimili, a possibili, et a falso.* 3rd edition. London, 1645.
  The Ancient Religion of the Gentiles, and the causes of their errors considered: the mistakes and failures of the heathen priests and wise-men in their notions of the deity and matters of divine worship are examined; with regard to their being altogether destitute of divine revelation. London, 1705.
  Autobiography. London, 1870.

Hobbes, Thomas: *English Works.* Edited by Sir William Molesworth. 11 vols. London, 1839–1845.

Hooker, Richard: *Works.* The third American edition. 2 vols. New York, 1857.

Lowde, James: *A Discourse concerning the Nature of Man, both in his natural and political capacity: both as he is a rational creature and a member of a civil society . . . with an examination of some of Mr. Hobbes's opinions relating hereunto.* London, 1694.

Malebranche, P.: *Treatise concerning the Search after Truth.* Translated by T. Taylor. 2 vols. 2nd edition. London, 1700.

Norris, John: *Cursory Reflections upon a Book called an Essay concerning Human Understanding: with a reply to the Remarks made upon them by the Athenian Society.* (Printed as an appendix to the third edition of: *Practical Discourses upon the Beatitudes of our Lord and Saviour Jesus Christ.* Vol. 1.) London, 1694.

Prideaux, Humphrey: *A Letter to the Deists: showing that the gospel of Jesus Christ is no imposture, but the sacred truth of God.* London, 1697.

Proast, Jonas: *The Argument of the Letter concerning Toleration briefly considered and answered.* Oxford, 1690.
  A Third Letter concerning Toleration, in defense of The Argument of the Letter concerning Toleration briefly considered and answered. Oxford, 1691.
  A Second Letter to the Author of the Three Letters for Toleration: from the author of The Argument of the Letter concerning Toleration briefly considered and answered, and of the Defense of it: with a postscript taking some notice of two passages in The Rights of Protestant Dissenters. Oxford, 1704.

Pufendorf Samuel: *Of the Law of Nature and Nations.* Oxford, 1703.

The Whole Duty of Man, according to the law of nature. Translated by Andrew Tooke. London, 1716.

Shaftesbury, 1st Earl of: *Some Observations concerning the Regulations of Elections for Parliament, found among the Earl of Shaftesbury's papers after his death, and now recommended to the consideration of this present Parliament.* London, 1689.

Shaftesbury, 3rd Earl of: *Characteristics of Men, Manners, Opinions, Times.* Basil, 1790.

Stillingfleet, Edward: *A Letter to a Deist, in answer to several objections against the truth and authority of the Scriptures,* London, 1677.

A Discourse in Vindication of the Doctrine of the Trinity: with an answer to the late Socinian objections against it from Scripture, antiquity, and reason. London, 1697.

The Bishop of Worcester's Answer to Mr. Locke's Letter concerning some passages relating to his Essay concerning Human Understanding mentioned in the late Discourse in Vindication of the Trinity. London, 1697.

The Bishop of Worcester's Answer to Mr. Locke's Second Letter, wherein his notion of ideas is proved to be inconsistent with itself and with the articles of the Christian faith. London, 1698.

Toland, John: *Christianity not Mysterious.* London, 1696.

Tyrrell, James: *A brief Disquisition of the Law of Nature, according to the Principles and Method laid down in the Rev. Dr. Cumberland (now Lord Bishop of Peterborough's) Latin Treatise on that subject.* London, 1701.

Whichcote, Benjamin: *Works.* 4 vols. Aberdeen, 1751.

Willis, Richard: *The Occasional Papers.* London, 1697.

Wollaston, William: *The Religion of Nature Delineated.* 8th edition. London, 1759.

Wynne, John: *An Abridgement of Mr. Locke's Essay concerning Human Understanding.* Boston, 1832.

Secondary works:

Alexander, S.: *Locke.* (*Philosophies Ancient and Modern.*) New York, [1908].

Barker, H.: *Locke.* Article in Hasting's *Encyclopedia of Religion and Ethics.* Vol. VIII, pp. 116–120.

Benn, Alfred W.: *The History of English Rationalism in the Nineteenth Century.* 2 vols. London, 1906.

Berkeley, George: *Works.* Edited by A. C. Fraser. 4 vols. Oxford, 1901.

Bourne, H. R. Fox: *The Life of John Locke.* 2 vols. London, 1876.

Carlyle, R. W. and A. J.: *A History of Medieval Political Theory in the West.* 3 vols. New York, 1903.

Curtis, Mattoon Monroe: *An Outline of Locke's Ethical Philosophy.* Leipzig, 1890.

Dunning, William A.: *A History of Political Theories.* Vol. 2, *From Luther to Montesquieu.* New York, 1905.

Figgis, John Nivelle: *The Divine Right of Kings.* 2nd edition. Cambridge University Press, 1914.

Fowler, Thomas: *Locke.* (*English Men of Letters Series.*) New York, 1880.

Fraser, A. Campbell: *John Locke as a Factor in Modern Thought. Proceedings of the British Academy,* 1903–1904. London.

Gierke, Otto: *Political Theories of the Middle Ages.* Translated by F. W. Maitland. Cambridge University Press, 1900.

Gillett, E. H.: *The Moral System.* New York, 1874.

Gooch, G. P.: *The History of English Democratic Ideas in the Seventeenth Century.* (*Cambridge Historical Essays*, No. 1.) Cambridge University Press, 1898.

Graham, William: *English Political Philosophy from Hobbes to Maine.* London, 1914.

Green, Thomas Hill: *Works.* Vol. 2. London, 1900.

Hertling, Georg von: *John Locke und die Schule von Cambridge.* Freiburg, 1892.

King, Lord Peter: *The Life and Letters of John Locke, with extracts from His Journals and Common-place Books.* London, 1858.

Leland, John: *A View of the Principal Deistical Writers, that have appeared in England in the last and present century: with observations upon them: and some account of the answers that have been published against them.* London, 1837.

Maitland, F. W.: *The Constitutional History of England.* Cambridge University Press, 1908.

Patten, Simon N.: *The Development of English Thought: A Study in the Economic Interpretation of History.* New York, 1899.

Pollock, Sir Frederick: *An Introduction to the History of the Science of Politics.* Macmillan, 1897.
    Locke's Theory of the State. Proceedings of the British Academy, 1903–1904. London.

Reid, Thomas: *Works.* 3 vols. New York, 1822.

Robertson, John M.: *A Short History of Freethought, Ancient and Modern.* 2nd edition. 2 vol. New York, 1906.

Ruffini, Francesco: *Religious Liberty.* Translated by J. P. Heyes. (*Theological Translation Library.*) New York, 1912.

Seaton, A. A.: *The Theory of Toleration under the later Stuarts.* (*Cambridge Historical Essays*, No. 19.) Cambridge University Press, 1911.

Sidgwick, Henry: *Outlines of the History of Ethics for English Readers.* 5th edition, reprinted. London, 1916.

Sorley, W. R.: *John Locke.* In the *Cambridge History of English Literature*, Vol. VIII, Chapter 14. Cambridge University Press, 1912.

Stephen, Sir James Fitzjames: *Horae Sabbaticae.* 2 vols. London, 1892.

Stephen, Sir Leslie: *History of English Thought in the Eighteenth Century.* 2 vols. London, 1876.

ST. MARY'S COLLEGE OF MARYLAND LIBRARY
ST. MARY'S CITY, MARYLAND

DATE

MAY 1 '70   FEB

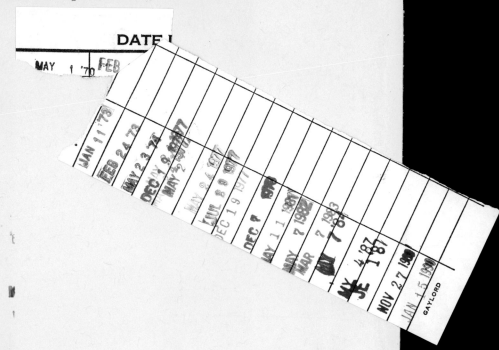

JAN 11 '73
FEB 24 73
MAY 2 3 74
DEC 8 1977
MAY 2 1977
MAY 26 1977
JUL 2 0 1977
DEC 1 9 1977
DEC
DEC
MAY 1 1 1981
MAY 7 1982
MAR 7 1983
JY 7 8
MY 4 '87
JE 1 87
NOV 2 7 1990
JAN 1 5 1990

GAYLORD